The
Diplomacy of
Human Rights

D1528616

The Institute for the Study of Diplomacy *concentrates on the processes of conducting foreign relations abroad, in the belief that diplomatic skills can be taught or improved and that the case study method is useful to that end. Working closely with the academic program of the Georgetown University School of Foreign Service, the Institute conducts a program of publication, teaching, research, conferences and lectures. An associates program enables experienced practitioners of international relations to conduct individual research while sharing their firsthand experience with the university community. Special programs include the junior fellowships in diplomacy, the Dean and Virginia Rusk midcareer fellowship, the Edward Weintal journalism prize, the Jit Trainor diplomacy award, and the Martin F. Herz monograph prize.*

The
Diplomacy of
Human Rights

Edited by
David D. Newsom

UNIVERSITY
PRESS OF
AMERICA

LANHAM • NEW YORK • LONDON

INSTITUTE FOR THE
STUDY OF DIPLOMACY

GEORGETOWN UNIVERSITY

University Press of America,® Inc.

4720 Boston Way
Lanham, MD 20706

3 Henrietta Street
London WC2E 8LU England

Printed in the United States of America

Co-published by arrangement with
the Institute for the Study of Diplomacy,
Georgetown University

Library of Congress Cataloging in Publication Data

The Diplomacy of human rights.

Includes bibliographies.
1. United States—Foreign relations—1945-
2. Civil rights.   I. Newsom, David D.   II. Georgetown
University.   Institute for the Study of Diplomacy.
JX1417.D57   1986   327.73   86-10981
ISBN 0-8191-5440-7 (alk. paper)
ISBN 0-8191-5441-5 (pbk. : alk. paper)

All University Press of America books are produced on acid-free
paper which exceeds the minimum standards set by the National
Historical Publications and Records Commission.

In pursuing a human rights policy, we must always keep in mind the limits of our power and our wisdom. A sure formula for defeat of our goals would be a rigid, hubristic attempt to impose our values on others. A doctrinaire plan of action would be as damaging as indifference.

Secretary of State Cyrus R. Vance
April 30, 1977

How we use our influence and how we reconcile political and moral interests are questions that call not for dogmatic conclusions but for painstaking, sober analysis—and no little humility.

Secretary of State George P. Shultz
February 22, 1984

CONTENTS

Preface

The Diplomacy of Human Rights is another in a series of publications by the Institute for the Study of Diplomacy on the *how* of diplomacy.

In both the Carter and the Reagan administrations, the consideration of human rights has been a significant element in the United States approach to international affairs. The speeches of Secretaries of State Vance and Shultz, reprinted in full in the appendixes, testify to the continuity of this concern.

Policies need to be implemented. This collection of essays seeks to go beyond the continuing debate over whether human rights issues should be emphasized in foreign policy to assume that such issues will continue to be a part of the diplomatic agenda of the United States and other democracies and to suggest, through actual cases, the measures by which such policies can be carried out.

The cases are far from inclusive of all countries and circumstances. There are significant omissions; we were not able in a timely fashion to find authors to address issues in either the Philippines or Central America. What we have is a sampling of regions and approaches that we believe illustrates the challenges, dilemmas, and effective approaches of this phase of diplomacy.

Controversy obviously surrounds this subject. Our intention is not to debate, but to inform. We are interested in what works and what does not. We seek to avoid judgement on policies and methods. We have, nevertheless, sought to include different points of view on both. They represent those of the authors.

We have tried, also, to include a variety of perspectives: that of the diplomat in the field, the staff member in the Congress, the bureaucrat in Washington, and the scholar.

Ambassador Francis J. Meehan provided valuable assistance at the development and editorial stages of this book while serving as research professor of diplomacy at the Institute for the Study of Diplomacy. In August 1985, he was appointed U.S. ambassador to the German Democratic Republic.

We are indebted to the J. Howard Pew Freedom Trust, which has supported the publications program of the Institute, and for the task of assembling and editing this book so ably performed by Margery R. Boichel.

I

Foundations of Human Rights Diplomacy

The Continuity of Concern

I speak today about the resolve of this Administration to make the advancement of human rights a central part of our foreign policy....

Secretary of State Cyrus R. Vance
April 30, 1977

Moral values and a commitment to human dignity have not been an appendage to our foreign policy but an essential part of it, and a powerful impulse driving it....

Secretary of State George P. Shultz
February 22, 1984

The Diplomacy of Human Rights: A Diplomat's View

David D. Newsom

Human rights are, inescapably, a controversial issue in diplomacy, but are likely to remain part of the international agenda of the United States and most Western democracies. Effective influence in this field can be exerted if there is a sensitivity toward the cultural and political environment, access to leaders. solid information, and solid support for the diplomatic effort.

Throughout modern times diplomats have been called on by their governments to intervene in other countries in the interests of the rights of populations and individuals. While some interventions arise from the initiative of the individual diplomat, most of these diplomatic actions are part of a determined policy of one country to advance human and political rights in another.

This publication emphasizes what the diplomat can do to promote human rights in another country. It assumes, within limits, that this objective will continue to be a part of the policy of the United States and of many Western democracies. The question of whether a country should make such judgements and seek to intervene in the internal affairs of another to defend individuals or to promote a different type of political system is, understandably, controversial. This study does not seek to deal with that controversy, already the subject of numerous publications. Still, the controversial aspects must be mentioned since they do bear on the boundaries of the diplomatic task.

Concern over individual and collective human rights has been a part of the diplomatic agenda of the United States from its earliest days. These diplomatic efforts spring from a deep impulse in the American society. If there is controversy, it is over the effectiveness of U.S. actions and over the types of situations in which we should bring our official influence to bear.

3

United States diplomacy in the human rights field suffers inevitably from the contradictions between promise and fulfillment. Rhetoric and actions of the United States in support of individuals and in favor of freedom and democracy can raise hopes and create expectations that, in many cases, can not be fulfilled.

There is nevertheless strong support in the United States for the expression of official concern over the denial of human rights to individuals and populations under the domination of the Soviet Union, even if such expression may not be effective. This concern increased after World War II with the flight to this country of numerous exiles from Eastern Europe who have kept alive the pressures on the United States to take an interest in the fate of those that have been left behind.

There has been relatively little disagreement over the correctness of this country's policies that seek the freedom of dissidents in the Soviet Union and Eastern Europe, support the emigration of Jewish communities, and press for a lessening of the Soviet grip on Eastern Europe. Added to this has been the desire in this country to afford a refuge, not only to those who were victims of Soviet domination, but to those religious and ethnic communities in Europe and around the world that may still be in danger of further persecution.

The pursuit of human rights issues in the Soviet Union and countries in Eastern Europe is accepted as an appropriate and necessary aspect of our diplomacy. If there are disagreements in this area, it is either over the effectiveness of our diplomacy or over whether what we do in this area is consistent with other objectives we may have in our relations with the Soviet Union. One debate in which both issues were present was that over the Jackson-Vanik amendment, which linked most-favored-nation treatment in trade to Jewish emigration from the Soviet Union and Eastern Europe.[1] This amendment has been a significant factor in the implementation of human rights diplomacy in these areas since its enactment in January 1975.

A series of largely domestic events in the last quarter century has made the issue of human rights in countries beyond the Soviet orbit increasingly live in the national debate and has placed greater pressures than ever on the diplomacy of the United States. These events included the civil rights movement, the radical student movements, the increasing lack of confidence in government growing out of Watergate, the growing power of committees in Congress, the unease over the identification with dictatorial regimes, particularly in Latin America, and the trauma of Vietnam. All of these created a strong impetus toward an institutionalized global human rights policy expressed through legislation and executive policy. Our diplomacy abroad became the cutting edge of this new national emphasis.

Although there was wide support in Congress and in the public for this emphasis, there were many voices in opposition. They saw our active concern over human rights in noncommunist nations threatening other interests, particularly security and trade.

Controversy has swirled around the official attitude toward "friendly" nations that share our opposition to communism, but whose governments are guilty of human rights violations. One pair of conservative columnists, for instance, has characterized U.S. human rights policy as "equating sporadic villainy inside friendly governments with the organized oppression of the Soviet police state." Those primarily concerned with human rights in the Soviet context have for many years felt that faults in the non-Soviet countries have been exaggerated, while the Soviet Union has escaped serious criticism, particularly by Third World nations. This school is also concerned that the weakening of anti-Soviet regimes by human rights pressures could adversely affect our global strategic balance. The controversy over human rights policies raged particularly in the Carter administration, especially over policy toward Iran.

Another country that is still at the center of policy controversy is South Africa. While there is general agreement on the unacceptability of apartheid, there is a feeling among many Americans that South Africa's strategic location and strong opposition to Soviet activities in the Southern Africa region should make it exempt from strong pressures from the United States.

In such nations, those resisting official U.S. pressure to change their internal policies looked for and found influential voices in the United States that would support a more tolerant view of their practices. Such signals sometimes tempted governments to resist the pressures for change in the hope that a new administration or a different mood in the U.S. would make unnecessary what they saw as difficult if not dangerous political moves. The U.S. diplomacy of human rights was thus often limited in what it could accomplish.

Controversy has also existed over what sanctions to apply in support of human rights diplomacy, particularly economic sanctions. As Patrick Flood's case history on Argentina demonstrates, strong resistance developed to the use of Export-Import Bank credits as a tool of leverage against Argentina. U.S. businesses involved argued that the application of such sanctions robbed U.S. business of major contracts without actually affecting the human rights policies of the Argentine government.

The strong national support for human rights policies that will put pressure both on Soviet regimes and the authoritarian regimes of non-Soviet countries was demonstrated, however, with the advent of the Reagan administration. Despite efforts by some to move away from an active United States involvement in human rights issues in non-Soviet countries, the new administration found that both laws and public attitudes compelled it to continue an active human rights policy around the world.

The effectiveness of U.S. diplomacy in the field of human rights has been aided by the fact that most nations are sensitive to how the outside world looks at their internal practices. Idi Amin and Bokassa were exceptions to this rule. Most nations respond to charges of mistreatment of their citizens either with genuine efforts to correct abuses or cosmetic actions to divert attention, or by defending what they are doing. International pressure helps focus attention on the abuses. Governments, however, will not readily submit to changes that may threaten their political power. Where improvements are possible without running this risk, the chances are likely that improvements can be made. Where the abuses are deemed essential for the retention of power, changes are less likely.

The Diplomatic Tools

Effective diplomatic action in support of human rights in another country involves both the individual actions of the diplomat and those policies and measures of the diplomat's country that can provide leverage and inducements for change.

In an ideal world, the diplomat would like to see change result from such efforts. In many regimes, as will be discussed below, change may not be possible, at least in the short term. The diplomat must then consider whether it is in the interest of his or her country to recommend "distance" from the regime. Public statements and policy actions can lessen the degree to which the diplomat's country is publicly identified, both at home and abroad, with the policies of the offending regime. Distancing is not necessarily "walking away" from an issue. It may serve to make our policies and principles more credible with others. The pressure of the resulting isolation can sometimes influence an internal situation.

"Distancing" can also give a signal of the seriousness of U.S. intentions to other countries where similar violations exist.

Where a U.S. diplomat determines that influence is possible, there are a number of tools available:

1. *Access.* A diplomat cannot effectively influence the actions or decisions of another country without access to that country's leaders, decision makers and opinion molders. The diplomat of the United States often has the advantage that, even if the host country is not sympathetic with the efforts being made, high officials are available because relations with the United States are important for other reasons. The ability to meet with human rights organizations and the political opposition is also important, both to gain information on the circumstances in the country and to give a signal that the United States is not wholly committed to the position of the government in power.[2]

The diplomat must weigh carefully the degree to which he presses for access either to government officials or private organizations. There are limits in both cases. There may be only limited time or opportunities for discussions with senior leaders; the agenda must be carefully constructed. Contacts with human rights organizations or opposition groups in authoritarian countries may be firmly opposed by the government—or, if carried out, can create serious barriers in relations with the authorities on other matters.

2. *Public Statements.* Depending on the objective of the diplomatic efforts, the diplomat abroad may wish to speak out on the human rights situtation in the host country or encourage the home government back in the capital to do so. Herein lies the heart of the debate over "quiet diplomacy." The diplomat must weigh whether a statement will move a government to take action or will increase its sensitivity to outside pressures and make other diplomatic efforts more difficult. Generally, public statements are used in the diplomacy of human rights when it appears that quiet efforts may not bear fruit or when the objective is more to "distance" the United States from a foreign regime than it is to influence that regime. The impact of such statements is of course enhanced if they are made at the presidential level or cabinet level. Official statements can be given further strength by special efforts to make them known internationally through the Voice of America and the other media of USIA.

3. *Legislation.* For the United States diplomat the existence of legislation requiring annual reports on the human rights situations in individual countries and requiring a consideration of human rights and emigration in questions of foreign assistance and trade provides both a problem and an opportunity. The problem arises when foreign governments consider that the application of U.S. legislative sanctions or requirements (such as the annual reports to the Congress) constitutes an unacceptable intrusion into their internal affairs. U.S. laws may represent a genuine political problem for foreign leaders if actions are taken in the face of such pressures. It is possible, however, for the diplomat to use the existence of legislation as an indication of the general feeling of the American people on an issue. If this is presented without the suggestion of a threat, it can assist in supporting diplomatic efforts to make progress on a human rights problem (as discussed in the case on Indonesia).

U.S. laws can be more effective in abeyance than in application. It is difficult to find cases where the actual application of the laws has led to changes in another country's human rights practices. Knowledge of a U.S. law, however, can sometimes help a faction within a foreign government arguing for more liberal practices. (The principal laws relating to the international aspects of human rights are discussed in the essays by John Salzberg and Lynne Davidson and listed in Appendix D.)

4. *U.S. Programs.* The legislation enacted during the 1970s provided U.S. administrations with the authority and, in some cases, with a mandate to apply human rights criteria to programs of military assistance, military sales, police assistance, export credits, trade, and economic assistance programs that did not fall in the category of "basic human needs." These were obvious tools of pressure on foreign governments. The legislation in many instances, however, left the interpretation of given situations to the discretion of the administration. During the Carter administration, major interagency machinery was established to monitor and manage the application of human rights legislation and executive policies. Much of the diplomacy of the period was devoted to

explaining the rationale for U.S. actions to affected countries and to other nations that had an interest in the U.S. programs.

The tying of U.S. programs and actions to human rights considerations is an obvious form of pressure. It is not within the scope of this study to pass judgement on the effectiveness of the use of these measures to advance the cause of human rights. Both the Congress and the public, it seemed, wanted U.S. money to be used under conditions that were consistent with our own professed ideals. At the same time, the administration of these policies encountered strong opposition from those who resisted penalties for "friendly" and strategically placed countries and from businesses which felt that opportunities were lost to others because of these policies. There have also been positive U.S. programs related to the human rights emphasis designed to train officials, police and others in correct attitudes and actions; these, in general, have received less attention and less opposition than "negative" actions.

5. *Consultation with Like-minded Governments.* Many Western European democracies share the concern of the United States over human rights violations both in Eastern Europe and in the Third World. They are less inclined to use economic and military programs for pressure, but they are often prepared to support the United States with diplomatic efforts. Human rights issues have become in recent years an important part of our agenda of diplomatic consultation with allies, including Japan. Diplomats from such countries have often been helpful to United States diplomats in reinforcing the international concern in specific situations. (The response of other governments to U.S. human rights diplomacy is discussed in chapter 4 by R. J. Vincent.)

6. *Multilateral Banks.* Another area of pressure created by the legislation in support of U.S. diplomacy relates to actions in the multilateral lending agencies—the World Bank, the Inter-American Development Bank, the Asian Development Bank, and the African Development Bank. It was the clear sense of Congress that the United States should not support any loans by these agencies to countries that were violators of human rights principles, except where it could clearly be shown that the loans would support projects related to "basic human needs." In practice, the only activity of these agencies over which the United States has a veto is the "soft loan" window of the Inter-American Bank. Actions in other banks are limited to voting or abstaining. The United States has not ever been able to get sufficient support from other members of the banks to stop any loans. In some cases, the threat of U.S. opposition has led countries to withhold or withdraw applications.

To U.S. diplomats in developing countries, this "tool" has been, in many ways, the least effective. The use of the banks as instruments of pressure has been seen as "politicizing" the banks. Such actions are often resented particularly by those technocrats and managers in offending countries who are potential allies on many human rights issues. The task of bilateral diplomacy in this phase of the human rights policy has been to seek to explain and defend the action of the United States in taking action against a loan.

7. *International Organizations.* The United Nations organization, both in the General Assembly, the Security Council and in the specialized agencies dealing with human rights, has established a strong body of precedents in support of efforts to improve human rights. Of particular importance have been the United Nations Commission on Human Rights, the organizations that have grown out of the Helsinki accords, and the Inter-American Commission on Human Rights. The involvement of an international organization in the survey of a human rights problem in a country is often one way out for a government seeking to improve its international image. Turning to an international organization, such as the Inter-American Commission on Human Rights (see the essay on Argentina) can provide a more politically acceptable way for a government to acknowledge and deal with an internal human rights problem than actions taken under pressure from a single outside government.

8. *Private Organizations.* Private organizations, some of them international in scope, provide another source of impartial observations of human rights problems. Reports by such organizations as the International Commission of Jurists and the International Committee of the Red Cross have played important roles in bringing human rights violations to the attention of a country's leaders and providing them a basis on which to make improvements. Other organizations, such as Amnesty International, do not deal with governments but create pressures through arousing the concern of private citizens in the United States and abroad. (A list of the principal human rights organizations involved in this way appears in Appendix E.)

Problems and Limitations of Human Rights Diplomacy

1. *The High Stakes.* Efforts to curb human rights violations in authoritarian countries often represent a direct challenge to the tactics that keep a leader in power. In nations where violations occur, life is often byzantine and brutal. The stakes are high. Rulers condone the killing and torturing of their fellow citizens by their security and police services because they fear a threat to their own power. Outside involvement in discouraging such practices strikes directly at the most basic concern of a political leader: his or her survival.

Human rights issues arise also in countries where the ruler is being challenged—or feels so—by terrorist acts. Terrorism begets terrorism. The security services may initiate it or may respond in kind. In either event, the ruler's survival depends on the loyalty of the military and security services; in turn the leader assumes an obligation to protect them from civil retaliation. Any effort from outside to encourage curbs on the activities of the security services is likely to encounter this reality.

2. *A Choice of Evils.* While it is tempting to believe that the outside efforts of

a country such as the United States may result in the establishment of more democratic policies, there may be no political alternatives in a country that realistically promise this result. The opposition may have the same attitude toward ruling as the party in power. They may speak more democratically because they are out and the others are in, but that does not change their basic way of looking at the acquisition and use of power.

The opposition in repressive regimes may be just as tough and often as unscrupulous as those in power. Their intention is, naturally, to enlist the United States in their own struggle against the government. They may or may not represent a preferable alternative from the standpoint of the United States. What they say or what they tell others about the practices of the group in power and their own alternative policies must be carefully weighed. A U.S. diplomat seeking to influence a human rights situation must avoid either romanticizing the opposition or becoming too closely involved with a single group in a complex situation.

3. *Ambiguous Support for Policies.* Many nations, especially in Latin America, seek the approbation of the United States for their internal policies. Where serious internal conflicts arise, both conservatives and liberals from these countries seek allies in the United States, particularly among key elements in the Congress and the administration in power. The United States, in effect, becomes the judge and jury of another country's internal struggle; the verdict is rendered in aid and arms sales. In such cases, as Nicaragua illustrated, positive changes cannot be encouraged unless there is united support in Washington.

The commitment of a president of the United States to human rights becomes essential if this country's policies in this area are to be effective. President Carter, in general, gave that commitment, although the signals were mixed. His comments in December 1978 praising the Shah of Iran as a strong advocate of human rights were obviously rhetoric inconsistent with a firm policy. As with any president, he was required to balance considerations of human rights with other objectives of national policy.

The Reagan administration, starting with a more tolerant attitude toward authoritarian regimes, gradually shifted to a human rights policy not different in many respects from that of the Carter administration. In both administrations, for the sensitive observer in a troubled land, there were mixed signals.

An ambassador can take some steps on personal initiative. There can be visits to opposition representatives and discussions with government leaders. His or her influence and credibility are limited, however, unless there is firm support from high levels in Washington.

4. *The Need for Flexibility in Applying Sanctions.* Ideally, a government should be able both to penalize and reward in support of diplomatic efforts to improve human rights. In the case of the United States, it has been much easier to penalize than to reward. The action to terminate an assistance program, to refuse a loan, or to deny military sales is simple and negative, even though

individual decisions may be controversial. It has proved more difficult in practice to reward by reshaping assistance programs. The inflexibility of the appropriations process and the cumbersomeness of the administration of U.S. aid programs generally have tended to defeat efforts to "fine tune" assistance in response to changes in human rights situations.

5. *The Need for Information.* One of the most important adjuncts to effective diplomacy in the human rights field is the determination of correct facts. In circumstances in which emotions are high, political futures are at stake, and exaggerations are common, seeking out the facts can be difficult, if not at times impossible, for a foreign diplomat. The search for information is, itself, sensitive. Sources must be protected and yet credibility must be established—especially if an ambassador is to discuss a precise situation with local authorities. It is often necessary to turn to other countries' diplomats or to international organizations to widen the base of information on which U.S. actions are taken.

6. *Where to Make the Appeals.* The effectiveness of diplomatic approaches on sensitive subjects is often determined by the channels used. The United States ambassador in the field may have the best access to key political leaders in the country. Demarches made to the country's ambassador in Washington may suffer the disadvantage of being reported through unsympathetic channels in the capital and, perhaps, not even reaching the decision makers. On the other hand, there are situations in which the influence of the country's ambassador in Washington is substantial; his appraisal of the Washington scene and of the intentions of the United States government may be an important key to improved policies. In making decisions on how to proceed on a given case, the first choice is an important one—between the ambassador of the United States in the field and the ambassador of the country concerned in Washington. Both may be employed when it is reasonably certain that the messages they convey will be complementary and not contradictory.

Conclusion

As this is being written, the world is observing improvements in the relations between the governed and the governors in many countries and challenges to traditional oppression in others. The changes in such countries as Argentina, Brazil, and El Salvador undoubtedly result primarily from internal forces. There is little doubt, however, that the efforts from outside, including those of the diplomats of the United States and other democracies, played a role in heightening the internal awareness of the issues and in establishing the pressures that led to change. The diplomacy of human rights is complex, controversial, sensitive and not always rewarding. The patterns of change now being observed, however, suggest that it may be more effective than is realized at the time the various pressures of such diplomacy are applied.

To illustrate further the attributes of this special brand of diplomacy—in which one nation seeks to correct the faults it sees in another—this publication includes a series of case histories of individual country situations.

Notes

1   Section 402 of the Trade Act of 1974, as amended.

2   See the Institute for the Study of Diplomacy publication *Contacts with the Opposition*, Martin F. Herz, ed., 1979.

Chapter 2

A View from the Hill: U.S. Legislation and Human Rights

John P. Salzberg

The apparent unwillingness of U.S. administrations in the 1960s and 1970s to take into account serious human rights violations in other nations led to legislation forcing the hand of the executive. The author was a key staff member in the House of Representatives subcommittee that helped create the legislation and the pressure for its passage.

The development of human rights as an important element in U.S. diplomacy may largely be attributed to congressional initiative. Prior to the 1970s U.S. diplomacy treated human rights as a peripheral matter. In the late 1960s and early 1970s members of Congress were troubled by many situations abroad in which they felt U.S. policy was contributing to human rights violations. "Tiger cages," political prisoners and other indications of repression were a major element in the growing congressional opposition to U.S. armed support for the South Vietnamese government. In response Congress adopted legislation opposing aid to governments that hold political prisoners.

In the 1960s the democratic Greek government was overthrown by a military junta. The European allies of the United States distanced themselves from the junta and the junta withdrew from the Council of Europe to prevent its expulsion. In contrast, the United States negotiated with the junta for home-porting facilities for its navy. During the conflict that established Bangladesh, the Kissinger tilt toward Pakistan in the face of reports of genocidal practices dramatized for many persons an indifference to human rights by the Nixon administration. Many other examples can be cited: U.S. ties with dictatorships in Latin America (e.g., Somoza in Nicaragua) and, in 1973, support for the overthrow of a democratic government in Chile and the installation of a repressive regime; as well as alliance with dictatorships in other regions of the world, as in the case of South Korea and the Philippines.

Support for a repressive regime by the superpower United States has more than a marginal influence on the regime's viability. United States support in the form of military and economic assistance provides substantial staying power for such a regime. Even in situations where tangible U.S. aid is arguably insubstantial, U.S. diplomatic identification with a regime provides significant symbolic support for the regime and its repressive practices. This support in itself helps to solidify domestic and regional elements in favor of the regime. The United States, as a superpower, in either situation is seen as an accomplice in the repression. It was questionable relationships of this sort between the U.S. and repressive regimes that sparked congressional concern for human rights and U.S. foreign policy.

The first legislation directly related to human rights concerns, in 1973, was a ban on any U.S. official involvement in the training and equipping of foreign police forces.[1] Prior to this, the Agency for International Development had an active police program, based on the belief that a humane police service was essential to development and democracy.

Congress, by 1973, after Chile, Vietnam, and reports of police excesses in other countries with which we were identified, prohibited further assistance. Unlike later legislation, this did not seek to promote human rights by permitting assistance if abuses were corrected. It was clearly intended to distance the United States from abuses.

In the next two years, the active interest of a subcommittee of the House Foreign Affairs Committee, originally under Democratic Congressman Donald M. Fraser of Minnesota, spurred the drive for legislation. As a result, beginning in 1974, a series of amendments to the foreign assistance legislation required the United States to show a positive impact on human rights in countries to which we were providing aid. Because of the mistrust of the executive, even after Carter's election, the legislation became increasingly specific.

The Fraser Subcommittee

Congressman Fraser was a pivotal figure in Congress in articulating concerns about human rights. He believed strongly that how a government treats its own people should be an important element in shaping U.S. bilateral relations. From 1973 through 1978 as chairman of the Subcommittee on International Organizations and Movements (later renamed the Subcommittee on Human Rights and International Organizations), he made human rights and U.S. foreign policy a major focus of the subcommittee's attention. After an initial series of fifteen hearings in 1973, the subcommittee adopted in 1974 a report entitled "Human Rights in the World Community: A Call for U.S. Leadership."

The subcommittee report was significant in enunciating the enduring ethical principle of U.S. responsibility for the international protection of human rights. The report provides the following rationale for this principle:

Protection of human rights is essentially the responsibility of each government with respect to its own citizens; however, when a government is itself the perpetrator of the violations, the victim has no recourse but to seek redress from outside his national boundaries. Men and women of decency find common cause in coming to the aid of the oppressed despite national differences. Through their own governments and international organizations, they have both the opportunity and responsibility to help defend human rights throughout the world.

The report contained twenty-nine recommendations regarding human rights as a factor in U.S. foreign policy, as well as ways and means of protecting human rights through international organizations. It called upon the Department of State to treat human rights factors "as a regular part of U.S. foreign policy decision making" and said the department should discourage human rights violations through private and public diplomacy, withdrawal of military aid and certain economic aid programs. It recommended that the department be organized to facilitate greater attention to human rights in policymaking.

The adoption of the subcommittee's report marked only the threshold of its work. The complexity of the issue and the strong resistance within the Nixon administration to giving human rights the desired priority underlined the necessity for continuing congressional monitoring. A subcommittee with authority to conduct hearings was the most effective means of continuing this monitoring process. From 1973 through 1978 the Fraser subcommittee held more than 150 hearings with more than five hundred witnesses. These hearings focused on U.S. relations with governments in all continents and of varying political ideologies. At least several hearings were held on each of the following countries: Chile, Nicaragua, El Salvador, Argentina, Cuba, the Philippines, South Korea, Indonesia, South Africa, Israel and the USSR. The subcommittee received testimony from international human rights nongovernmental organizations, representatives of religious organizations and others with expertise in the country concerned. Frequently the public witnesses had recently returned from the country under study and had direct knowledge of the human rights conditions. The subcommittee also heard testimony from nationals of the country—lawyers, political opposition figures, church and other nongovernmental representatives—who not only had firsthand knowledge but in some instances were themselves victims of repression. To provide balance, the subcommittee often had witnesses who defended the human rights record of the foreign government under scrutiny.

In addition, the subcommittee requested testimony from the Department of State, usually at or near the conclusion of a hearing series. The department representatives would be asked to comment on the allegations made by previous witnesses and to describe how the department was attempting to ameliorate human rights conditions in the country under study or, at a minimum, how the United States was dissociating itself from the repressive practices.

The hearing process had an educational influence on the Department of State officials who testified or assisted in preparing the testimony. Moreover, the hearing process in some instances led to significant policy developments. A subcommittee hearing on a particular country often led to visits to Congressman Fraser by the U.S. ambassador to that country or department officials. The ambassadors would recount the diplomatic initiatives being taken to address the problems posed in the hearings. For example, the Fraser subcommittee held a series of hearings on Indonesia's long-term political prisoners. At the time of the hearings, in 1975, it was alleged that more than 30,000 prisoners had been held for more than ten years without being charged or tried.[2] Following these hearings our embassy undertook extensive discussions with the Government of Indonesia. These talks facilitated the release of almost all the prisoners.[3]

The initiatives such as the one just cited were genuine efforts at ameliorating human rights conditions—prisoners were released or put on trial, torture was diminished, etc. The short-term problem from the subcommittee's perspective was that the initiatives were taken within the confines of a bilateral relationship that closely identified the U.S. with the foreign government and therefore subjected our diplomacy to charges of complicity. Moreover, ameliorative proposals from congressional sources did not fundamentally change the government's repressive nature. The responses by the governments were often criticized as being cosmetic, giving only the appearance of human rights improvements, e.g., political prisoners were released but others would soon be arrested. However, given the difficulty of achieving any progress in human rights, the Fraser subcommittee's success in encouraging new initiatives by the Department of State represented a significant development in the diplomacy of human rights. Precedents were established by the department and its embassies of raising human rights issues with host governments; diplomatic skills were developed and an understanding and appreciation of human rights as an integral part of U.S. diplomacy evolved. When an administration took office with human rights as an accepted centerpiece of its policy, these precedents and the experience gained by the career Foreign Service officers would facilitate the continuation and strengthening of this new policy.

In response to the Fraser subcommittee hearings and report, the Department of State also adopted some organizational changes to increase the consideration given to human rights factors. Several specific recommendations contained in the subcommittee's report were adopted—establishing a Human Rights Office in the Bureau of International Organization Affairs, creating the post of assistant legal advisor for human rights, and designating human rights officers in each of the regional bureaus.

It was also apparent from the hearings that there was a need for someone in the department to have overall responsibility for human rights. On July 10, 1974, Chairman Fraser wrote to Deputy Secretary of State Robert W. Ingersoll, "The Department should (also) have someone at the policymaking level to insure that human rights factors are given reasonable consideration....It is particularly necessary to have someone with overall responsibilities who would oversee developments in human rights and decision making in this area." On August 14 Mr. Ingersoll wrote back indicating that he planned to have an officer in his office to "insure full consideration of human rights factors in decision making." The office was later to become the Bureau of Human Rights and Humanitarian Affairs headed by an assistant secretary of state.

Human Rights Legislation

Despite these organizational changes by the department, Congressman Fraser was not satisfied that real changes in policy had been made. During the mark-up of the foreign aid bill in 1974, Congressman Fraser questioned Deputy Secretary Ingersoll on how the administration had implemented the Abourezk amendment. This was a non-binding amendment calling for the prohibition of foreign aid to governments with political prisoners.[4] Fraser specifically referred to political prisoners in South Korea and asked what the administration had done to implement the amendment. A disappointing response led Fraser to introduce an amendment (Section 502B of the Foreign Assistance Act) which affirmed "the sense of Congress...that, except in extraordinary circumstances, the President shall substantially reduce or terminate security assistance to any government which engages in a consistent pattern of gross violations of internationally recognized human rights." The burden was put on the president to prove the existence of "extraordinary circumstances" that would justify any continuation of assistance.

This amendment, enacted by Congress in December 1974, became the yardstick for the Fraser subcommittee's consideration of human rights policy. Military aid was singled out because armed forces in repressive governments often were responsible for violations of integrity-of-the-person rights—e.g., prolonged detention, torture and killing. Congressman Fraser used language taken from UN resolutions to underline U.S. responsibility under international law to protect human rights. This legislation also covered grant military training and security assistance for police and civil law enforcement authorities.

Flowing from this legislation and the Fraser-Ingersoll exchange, the Department of State began to ask U.S. embassies to prepare reports on the human rights conditions in affected countries. This practice began with the Bureau of East Asian and Pacific Affairs—the bureau that Ingersoll had headed before becoming deputy secretary. Soon thereafter all regional bureaus required reports from their embassies. These reports were completed in November 1975 and consisted of a short summary and a country-by-country analysis. Secretary Henry Kissinger, however, decided not to release these reports. Instead, a report was issued declaring that all states violated human rights and that it would not be in the interests of the United States to single out any individual states. This action led members of Congress to question Secretary Kissinger's good faith in implementing Section 502B of the Foreign Assistance Act.[5]

The 1974 amendment was the first in a series of amendments that related human rights to U.S. or international assistance programs. In 1975 Congressman Tom Harkin offered an amendment[6] to the bilateral economic development aid bill that prohibited such aid to governments that, as defined in the 1974 amendment, engage in a "consistent pattern of gross violations of internationally recognized human rights," unless the aid directly benefited needy people. Economic aid, as much as military aid, demonstrated U.S. political support for a particular government. Moreover, in the case of one gross violator, Chile, the Nixon and Ford administrations had, in the view of the subcommittee, undermined a congressional ban on military aid by increasing economic aid. The Harkin amendment sought to diminish the use of economic aid as political support for repressive governments. Congressman Harkin and others went on to link human rights with other forms of bilateral and multilateral economic aid. With respect to multilateral institutions, U.S. delegates were required to vote no or abstain on loans to governments with unsatisfactory human rights records unless the aid directly benefited needy people.

In 1977, the "gross violations" language of sections 502B and 116 of the Foreign Assistance Act was extended to programs under the Food for Peace Act (PL-480) and in 1978, to the Overseas Private Investment Corporation and the Export-Import Bank.

In addition, Sections 701 and 703 of the International Financial Institutions Act of 1977 established goals and standards concerning human rights and basic needs to be pursued and applied through the voice and vote of the United States in the four principal multilateral development institutions in which the United States participates: the World Bank,[7] the Inter-American Development Bank, the Asian Development Bank, and the African Development Fund. The law further requires the United States to urge these institutions "to channel assistance" to countries that do not violate human rights and to oppose assistance by these organizations to countries whose governments engage in a consistent pattern of human rights violations unless the assistance is "directed specifically to programs which serve the basic human needs of the citizens of such country."

Each of these pieces of legislation also calls for periodic reports to the Congress on implementation.

All the legislation before 1977 linking aid and human rights had been negative inasmuch as it sanctioned violators with aid cut-offs. But thereafter a more positive approach was sought. In 1977, Congressman Fraser introduced an amendment, Section 116(e) of the Foreign Assistance Act, which authorized $750,000 for "programs and activities which will encourage or promote increased adherence to civil and political rights...in countries eligible for assistance." Such activities included programs of teaching, visits, information, legal services, research and workshops. These programs have assisted nongovernmental organizations, both in the U.S. and in developing countries, that are actively involved in promoting human rights. Government agencies of developing countries have also been assisted. In Fiscal Year 1984, $3,102,965 was spent on these continuing activities.

Despite the progress achieved by the hearings and the legislation adopted in 1974 and 1975, the Nixon and Ford administrations did not change their policies with respect to human rights issues sufficiently to satisfy the proponents of a more active human rights policy in the Congress. Military and economic aid continued to such highly criticized regimes as those in Chile, Nicaragua, El Salvador, the Philippines and South Korea. Congress decided that more stringent general and specific country legislation was required to achieve its objectives. Legislation prohibiting or limiting military and in some cases economic aid was adopted. Legislation directed at Chile prohibited military aid and limited economic aid;[8] legislation for South Korea linked military aid and human rights.[9] Congressman Fraser, who was one of the sponsors of the legislation for Chile and South Korea, regretted the need for specific country legislation. He realized that the executive branch rather than the Congress was in a far better position to "fine-tune" responses to a country's human rights performance. Congress could not quickly lift or reimpose a ban on aid. However, the administration's resistance to congressional concerns impelled congressional action.

The 1974 legislation linking human rights and security assistance (Section 502B of the Foreign Assistance Act) was transformed in 1976 from non-binding legislation to a requirement that except in extraordinary circumstances security assistance be prohibited to governments engaged in gross violations of human rights. The legislation also required that military aid programs be formulated and conducted in a way that would avoid identification of the U.S. with repressive regimes. The legislation went beyond the confines of military aid programs: it stated that human rights was "a principal goal" of U.S. foreign policy, and required an annual public report to Congress regarding the observance of human rights in each country receiving security assistance. Later, the human rights reports were required of all countries.

Finally, in 1977, legislation mandated the appointment of an assistant secretary for humanitarian and human rights affairs in the Department of State.

In 1977 the Carter administration took office with a commitment to make the observance of human rights throughout the world a principal goal of U.S. foreign policy. It did not generate its human rights policy out of "whole cloth," however. Congress had adopted the legislation for this policy. The Fraser hearings had provided an educational forum for diplomats as well as the American public to develop an understanding and appreciation of the importance of human rights for U.S. long-term interests. The institutional mechanisms within the bureaucracy had been developing to accomplish this goal as well. The stage had been set for the pursuit of an effective human rights policy.

Notes

1 Section 660 of the Foreign Assistance Act of 1961, as amended. Citations of specific legislation are gathered in Appendix D, which lists the principal congressional enactments relating to human rights.—Ed.

2 Reports of the number of prisoners still held varied from 30,000 to as high as 100,000.

3 For an account by the U.S. ambassador at the time, see the case history on Indonesia in chapter 9.—Ed.

4 Section 32 of the Foreign Assistance Act of 1973.

5 During this period the Congress chose not to define any more clearly what was meant by "a gross violator," and the Executive resisted efforts to prepare a list of such countries.

6 Section 116 of the Foreign Assistance Act of 1961, as amended.

7 Formally, the International Bank for Reconstruction and Development and its affiliates, the International Finance Corporation and the International Development Association.

8 Earlier legislation expressing concern for human rights in Chile is contained in Section 35 of the Foreign Assistance Act of 1973.—Ed.

9 Other countries at which such legislation was directed in the ensuing years included Argentina, Cambodia, Cuba, El Salvador, Guatemala, Haiti, Nicaragua, South Africa, Uganda, and Vietnam, among others.

Chapter 3

The Tools of Human Rights Diplomacy with Eastern Europe

Lynne A. Davidson

Lynne Davidson, a staff member of the U.S. Commission on Security and Cooperation in Europe, sets forth the principal instruments available, both domestic and international, to support diplomatic efforts involving human rights violations in the East-West context.

This study is not a comprehensive evaluation of human rights conditions in the seven Warsaw Pact countries. Nor is it a critique of any one administration's policy decisions in the area. Rather, from my perspective as a staff member of the U.S. (Helsinki) Commission on Security and Cooperation in Europe, an independent advisory agency of the U.S. government under the chairmanship of Congressman Dante B. Fascell (D-Fla.),* I shall discuss something of what I have learned about the practical conduct of East-West human rights diplomacy.

In accordance with its mandate to monitor and encourage compliance with the human rights and other provisions of the 1975 East-West Helsinki agreement, the Helsinki Commission has played a pivotal role in East-West human rights policy formulation and coordination within the U.S. government under the Ford, Carter and Reagan administrations. Due to the nature and extent of their expertise, commissioners and staff have served as key members of U.S.

The views expressed here and in chapters 13 and 15 are those of the author and do not necessarily reflect those of the U.S. (Helsinki) Commission on Security and Cooperation in Europe.

* Congressman Fascell chaired the commission from June 1976 to April 1985. The current chairman is Senator Alfonse D'Amato (R-N.Y.) — Ed.

delegations to all multilateral meetings of the Helsinki signatory states. The commission has also cooperated closely with nongovernmental organizations (NGOs) interested in promoting human rights within the East-West context, bringing their particular concerns to government attention while making government information on human rights in Eastern Europe and the Soviet Union more accessible to the private sector.

There are some decided advantages to working in the East bloc area compared to other parts of the world. U.S. diplomats and officials whose jurisdictions lie in the Soviet Union and Eastern Europe do not have to contend with as much disagreement among the branches of government, the political parties, the press and public over the existence, nature and underlying causes of human rights abuse in the East bloc. As President Ford learned during the 1976 presidential campaign when he badly misspoke himself on the subject of the Soviet Union's domination of Poland, Americans widely believe that the peoples of Eastern Europe and the Soviet Union are *not* free and consider human rights violations to be endemic to the political systems under which they are forced to live. Furthermore, there is a popular view in the United States that, if only to be true to our own historic tradition and system of values, the U.S. government ought to support the peaceful efforts of Eastern human rights advocates.

The Helsinki Commission's experience has shown that the conduct of an effective U.S. human rights policy toward the various East bloc countries must incorporate and integrate the following practical elements:

1. Constant monitoring of human rights conditions and systematic government reporting on human rights trends over time and in relation to the specific human rights commitments each East bloc country has made.

2. Full and coordinated use of international and domestic human rights mechanisms.

3. Cooperation among the executive and legislative bodies having human rights interests and responsibilities in the East bloc area and open communication with responsible nongovernmental organizations active in this field.

4. A frank, constructive and sustained exchange of views with the respective East bloc governments, whether on a bilateral basis or by means of multilateral mechanisms.

5. Close coordination and concerted action with NATO allies and consensus-building with the neutral and nonaligned governments of Europe.

Unfortunately, in most circumstances, the United States and other countries can do little more than condemn human rights violations once they have occurred. In the East, the decision to take repressive action depends primarily on intra-bloc and internal imperatives, which are perceived by the leadership to override international consequences. In such cases, the actions of the United States and other outside parties have no *determining* influence but may—if appropriately chosen and efficiently implemented—exert a restraining force.

Before taking any positive action in the human rights area, East bloc officials make the cold calculation: would a positive gesture serve their interests *more than would failure to take that step*? There is no such thing as a gratuitous humanitarian gesture in the East bloc context. It is in circumstances where (1) an East bloc regime does not perceive an immediate threat to power and where its own interests may be served by showing sensitivity to international human rights concerns, and (2) where there is considerable Western leverage and a willingness to use it in a concerted manner to achieve human rights goals, that the most successful human rights diplomacy can be carried on by Western governments.

Tools of the Trade

International Instruments

Increasingly, it has proven advantageous to pursue East-West human rights diplomacy outside the highly politicized superpower relationship and within a broader context. An orchestrated multilateral approach has the virtue of increasing leverage by compounding the political cost to the Eastern governments of human rights violations, while heightening their incentive to make progress.

By their own admission, the value systems of East bloc governments are fundamentally different from those of Western democracies. East bloc state/party systems subordinate human rights to the interests of the state and define them largely in socioeconomic as opposed to civil and political terms. This presents countless opportunities for East bloc diplomats to draw their Western counterparts into debates over "apples and oranges." Such empty exchanges invariably are accompanied by indignant Eastern protestations that human rights efforts by Western governments are simply arrogant attempts to impose our value system on their societies.

Nevertheless, as signatories to international agreements, East bloc governments also have committed themselves to respect the freedoms of thought, conscience, association, expression, belief and religion, as well as civil, political, cultural, minority and trade union rights.

International human rights documents necessarily contain compromise language acceptable to the broadest possible range of signatories. Naturally, Eastern countries try to manipulate every qualified phrase and interpret these texts in a self-serving manner. Very often, human rights exchanges between representatives of East and West resemble Humpty Dumpty's absurd conversation with Alice, in *Through the Looking Glass*: " 'When I use a word,' Humpty Dumpty said, in a rather scornful tone, 'it means just what I choose it to mean, neither more nor less.' "

Therefore, when interceding with East bloc counterparts on humanitarian matters, familiarity with the text and negotiating history of relevant human rights documents, and with the agreed procedures governing the operation of the international mechanisms associated with them, is essential.

The East bloc countries are party to most of the agreements that constitute the body of international law on the subject of human rights: the Charter of the United Nations; the Universal Declaration of Human Rights; the International Labor Organization conventions, particularly the Convention on Freedom of Association and Protection of the Right to Organize (#87) and the Convention on the Right to Organize and Bargain Collectively (#98); the International Covenants on Civil and Political Rights and Economic, Social and Cultural Rights; and, the International Convention on the Elimination of All Forms of Racial Discrimination. (It must be pointed out, however, that the key ILO conventions respecting human rights, the two covenants and the Convention on the Elimination of Racial Discrimination, although in accord with U.S. law and practice, have not been formally ratified by the United States for arcane constitutional reasons pertaining in large part to states' rights. Our country gratuitously has left itself open to international criticism on this score and has deprived officials engaged in human rights diplomacy of the full use of these important tools.)

By direct reference to the U.N. Charter, the Universal Declaration of Human Rights and the covenants, and by general reference to fulfilling in good faith the obligations assumed by participating states under international law, the Final Act of the Conference on Security and Cooperation in Europe (CSCE)—a nonbinding statement of international political intent—incorporates the substance of all of the aforementioned instruments of human rights diplomacy and applies them specifically to the East-West context.

The Helsinki Framework

The U.S. government's pursuit of an active human rights policy toward the East bloc as a region can be dated to the adoption of the Final Act on August 1, 1975 in Helsinki, Finland by the leaders of thirty-three nations of Eastern and Western Europe, plus Canada and the United States. Seen as the capstone of détente policy, the Final Act placed respect for fundamental human freedoms squarely within the East-West framework as a basic element of government-to-government relations. According to the Helsinki accords, a state's humane treatment of its citizens is deemed as significant as respect for a neighbor's frontiers or willingness to settle disputes peacefully. A second important precept of the Final Act is that the internal conduct of a state in the field of human rights becomes to a degree the international responsibility of all the participating states in the CSCE.

The Final Act's unique follow-up provisions call for periodic major review meetings—such as those held in Belgrade, Yugoslavia (1977–78) and Madrid, Spain (1980–83)—and for other spin-off fora, such as experts' meetings on particular facets of the Helsinki accords. The follow-up meetings provide opportunities for the signatory states to exchange views on the state of the Final Act's implementation and to adopt by consensual agreement new commitments which strengthen and expand upon the original Final Act provisions. Insofar as the Final Act lacks an enforcement mechanism, the periodic review meetings are an important means by which a signatory state may be taken to task before the court of world public opinion for the violation of Helsinki standards.

From the beginning, the West has acknowledged that full implementation of the Helsinki accords' human rights provisions realistically cannot be accomplished overnight and that Helsinki necessarily will be a long-term process. Open, democratic societies have comparatively little difficulty honoring Helsinki commitments—for them, fostering the flow of information, ideas and people across East-West frontiers and giving free rein internally to the exercise of human rights and fundamental liberties is the natural order of things. By contrast, the closed Communist systems of the East bloc are notoriously resistant to reform. Therefore, in evaluating the compliance records of East bloc countries, we look for patterns of conduct over time—rather than particular instances of compliance or noncompliance—as the true measure of Eastern good faith.

Generally speaking, in the years since the Helsinki accords were signed, East bloc human rights behavior has registered on the "bad to worse" end of the scale. Rare improvements in human rights conduct have been largely grudging, dilatory, cosmetic and calculated to serve *other* than humanitarian interests, generally signifying only temporary movement from the "bad" to the "less bad."

While giving full weight to the dominating Soviet presence, interests and influence in the region, we must remember that the human rights behavior of East bloc countries also has been conditioned by their own history, geopolitical situations, styles of leadership and each regime's perception of the national interest. Since Helsinki, the United States to some degree has tied development of bilateral relations with the various East European countries to good faith participation in CSCE and adherence to human rights pledges. By the same token, the Helsinki umbrella has afforded East European regimes greater latitude in establishing relationships with Western nations independently of the Soviet Union.

The Domestic Framework

In 1973, chiefly as a consequence of the controversy over our foreign policies toward repressive Third World countries, the U.S. Congress—in parallel to the international negotiation of the Helsinki accords—began to erect a domestic legislative framework to ensure that human rights considerations become an intrinsic component of global U.S. diplomacy. Through subsequent amendment of the Foreign Assistance Act of 1961, Congress made executive enforcement of human rights policy a requirement of U.S. law, and the State Department became legally bound to publish annually reports on human rights practices in countries throughout the world. Later, Congress passed the Jackson-Vanik amendment (Section 402) of the 1974 Trade Act, linking freedom of emigration to a Communist country's rights to have normal trading relations with the United States. [See the earlier chapter by John Salzberg and Appendix D for further legislative details.—Ed.]

In 1976, the creation by Congress of the U.S. (Helsinki) Commission on Security and Cooperation in Europe gave the conduct of East-West human rights diplomacy a unique institutional foundation within the U.S. government. The bipartisan commission was comprised of six members of the House of Representatives (including the chairman) and six from the Senate (including the co-chairman), and one member each of the State, Commerce, and Defense Departments.* The commission's seminal studies of the human rights records of East bloc signatory states laid the conceptual groundwork for all subsequent compliance reviews. To assist the commission in carrying out its monitoring duties, the law requires the president to submit to it semiannually a report on CSCE implementation by each of the East bloc signatory states.

Also in 1976, by further amendment of the Foreign Assistance Act of 1961, a coordinator for human rights and humanitarian affairs was established in the State Department. At the urging of Helsinki Commission Chairman Fascell, in 1977, President Carter signed subsequent legislation to upgrade the department's small human rights office into a bureau and elevate the human rights coordinator to assistant secretary level. In addition to the commission and the Bureau for Human Rights and Humanitarian Affairs, the Regional Political-Military Affairs Office of the European Bureau (responsible for NATO and CSCE affairs) and the respective East European and Soviet affairs desks at the State Department; the National Security Council's Soviet/East European affairs staff; elements of the United Nations Human Rights Commission and the International Labor Organization; congressional committees and subcommittees with legislative responsibilities involving human rights, bilateral trade and other matters with East bloc countries all have played significant and interdependent roles in developing and implementing our East-West human rights policy.

In addition to the work of official bodies, scores of nongovernmental organi-

---

* To underscore the bipartisan and bicameral nature of the commission, on March 27, 1985, President Reagan signed into law new legislation providing at the beginning of each Congress for a rotation of the Helsinki Commission chairmanship and co-chairmanship between the House and Senate. Accordingly, a new chairman from the Senate, Alfonse D'Amato (R-N.Y.), and a new co-chairman from the House, Steny H. Hoyer (D-MD), assumed the leadership of the commission on April 15, 1985. The number of commissioners from each chamber was increased from six to nine. — Ed.

zations (NGOs) monitor human rights conditions in the East bloc, publicize rights violations, exert public pressure on offending governments and provide invaluable support to U.S. diplomatic efforts. These organizations may be supranational and have a global human rights interest, like Amnesty International, or they may be U.S.-based and focussed specifically on East-West issues, such as the private Helsinki Watch in New York. NGOs may be geared toward religious, ethnic, national or labor rights concerns, such as the National Conference on Soviet Jewry, the American East European Ethnic Conference, the Joint Baltic American National Committee, or the Committee in Support of Solidarity. Groups organized along professional lines, such as the Committee of Concerned Scientists, Inc. or the American Psychiatric Association's Committee on the Abuse of Psychiatry and Psychiatrists, speak out for their persecuted colleagues in the East. Also, citizens may become personally involved in East-West human rights advocacy due to the victimization of a family member or friend. [See also Appendix E.—Ed.]

Consistent with the U.S. tradition of "open government," and with the Helsinki Final Act's express acknowledgment of the relevant and positive contributions private organizations and citizens make to the Helsinki process, the Helsinki Commission has successfully encouraged successive U.S. administrations to afford nongovernmental organizations opportunities to take an active part in the formation and conduct of human rights policy vis-a-vis the East bloc. For example, both at the Belgrade and (more extensively) Madrid CSCE review meetings, the Helsinki Commission ensured that NGO representatives and citizen experts served as advisors to or members of the U.S. delegations. Their presence demonstrated to the other signatory countries the interest in CSCE among a wide cross-section of the U.S. public.

Bilateral Instruments

The U.S. and other governments have employed a variety of bilateral foreign policy instruments, including high-level visits, cultural and scientific exchanges, and trade and other forms of economic cooperation to pursue human rights objectives. Dangling the carrot of increased U.S. cooperation, exchanges and trade, or, conversely, wielding the stick of their restriction or curtailment, signals U.S. approval or disapproval of the human rights practices of a given East bloc country.

However, the United States and other countries cannot respond effectively to repressive action on the part of Eastern countries if they, singly or collectively, lack sufficient leverage to affect the situation, or, having such leverage, lack the determination to use it because other foreign policy or domestic interests seriously conflict and take precedence. When egregious human rights violations are committed by an East bloc government, a U.S. failure to apply penalties, even when leverage is minimal and the effect largely symbolic, may cause the offender regime to conclude that the U.S. commitment to human rights is not credible and/or that the regime can act repressively with *political* impunity. Hence, President Reagan's unconditional lifting, for domestic reasons, in April 1981 of the grain embargo, which had been imposed on the Soviet Union by President Carter as a consequence of the invasion of Afghanistan, sent the wrong signal to the Soviet Union at a time of increasing internal repression in the USSR and the growing threat of a Soviet invasion of Solidarity Poland.

Economic leverage is generally regarded as the most powerful means by which the United States can influence East bloc behavior. The expansion of bilateral trade and economic cooperation, consistent with the Helsinki accords' provisions, constitutes an important component of our political relations with the various East bloc countries. But our ability to use the economic tool to improve the human rights situation in a particular country is conditioned and limited by a number of factors: 1) the dependence of the country's economy on foreign trade generally; 2) the amount of U.S. involvement in the country's foreign trade; 3) the country's ability to turn to trading partners other than the United States; and 4) the willingness of other governments having a significant economic impact on particular East bloc economies to use economic leverage in concert with the United States.

These factors are interrelated and circumstances vary greatly among the countries of Eastern Europe and the Soviet Union. Although the U.S. has made up a very small proportion of Soviet trade, it has played a more significant role in the economies of some East European countries. Where U.S. economic ties have been fairly significant, as with Poland, Hungary and Romania, the application of economic leverage has led to the resolution of humanitarian problems.

It is important to remember that many West European countries (Italy, Finland, France and the Federal Republic of Germany, in particular) conduct more trade with the East than does the United States. The cost to the United States of imposing the economic stick is not very great except with respect to grain and perhaps a few other products. West European countries that trade more heavily with the East have a much bigger stake in East-West commerce. They have greater leverage, but also a much greater hesitancy to use it as a negative incentive. Hence, our ineffectiveness in persuading NATO allies to participate in meaningful economic sanctions against the USSR—particularly those related to construction of the export gas pipeline from Siberia to Western Europe—and against the martial law regime in Poland.

Conclusion

Certainly, human rights work with the East bloc would seem to present a challenge worthy of Sisyphus. But a great deal has been accomplished already. In less than a decade human rights diplomacy has become a fact of daily life in the conduct of East-West relations. In a few short years, the United States and other Western nations have gone from asking *whether* we should pursue an active human rights policy toward the East, to debating *how* most effectively to go about it. The Helsinki process as a whole and the galvanizing influence of the Helsinki Commission within the U.S. government in particular have ensured that the victims of East bloc repression are now not so easily dispatched, unnoticed and unremarked, to the Gulag—an accomplishment almost inconceivable ten years ago and one that should not be underestimated or taken for granted today. The West's persistent, concerted and compassionate efforts have led to some positive results. These hard-won successes—even if they have not produced systemic change—have made profound differences in the lives of individuals.

Our fundamental humanitarian objective was perhaps put most succinctly by physicist Yuri Orlov, founder of the Moscow Helsinki Group and a prisoner of conscience since 1977: "By our efforts, we increase the probability that in the end we shall be successful."

Chapter 4

The Response of Europe and the Third World to United States Human Rights Diplomacy

R. J. Vincent

The perspectives of Europe on human rights issues are similar to those of the United States, but the emphases in diplomacy may differ. The Third World perspective is often quite different from that of either the United States or Europe. Professor Vincent tells why.

In contemporary international politics the making of diplomatic points about human rights is most closely associated with the foreign policy of the United States, especially during the Carter administration. But the arrival of the issue of human rights in international society is not the result of American preoccupations alone. After the First World War, to take but two examples, the minorities treaties and the establishment of the International Labour Organization showed a general recognition that the society of states should concern itself with the interests of groups and individuals outside the world of states. And at the end of the Second World War, the attention given to human rights in the Charter of the United Nations was a more explicit recognition that international society should make the rights of individuals and groups other than states one of its great purposes.

This has not disposed of the principle of nonintervention, which, as the states-members of the United Nations tirelessly point out—especially in response to the enthusiasms of others for human rights—is still a central principle of the international legal order. The new states of the Third World that have just gained their sovereignty, and thus their entitlement to the protection of the principle of nonintervention, are highly sensitive to what they perceive to be the 'cultural imperialism' lying behind the mask of human rights. The old states of Europe, conscious of their loss of autonomy with the rise of the new super-powers, tend to be skeptical of the ideological zealotry of both those powers at the same time as being anxious to preserve their traditional liberties. And the superpowers themselves, especially when reacting to the dogma of the other, are quick to insist on their sovereignty: the United States to protect its unique institutions from an inferior international law, the Soviet Union to preserve intact its exclusive competence when it comes to the implementation of what it accepts as the international law of human rights.

The impact of human rights on contemporary international politics, then, can be rendered partly in terms of the advance of cosmopolitan values on the redoubt of state sovereignty, and partly in terms of the attempt by some powers to gain ideological advantage at the expense of others. This ambiguity dogs the path of any state taking up the issue of human rights in foreign policy. What to the initiating state is the selfless pursuit of universal values is interpreted by outsiders as the attempt to camouflage self-interest.[1] The horns of the dilemma this presents are particularly sharp for the United States. If it neglects the idealistic element in its tradition, the sense in which its revolution was the beginning of emancipation for all humankind, it erodes the domestic legitimacy of its foreign policy. But if it carries its tradition abroad in the spirit of Woodrow Wilson's commitment to democratic values everywhere, it runs into the charge of disregarding the traditions of others that are said to have an equal stake in international society.[2]

The object of this chapter is to ask how the United States has fared on the latter horn of the dilemma by observing and commenting on the reception of the American commitment to human rights among its Western European allies, where it might look for some understanding, if not for wholehearted support, and in the Third World, where the new revolutions invite skepticism towards the continuing appeal of the old ones.

I

In Western Europe, especially among its fellow members of the Atlantic alliance, the United States might expect to find some common ground with its own official view of human rights. For here is the source of the liberal tradition on which its own revolution was founded, and also the place where the principles derived therefrom seemed, in the Cold War, most under threat. In-deed, the Cold War itself could be interpreted as at root a disagreement between East and West about human rights, in which being Western was more fundamental than being American or European. So whenever the Western allies were gathered together to discuss human rights among themselves or with others, the surprise was when they failed to agree on basics, not when they agreed. It was natural that they should line up behind civil and political rights of individuals against the Eastern preference for economic and social rights, for liberty and property against equality and welfare.

We might examine the quality of this solidarity in three arenas: East-West, as, for example, in the Helsinki process; North-South as, for example, in attitudes to economic development; and within Europe, as, for example, in attitudes towards the left in Western European politics.

As is well-known, the Conference on Security and Cooperation in Europe was not the result of a Western initiative. It took place when the West had finally persuaded itself that the Soviet desire for formal recognition of its post-war position in Eastern Europe was no more than the description of an established fact. And within the West, it was the Europeans who led in believing that such matters as family reunification, liberalization of travel, freer flow of information, and better conditions for journalists might be pushed at Helsinki as the Western side of the bargain. When the Final Act was signed on August 1, 1975, the response in the United States was not overwhelming, and the State Department "played down the conference as an exercise which was primarily of interest to the allies of the United States...."[3]

As the Helsinki Final Act became the Helsinki process with the follow-up conferences at Belgrade and Madrid, there was greater American appreciation that the accords were not simply a sell-out to the interests of the Soviet Union, and of the diplomatic embarrassment that the human rights provisions of the agreement might cause the Soviet bloc. And with greater American enthusiasm came greater European caution as, for example, in President Giscard d'Estaing's preference for quiet diplomacy in pursuit of human rights in the Soviet Union, and also in Chancellor Schmidt's preference for the concrete achievements of both German-German and German-Soviet détente over the ideological pronouncements of those with no relatives in East Berlin. More recently, only Mrs. Thatcher in Europe has matched the stridency of the Reagan administration's association of human rights with anti-communism.

There is no cause for allied alarm in these shifts of position. It may be compared to different individuals from the same team taking it in turns to lead the pack in the Tour de France. Moreover, it is part of the pattern of alliance politics that each member should be skeptical about the initiatives of others, and that each should present as an alliance interest its special preoccupation. There has been some of this during the Helsinki process, but generally the human rights objectives of the West have been similarly perceived, and the problems the subject has caused the Soviet Union, problems it cannot avoid having accepted the legitimacy of their discussion, have been a payoff for all the Western powers. This is not an area in which the United States can make the conventional leader's complaint about the loyalty of the followers, nor the Europeans the conventional follower's complaint about the arrogance of the leader. Though we might add that this is an area of public diplomacy where principles may be agreed upon without private sacrifice.[4]

In their attitudes to the place of human rights in North-South relations, there is revealed a more substantial difference between Americans and Europeans than in their differences of tactics on the East-West chessboard. Both the United States and the European countries have long-standing policies of economic aid to developing countries. In both places, the economic professionals have been skeptical of the intrusion of the lawyers' concern with human rights into their province of development.[5] But the lawyers have made more progress in the United States than in Europe. Thus, for example, the amendments to the United States Foreign Assistance Act requiring that aid not be given to any country "the government of which engages in gross violations of internationally recognized human rights."[6]

In the European Community's development cooperation agreements with the African, Caribbean and Pacific (ACP) countries, the commitment to civil and political rights as a prerequisite for aid has been resisted by the developing states. In Lomé III,[7] for example, there is emphasis on the right of all participating states to determine their own political, economic and social systems. Moreover, while the EEC is committed to promoting ACP economic development, the shape of domestic development is a matter for those countries alone.[8] This may be merely a measure of the negotiating power of the ACP countries at Lomé, compared to the unilateral engagements of American legislation. But there is also more of a disposition in Europe to consider economic development as an end in itself that should not be disrupted by too much attention to the politics of human rights. This is best illustrated by Swedish aid policy, which has been described as "moralistic or even sanctimonious" in tone, not on behalf of the classical western liberties, but rather in pursuit of "conditions for development characterized by economic and social equalization."[9]

This difference reflects a disagreement about the definition of human rights between the United States and Europe that has its impact in our third arena—within Western Europe. For, whereas official recognition in the United States of the importance of economic and social rights (making development aid an obligation, not an act of charity) featured briefly in the Carter administration, there is a deeper European commitment to the importance of these rights as evidenced by the signature of the European Social Charter in 1961.[10] This openness to accepting as part of the definition of human rights the view of them favored by the Eastern bloc marks off Europe from the official United States. For while the Europeans have reached out for a definition of human rights that may apply to everyone regardless of their political circumstances, in the United States the tendency is more to take human rights as ideological armament for the war with the East, to see them as the weapons with which to change political circumstances in a particular direction.[11] This, in a realist interpretation, may merely result from the different geopolitical positions of the United States and Western Europe, location and relative power predisposing doctrine. But it might also be interpreted as the contemporary manifestation of the traditional divide between an American revolution that was fought to constitute liberty against oppression, and a French revolution that was fought to establish freedom from want.[12] The "welfare ethic" in European politics, which troubles Americans as a sign of incipient softness towards communism, is within Europe part of an indigenous tradition established long before the Soviet Union took up the cause.

There are, then, strategic differences between the Americans and Europeans on human rights and not merely tactical ones. But the extent to which they emerge has depended on the situation. In the Helsinki process, the liberty party has been dominant, and the members of the Western coalition have got from it roughly equal satisfaction. But in North-South relations, and also in relations between the United States and Western Europe, the division within the Western human rights tradition between liberty and equality has been more exposed. In these circumstances, a foreign policy of human rights assembles no automatic Western coalition, and may lead professional diplomats to regret the inclusion on their agenda of so contentious an issue.

II

While between the United States and Western Europe the common bond of liberal political theory is substantial enough to make their collaboration on the issue of human rights at least a continuing possibility, the connecting bridge between the United States and the Third World is more rickety. It is not that their theoretical starting places are completely alien from each other, for we shall shortly see that the Third World conceptions of human rights are informed by a principle of self-determination which can itself be traced from a Western root. But the collectivism of the Third World interpretation of this doctrine sets it against the individualism that still unites Americans and Europeans.

Third World doctrine on human rights, as principally developed at the United Nations, can be described in terms of three layers of interpretation of the principle of self-determination. This principle, written into the Charter of the United Nations, meant first of all for the Third World freedom from colonial rule. This was a precondition for the enjoyment of all other human rights. Once the nation had been delivered from external oppression, then there might be the possibility of internal liberty, but the first freedom was that of the group. Then, in the second layer of interpretation of the principle of self-determination, the obstacle to freedom is also external: it is the racial discrimination still practiced by those maintaining a colonialist disposition, especially in and towards South Africa. And the third layer of interpretation reached in the Southern doctrine of self-determination is the economic and social one. Here, once more, it is the external obstruction of the old international economic order that stands in the path of the realization of the Third World right to development.

Human rights, in these interpretations, impose obligations on the First and Second Worlds (and especially the former) and make the Third World the beneficiary of their fulfillment. So the Western, and especially the American, notion of a place for human rights in its diplomacy, confronts immediately the Third World view that it is the West, and especially the Americans, that have duties in this area, not them, and that the international system itself is a barrier to the establishment domestically of regimes of human rights.

This is at least a plausible view, and it is one that the more sensitive observers of human rights in the West have taken seriously.[13] But if it were taken literally, as well as seriously, it would withdraw the whole domestic experience of politics in the Third World from any external moral scrutiny. And this is an extreme to which Third World countries have rarely gone. For while they have not hesitated to deploy their doctrine of human rights to extract what they can from those they see as the delinquent powers, when it is their records that are under scrutiny they have generally sought to defend themselves in terms of principles they share with their critics rather than invoking their right to apply whatever domestic standards they choose. The question for both critics and criticized has, in practice, been how to take account of the views of the other and what weight to give them, rather than simply to take them or leave them. It has been a question of how to manage the question of human rights in international relations. Let us consider, firstly, the general position of the United States on human rights in the Third World, and then three different kinds of Third World reaction to its human rights advocacy.

We have seen that, going back to the Founding Fathers, the idea that American foreign policy should be guided by principle and not be merely the reaction to circumstance is deeply embedded in American political culture. So when President Carter said at his inauguration that "because we are free, we can never be indifferent to the fate of freedom elsewhere," we knew that we had heard this before. What was different about the Carter administration was its explicit adoption of human rights both as a standard by which to judge the conduct of others and as a set of principles that was to guide its own foreign policy. In a speech at Athens, Georgia, in April 1977, that was to become famous, Secretary of State Vance spelled out the criteria.[14] The scope of United States concern included the integrity of the person (freedom from torture, inhumane punishment, arbitrary arrest), the fulfillment of basic needs (food, shelter, health care, and education), and the classical civil and political liberties (freedom of thought, religion, speech, movement). In the Reagan administration this scope narrowed to the first and third concerns, and human rights became again a stick with which to beat others rather than a basis for self-reproach.

American foreign policy with regard to human rights, even during the

Reagan administration, has not been a matter of announcing some doctrinal position to the world and then expecting the world to act on it. In the practice of its foreign policy, the United States has not been as insensitive to the different views of others as some of its critics have maintained. It is, after all, part of the craft of diplomacy to find the local formula by means of which to convey the preoccupations of one member of international society to another. But the effort has met with varying success, and we may consider here three different kinds of Third World reaction to the human rights policy of the United States: contempt, cynicism, and accommodation.

The contemptuous reaction of the Third World to United States policy was illustrated by Argentina and Brazil during the Carter administration. When, in February 1977, Secretary Vance announced a reduction in military assistance to Argentina because of its human rights record, the regime responded with the charge that this was an interference in its internal affairs, and to convey its displeasure it rejected the aid still remaining in an already appropriated fund. Brazil responded similarly to an adverse report on its human rights record prepared by the State Department, telling the United States to keep its military assistance, and going on to abrogate a series of military agreements with the United States.[15] Contempt here sprang from offended pride. It was not merely that the United States was interfering. Much of the Latin American approach to foreign policy had been built on the response to the interference of the United States. It was more the personal insult involved in the criticism of domestic conduct: one prince calling another names for his treatment of his family.

A second class of reaction has been the cynical one, illustrated by Iran, South Korea, and the Philippines. There are three aspects to this. There is firstly the notion that the United States is the great power on whose support a client depends. If the United States requires some changes in the policy of the client in order to legitimize its policy at home, then the client may concede the changes as the price of alliance. An example of this is the Shah of Iran's response to the Carter administration's human rights policy: releasing some prominent political prisoners, improving prison conditions and allowing the Red Cross to visit some of them, and reducing the incidence of torture.[16] We may call this cynical because it reflects neither any indigenous determination to improve, nor willingness to move far beyond the changes necessary for the payment of alliance dues.

Next there is the higher cynicism of some of those countries that are host to American bases, in exchange for the leasing of which military and economic assistance might be called "rent."[17] And if the relationship between the United States and the state in which the bases are located can be reduced to this commercial minimum, then there is no basis for linkage to the human rights issue. Both patron and client recognize that security is the value that is being paid for through the bases, and the minor hypocrisies of the patron with regard to client human rights do not need to be taken seriously. This is sometimes represented as the situation that exists between the United States and the Philippines.[18]

Then there is the highest cynicism of a state in a position similar to the Philippines manipulating its geopolitical position to blackmail the patron power. So far from the great power's insisting on certain domestic proprieties if its assistance is to be sustained, the client state hints that it might look elsewhere for arms or aid if the current patron considers reducing them as a signal of attachment to human rights. South Korea, it is said, has used this threat on occasion to keep the United States in line.[19]

Our third suggested response was accommodation. Indonesia is one example of this response. David Newsom shows this in his chapter below. The anxieties of the United States regarding the number of political prisoners in Indonesia were pressed to some point with the relevant authorities, and as long as the question was handled sensitively the initiative was not futile. In this case, it seems, reward was thought to be as important as the threat of punishment—acknowledgement by the United States that the Indonesians were attempting genuinely to move in its direction. Such a policy carries its own dangers, for it might involve the congratulation of a regime with many skeletons still in its cupboard. Congratulations for this reason need not be effusive. Thailand is a similar case of an accommodating response to a friendly nation's susceptibilities, with subsequent acknowledgement by the United States that movement is taking place in the right direction.[20]

These three responses are not mutually exclusive. A country reacting to United States human rights diplomacy may be at the same time contemptuous, cynical, and accommodating. Indeed, the response in Latin America may be expected to be all three at the same time, given the history of hemispheric international relations. And we might add that, from the point of view of the advocate of human rights, even the cynical reaction is tolerable because it moves, or helps to move, the trend of affairs in the right direction (provided, that is, that South Koreans are not allowed to get away with turning the maxims of power politics on their head). In this regard, the doctrinal bastions built by the Third World countries on the question of human rights have not been sufficiently strong defenses against the doctrinal penetration of the great powers. They are plausible, and they have played the major part in the public diplomacy of human rights at the United Nations, but they have not snuffed out the Western concern with the basic rights of individuals everywhere.

This, however, is not a celebration of cynicism. If the United States is to have any expectation of a positive response abroad to the concern for human rights which comes from its domestic political experience, it must itself be consistently attached to them. For if, as Richard Ullman has pointed out, the United States winks at its own advocacy so that there is private disregard of its public principles, then the diplomacy of human rights becomes a pointless charade.[21]

III

On the basis of this brief survey, we should hesitate to come to Stanley Hoffmann's conclusion that there is an "extraordinary lack of public support for a human rights policy outside the United States."[22] There have been circumstances in which the Europeans have led on human rights, not followed, and the Third World countries have led in many aspects of the debate on human rights at the United Nations, where they have the numbers. Their leadership in these circumstances means their failure necessarily to follow the United States, which may be a cause for American concern.[23] Beyond parliamentary diplomacy, which has its own rules, whatever issue a great power chooses to take up in its foreign policy will be of interest to all the others, including other great powers, and we might expect a response in international society generally to anything the United States makes a point of. It is too facile to argue that the rise and fall of attention to human rights in the world as a whole correlates with the rise and fall of American power, but the two are not unrelated.[24] Whether the reaction to United States human rights diplomacy is contemptuous or accommodating, there has to be a reaction; the American initiative cannot simply be disregarded.

In the light of this we might ask ourselves in conclusion how the United States might make the most successful impact in behalf of the furtherance of human rights in the world. This is a question that has been much debated over the last decade, and it is not our intention here to examine all the measures from quiet diplomacy to war that might conceivably be taken. But our task in this chapter has been to assess the response to United States human rights diplomacy in Europe and in the Third World, and we might conclude with three observations about how to make that response a positive one.

The first of these has to do with what principles to adopt. True policy for the United States would be to shackle a realist perception of its impact on international politics to a conception of human rights which others can accept as fundamental without doing violence to their different ideologies. This would mean that the United States would be expected to lead on the issue, but others would not regard it as a denial of the uniqueness of their institutions to follow. The human rights placed at the center of policy should be basic rights in the sense of rights that everyone ought to enjoy—security, subsistence, liberty—regardless of political circumstances, and not simply a list of what we happen to be good at. And it should be shown that these basic rights are as much about their rights as they are about ours. The principle of self-determination, it should be argued, is not worth having without them. And to this conception of basic rights should be added a judgement about what in the world constitutes the worst offence to them. If American advocates of a policy of human rights showed more interest in the closing of a newspaper in Central America than they did in the wholesale loss of life in Central Africa, the constituency outside the United States whose sympathy is crucial for a successful human rights policy might be lost. Basic rights should be connected to worst cases.

Then the second way of aiming at a positive response in the world outside to a United States human rights policy is to come to the problem with clean hands, in order to avoid what is to a human rights policy the crippling charge of hypocrisy. It is not enough that the United States have a good domestic human rights record (not an unblemished one, which is impossible); its international policy must also stand up to scrutiny. Otherwise the South Korean or the Filippino argument about hypocrisy can be used to deadly effect. This is the point made by the people who argue, both in and out of the United States, that the first step to take in getting human rights into foreign policy is to meet any obligations that we have correlative to the human rights of others, as distinct from persuading others to live up to their obligations.

In the third place, when an issue is taken up, the United States should act in as wide a coalition as possible for identifiable goals whose achievement it is possible to recognize. The wide coalition does not mean that every time the United States ambassador mentions the issue of human rights at the Ruritanian foreign office it needs to have the Western alliance lined up behind it. More effective may be allied consistency in their separate representations—just as a thousand letters from individuals agitated about some human rights issue are more impressive than one letter with a thousand signatures. The clarity of the objective means resisting the temptation to attach oneself to human rights as a generalized formula for improvement in the world. The most impressive human rights campaigns, such as that for the abolition of the slave trade, have taken up a single overriding issue, have had the support of a wide coalition, and have been led by a great power. This may be the model that the United States should have chiefly in mind.[25]

It may be said that the injunction of selflessness expects too much of a mere state in a world of states whose concern in that society is to pursue its partial interests. The reply to this is that the pursuit of partial interests should not fly under the misleading flag of human rights. For the pursuit of the objective of human rights to have any credibility it must be shown to have some integrity apart from the mere interests of the pursuers. This, it barely needs stating, makes of human rights a low priority in the foreign policies of states. They are the business of the community of humankind not of the society of states. But what little can be done should not be blown away by partiality.

Notes

1 This is a characteristic Latin American theme in protest against the foreign policy of the United States. See Franciso, Orrego, "Latin America," in R. J. Vincent (ed.),

Foreign Policy and Human Rights: Issues and Responses (forthcoming from Cambridge University Press).

2 For two useful treatments of the American tradition, see Tracy B. Strong, "Taking the Rank with What Is Ours: American Political Thought, Foreign Policy and Questions of Rights," in Paula R. Newberg (ed.), *The Politics of Human Rights* (New York & London: New York University Press, 1980; and Arthur Schlesinger, Jr., "Human Rights and the American Political Tradition, *Foreign Affairs: America and the World 1978* (New York: Council on Foreign Relations, 1979).

3 Harold S. Russell, "The Helsinki Declaration: Brobdingnag or Lilliput?" *American Journal of International Law* 70, 2 (April 1976), p. 242.

4 For the view that this is the level at which the question of human rights ought to remain in international relations, see Adam Watson, *Diplomacy: The Dialogue Between States* (New York: McGraw Hill, 1983), p. 80.

5 See, e.g., Paul Streeten, *First Things First: Meeting Basic Human Needs in Developing Countries* (New York: Oxford University Press, 1981).

6 For useful extracts see *United States Foreign Policy and Human Rights: Principles, Priorities, Practice* (A Report of the National Policy Panel of UNA-USA, December 1979), Appendix B.

7 Third ACP-EEC Convention, signed at Lomé, Togo on 8 December 1984.—Ed.

8 See Carol Cosgrave, "Lomé III," *The World Today* 41, 2 (February 1985).

9 Goran Ohlin, "Swedish Aid Performance and Development Policy," in Bruce Dinwiddy (ed.), *European Development Policies* (New York: Praeger, 1973), pp. 56, 52.

10 See A. H. Robertson, *Human Rights in the World* (2nd ed., New York: St. Martin's Press, 1982), pp. 197-207.

11 This is to characterize the dominant tendency in official American attitudes. This generalization is not meant to cover all American attitudes. For a prominent American protest against the official tendency, see Henry Shue, *Basic Rights* (Princeton: Princeton University Press, 1980).

12 See Hannah Arendt, *On Revolution* (London: Faber, 1958), p. 68.

13 For sensitivity to cultural pluralism, see Kenneth W. Thompson (ed.), *The Moral Imperatives of Human Rights: A World Survey* (Washington: University Press of America, 1980). On Western duties, see Shue, *Basic Rights*.

14 See appendix B for text of this speech.—Ed.

15 See U.S. Library of Congress, Foreign Affairs and National Defense Division, *Human Rights Conditions in Selected Countries and the U.S. Response*, prepared for the Committee on International Relations, U.S. House of Representatives (Washington: U.S. Government Printing Office, 1978), pp. 31, 45.

16 See Richard W. Cottam, "Arms Sales and Human Rights: The Case of Iran," in Peter G. Brown and Douglas MacLean, *Human Rights and U.S. Foreign Policy* (Lexington: D.C. Heath, 1979) p. 294. [See also Chapter 7 below by David McGaffey on U.S. human rights diplomacy in Iran.—Ed.]

17 Richard P. Claude, "Human Rights in the Philippines and U.S. Responsibility," in Brown and MacLean, *Human Rights*, p. 238.

18 Ibid.

19 See David N. Ranard, "Korea, Human Rights and United States Foreign Policy,"

in Tom J. Farer (ed.), *Toward a Humanitarian Diplomacy* (New York and London: New York University Press, 1980), p. 209. [For another account of U.S. human rights diplomacy in Korea, see chapter 8 by William H. Gleysteen, Jr.—Ed.]

20 U.S. Library of Congress, *Human Rights Conditions*, p. 290.

21 Richard H. Ullman, "Introduction" to Jorge I. Dominguez et. al., *Enhancing Global Human Rights* (New York: McGraw Hill, 1979), p. 16.

22 Stanley Hoffman, *Duties Beyond Borders* (Syracuse: Syracuse University Press, 1981), p. 119.

23 See Daniel P. Moynihan, "The United States in Opposition," *Commentary* 59, 3 (March 1975).

24 Samuel Huntington, "Human Rights and American Power," *Commentary* (September 1981).

25 See Charles H. Fairbanks, Jr. with the assistance of Eli Nathans, "The British Campaign against the Slave Trade: An Example of Successful Human Rights Policy," in Fred E. Baumann (ed.), *Human Rights and American Foreign Policy* (Gambier, Ohio: Public Affairs Conference Center, 1982).

Chapter 5

Unilateral Human Rights Intercession: American Practice under Nixon, Ford, and Carter

Jeffrey D. Merritt

Human rights concerns have long been present in some form in every recent U.S. administration. Jeffrey Merritt shows how concerns and actions differ.

A government's principal duties are to protect the security, interests and rights of its own citizens—not of other nations' citizens. Few governments try, and still fewer are able, to protect human rights abroad. Because of its heritage and influence, the United States has sometimes been well positioned to intercede. Yet, after years of debate and experimentation, controversy continues as to whether, when, and how it should respond to foreign abuses.

This paper explores the phenomenon of unilateral human rights intercession[1] by examining the Nixon, Ford, and Carter administrations. To provide additional focus, the author briefly compares those administrations' responses to human rights violations in Brazil, Uganda, and the Soviet Union.[2]

U.S. officials face hard choices in addressing sensitive human rights problems while looking after other important American interests. Among the considerations ["factors"] policymakers must evaluate and juggle are:

—relevant domestic and international law;

—U.S. [bilateral] relations with "target" governments;

—international relations [involving "third" states], and U.S. national security;

—domestic politics and economics;

—the safety and interests of U.S. nationals;

—individual leadership qualities and needs.

Nixon Administration Response to Human Rights Violations

The Nixon administration did not weigh human rights heavily in its foreign policy decision making, believing the United States should deal with governments irrespective of how they treated their own citizens. President Nixon and National Security Adviser [later, Secretary of State] Kissinger saw little utility in public scoldings. Nor were they eager to engage in traditional ("quiet") human rights diplomacy. Top administration officials never explicitly rejected a right to intercede, but their words and actions reflected tolerance of "domestic jurisdiction" and "noninterference" arguments. Cautious U.S. diplomats lacked clear guidance as to what evolving international human rights law allowed or required them to do.[3]

Indeed, from 1969 to 1974 there was only one full-time human rights officer in the executive branch. The human rights officer had little impact on policy decisions of a bilateral nature. His primary responsibility was to monitor human rights issues at the United Nations. While the State Department claimed to weigh human rights together with other relevant considerations in making policy, critics charged that political, economic, and military considerations usually crowded out human rights. The administration conceded that State was not perfectly organized to deal with human rights questions, but resisted most congressional suggestions for greater bureaucratic attention to human rights. Reforms made in 1974 were largely cosmetic and had virtually no impact on policy at the top of the administration.

The upsurge in congressional human rights interest in 1973 and 1974 stemmed, in part, from disillusionment with Vietnam policy and Watergate "morality." It also grew from accumulated evidence that the administration rarely factored human rights into foreign policy and often condoned or supported brutish regimes. Washington's role in Chile's coup and repressive aftermath recalled U.S. backing for Greece's colonels, martial law regimes in South Korea and the Philippines, Iberian dictators, and several Latin American military governments. Its posture during bloody civil wars in Nigeria and Pakistan and its status-quo orientation toward southern Africa also contributed to a growing human rights clamor.

Ford Administration Response to Human Rights Violations

Secretary of State Kissinger's continued preeminence in foreign policy ensured that the Ford administration's approach to human rights differed only marginally from the Nixon administration's. Kissinger defended administration support for certain abusive regimes as essential for U.S. security, arguing that

you cannot implement your values unless you survive....Wherever we can, we are trying to nudge [these regimes] in a direction that is compatible with our values. But to pretend that we can simply declare our values and transform the world has a high risk of a policy of constant interventionism in every part of the world and then sticking us with the consequences.[4]

The Ford administration confronted an "activist" Congress that was increasingly determined to reverse the amorality of Watergate, Vietnam, and realpolitik. Congress adopted nonbinding legislation which directed that the president end military aid to governments engaged in "a consistent pattern of gross violations of internationally recognized human rights" unless "extraordinary circumstances" warranted such assistance.[5] When the administration balked at compliance—and also refused to submit comprehensive human rights reports on aid recipients[6]—Congress tightened the requirements.

Hearings sometimes exposed administration officials as insensitive apologists for abusive regimes. More often, reluctant or inconsistent testimony underscored the dangers of "clientism" and the need for greater human rights policy coordination within the administration. Modest steps were taken to strengthen a weak human rights bureaucracy, but the new office of Coordinator for Humanitarian Affairs was really "no factor" in administration policymaking. Proposals for strengthening the human rights component in U.S. foreign policy were routinely resisted by Secretary Kissinger,[7] and time ran out on the Policy Planning Staff's effort "to formulate criteria for more thoughtful and consistent implementation of human rights provisions in existing legislation."[8]

Public criticism of repressive regimes was rare and private diplomacy sporadic. Administration intercession was often limited to telling offending governments that Congress was annoyed and might take measures if violations continued. Even a private demarche suggesting congressional displeasure could land a diplomat in Kissinger's bad graces, as Ambassador David Popper, discovered after raising human rights issues with Chilean officials in 1974. Kissinger's widely circulated comment—"Tell Popper to cut out the political science lectures"[9]—undoubtedly chilled many a contemplated intercession over the next two years.

Carter Administration Response to Human Rights Violations

President Carter's decision to make human rights a central foreign policy theme was politically expedient, but it also reflected a sincere moral and religious belief. Secretary of State Vance articulated the need for the United States to be realistic about what it could hope to achieve in promoting human rights abroad: "In the end, a decision whether and how to act in the cause of human rights is a matter for informed or careful judgment. No mechanistic formula produces an automatic answer." Vance cited questions to be answered where intercession was contemplated: What is the nature of the violation? What are the prospects for effective U.S. action? What other U.S. interests need to be considered?[10] For insiders, Vance's speech raised as many questions as it answered. Time-consuming policy reviews also produced few pat prescriptions—and many headaches—for confused bureaucrats.

The problem of "consistency" bedeviled the administration, as it differentiated responses according to a violator's history, culture, and "demographics," as well as its relationship to the United States. Inevitably, there were resentments and charges of administration hypocrisy: Why criticize El Salvador but not South Korea? Why challenge Moscow but not Peking?

The administration conceded the imperfection of its policy, but always ruled out a "quick-fix human rights formula." Political considerations dominated the analytic process by which countries received attention.[11] National Security Adviser Zbigniew Brzezinski explained why some degree of selectivity and inconsistency was necessary if human rights were to be advanced.

...If, in fact, you are in a position, without damaging your other relationships, to make progress in the case of country A but not progress in the case of country B, should you therefore abstain from making progress in country A? I would say no.[12]

Tactically, the Carter administration preferred quiet diplomacy. Private discussions generally occurred at a higher level than in previous administrations, however.[13] The administration complemented traditional diplomacy with public criticism, symbolic actions, and foreign aid pressures. By 1978, officials spoke of a "sequential and calibrated diplomatic strategy,"[14] with public criticism or sanctions sometimes following the failure of quiet persuasion to produce positive change. Critics found the administration's tactics somewhat less than systematic, however.

The Carter administration sought to weave human rights throughout the entire bureaucracy. Under Patt Derian, the Bureau of Human Rights and Humanitarian Affairs [HA] usually took a "human rights advocacy" position in policy battles with State's regional bureaus and other executive departments. HA played an important role in decisions on economic aid—especially multilateral loans—but had much less clout on military assistance.

Congress pressed the generally sympathetic administration for an even greater emphasis on human rights. By 1979 human rights provisions were in legislation governing most U.S. foreign assistance programs. The administration tried, where possible, to use aid to induce human rights observance. But many critics—in and out of government—believed its overall approach was too punitive, especially in Latin America.

Carter admits that the United States "paid a price for its emphasis on human rights," namely the resentment of a number of repressive regimes. Aware that many detractors feel his human rights policies contributed to even greater losses—the replacement of "friendly" regimes in Iran and Nicaragua by governments hostile to the United States—the former President writes:

> There is no doubt that a few of these [oppressive regimes] could have been spared both embarrassment and the danger of being overthrown if they had strengthened themselves by eliminating the abuses. For those who did not survive, it may be that our emphasis on human rights was not wrong, but too late. Had America argued for these principles sooner, such foreign leaders might not have allowed themselves to become too isolated to correct the abuses without violence.[15]

Case Study Findings: Brazil, Uganda, and the Soviet Union

Brazil

In Brazil, a long-standing American ally of considerable strategic and political importance in the hemisphere, torture of political prisoners intensified in the aftermath of the military government's crackdown on political dissent and subversive activity. The Nixon administration rarely expressed public displeasure with these violations and, in fact, continued to lend Brazil military, economic, and diplomatic support. Charges that U.S. officials actually trained and supervised torturers have not been substantiated, however.

The Ford administration, believing the new Geisel government demonstrated a willingness to correct abuses by hard-line military elements, continued its military support of Brasilia and concluded a "consultation" agreement in 1976.[16] By questioning that agreement—and criticizing Brazil's human rights record—the Carter administration produced a nationalistic reaction. Brasilia reacted particularly sharply to the State Department's report on its conduct and cut several military ties. Visits to Brazil by the president (1978) and Mrs. Carter (1977) also highlighted the human rights issue.

Uganda

Idi Amin's January 1971 coup against Milton Obote's government plunged Uganda into a deepening morass of political/tribal killings. Although it did "rupture" diplomatic relations in 1973, the Nixon administration took few meaningful actions, outside of support for weak international efforts, to pressure Amin's government. Despite increasing evidence of massive violations, the Ford administration made no move to end economic transactions involving U.S. firms—dealings that were of vital importance to the regime's maintenance, but of little significance to the United States. It did, however, publicly demonstrate displeasure with Idi Amin and his policies.

President Carter's remarks critical of Ugandan killings triggered a new threat against Americans by Amin. Although the administration strengthened diplomatic and economic restrictions, it opposed congressional efforts to end trade with Uganda for a number of reasons—including the safety of those Americans.

Soviet Union

Restrictions against leading Soviet dissidents and would-be Jewish émigrés elicited only a mild response from the Nixon administration, which generally subordinated human rights concerns to the pursuit and maintenance of détente. Détente considerations also muted the Ford administration's criticism of Soviet violations. It opposed congressional efforts to link trade with Soviet emigration practices and chose not to publicly embrace Soviet human rights activists, including exiled author Alexander Solzhenitsyn.

By contrast, the Carter administration took several bold steps to support Soviet dissidents and made no concerted effort to repeal legislative restrictions on trade and credits, despite marked improvement in the rate of Jewish emigration. It consistently opposed linking human rights to arms control and "political" issues, but may actually have worsened relations by dramatizing the rights issue.

Conclusions and Discussion

This paper strongly affirms the political nature of unilateral human rights intercession. As Sandy Vogelgesang has correctly observed:

> Stripped of reference to the law or universal morality, promotion of human rights is a political exercise. At the broadest international level, it is about power: the challenge to the internal power of an oppressive government and the external imposition of power to change that government or its behavior.[17]

In each of the three cases cited, American officials balanced real and imagined political costs and benefits in responding to human rights abuse overseas. Their policy choices were sometimes further complicated by different concepts of morality and "justice." There cases suggest the crucial significance of the context—legal, moral, and, especially, political—in which an intercession is made. They also suggest the dilemmas inherent in trying to meet the requirements of various circumstances and interests while also striving for policy coherence and consistency.

Each human rights case and each intercession is unique. Yet patterns emerge which differentiate one administration's responses and decision-making priorities from another's. Other patterns show continuity in policy. Few would not expect to find that the Carter administration took a more "forceful" approach to intercession than the Nixon and Ford administrations. One would anticipate a similar result from *any* three cases.

Caution should be exercised, however, in generalizing overmuch the findings of three unique cases. While there is no "typical" human rights case, some cases clearly depart more from the norm. Uganda is such an "exceptional" case.

That caveat offered, the author concludes that the great majority of human rights cases would demonstrate—as does his larger study[18]—the preeminent importance of three among several considerations for interceding: domestic politics and economics; national security/international relations; and bilateral [interceder-target] relations. These considerations clearly dominated the full range of Nixon, Ford, and Carter administration intercessionary activity (i.e., human rights "policy"). Future administrations in a state-centric world system will probably also accord them as high a priority.

Even the most human rights-oriented government must place a relatively lower value on improving human rights abroad than upon protecting its own citizens' rights, interests, and lives—not to mention national security. An administration failing to comprehend this will not last long. By giving precedence to these largely "political" concerns over human rights, a major power like the United States understands that it may have to take morally ambiguous—or even morally repugnant—foreign policy actions in certain situations.

Domestic politics and economics

This paper's findings buttress Vogelgesang's conclusion that domestic political considerations are "the decisive determinants of U.S. foreign policy on human rights."[19] A human rights policy which lacks the support of the American people and their representatives cannot long be sustained.

There is, as William Maynes points out, "a liberal tradition of interest in the human rights of others deeply rooted in the American body politic."[20] Survey research and history suggest, however, that Americans support their government stressing human rights "more strongly in principle than in practice." A strong majority favors a cautious, case-by-case approach in which no damage is done to other U.S. objectives.[21]

America's shifting political tide brought changes in human rights policy during the seventies. Domestic politics frequently explained the unsystematic actions of both Congress and the Executive in the human rights field. Specific domestic requirements often determined the precise nature of an intercession.

Interceder-target (bilateral) relations

The more important country X is to the United States, and the more power/prestige X has in the world, the more significant U.S.–X relations normally will be as a factor in U.S. intercession with X. This is evidenced by the vastly different priorities given bilateral relations considerations in the Soviet and Brazilian cases (high priority) and the Ugandan case (low priority).

There are different philosophies as to how an interceder's relationship with a target *should* affect intercession, and certain realities as to how it *will* affect intercession in practice. Historically, Washington has interceded more forcefully with enemies than with friends. The Nixon and Ford administrations generally maintained this practice, but softened their approach to Moscow in the détente era. The Carter administration blurred the distinction by hardening its approach to "friends" such as Brazil.

A government's military, political, economic, and/or cultural "leverage" with a target will affect intercession, as will a target's ability to damage the interceder's interests. Washington's economic leverage with Uganda was relatively great, but its political influence poor. Whereas Brazil and the Soviet Union could inflict serious damage on U.S. interests, Uganda could not.

The ideological affinity/hostility of interceder and target may affect intercession. However ideological considerations per se did not inhibit the Nixon and Ford administrations' intercessions with right-wing regimes such as Brazil so much as realpolitik. Nor did ideology really account for the Carter administration's apparent focus on authoritarian regimes in Latin America. Contrary to some allegations, the Carter administration's sharpest ideological use of human rights was against the Soviet Union.

More than its predecessors, the Carter administration exploited the opportunity to discredit socialism/communism and extol democratic ideals in the Soviet case. Human rights disputes between Washington and Moscow often acquired an ideological flavor because of each side's stress on different types of rights—civil and political versus economic and social. Washington's challenge was to intercede effectively for individual dissidents or refuseniks without confronting Soviet ideology in a manner suggesting political interference.

National security; international (third-state) relations

National security considerations were extremely important in the Brazilian and Soviet cases because those countries had great regional and global strategic significance. National security stakes were less important in the Ugandan case.

National security is difficult to define, but has obvious links to domestic political perception. A human rights policy which does not sustain national security—or a people's sense of security—is itself unsustainable. If enough people believe national security is threatened by a particular policy or intercession, then national security becomes a factor even if the threat is illusory. In the Soviet case, for example, popular perception that the Carter administration's human rights broadsides were creating a security threat sometimes overshadowed the reality that Moscow's stance on arms limitation and war/peace issues was minimally affected by human rights.

International relations considerations were important in each case. Tensions created by intercession in the Brazilian and Soviet cases affected broader alliance relations. U.S. policy toward Ugandan violations was influenced by political realities in East Africa. That policy, in turn, influenced the attitudes and actions of other African nations as well as world opinion.

There is no obvious equation between human rights intercession and international political relations. Some nations will approve or benefit from a U.S. action; others will disapprove or suffer from it. The target's own relationships with other nations will likewise be affected in a variety of ways.

The Nixon administration's realpolitik approach to human rights was based, in part, on a desire to ensure regional and international stability favorable to U.S. interests, to reduce East-West tension, and to end America's Vietnam involvement. The Carter administration's approach "sought," in Brzezinski's words, "to reduce the identification of the United States with repugnant regimes as a means of reaffirming America's leadership of the world and advancing our goals of opposing Soviet influence and power."[22]

Leadership/personality

People decide whether and how to intercede in a particular human rights case. Any sound analysis of an intercession must, therefore, examine who made it and who decided upon it. What perspectives, backgrounds, and prejudices did policymakers bring to such decisions? What did they have to gain or lose personally and professionally from a particular course of action?

Hundreds of individuals shaped U.S. intercessions in the Brazilian, Ugandan, and Soviet cases, but four had an especially profound impact. President Nixon and Dr. Kissinger fostered a climate of caution and disinterest regarding human rights. President Carter's native enthusiasm for human rights—dovetailing smartly with domestic political requirements—dictated a bold approach to intercession. Idi Amin affected U.S. policy by sheer force of personality.

Uganda was an extreme case of a target's leadership confounding interceders' rational policy choices. The caution exhibited by all three administrations may suggest how interceders respond to gross violations committed by psychopathic leaders.

Americans' safety and interests

With the possible exception of national security, there is no more important consideration for U.S. policymakers in certain intercessionary situations than the safety of Americans living in the target state. As the Ugandan case illustrates, actual or imminent violence against Americans is top priority for

Washington. In most cases, however, danger to Americans will be minimal, and the safety factor far less important as a consequence. Abuse of other American interests by the target may also affect U.S. human rights actions.

Domestic and international law

Legal considerations carried far less weight than political considerations in the three case studies. One would anticipate similar findings in other cases. Most intercessions require no legal justification. However, interceders may try to legitimize their actions in an effort to smooth relations with a target sensitive about political interference.

The legal climate for intercession improved during the seventies. Domestically, Congress moved to prohibit foreign assistance to human rights violators and to require executive branch assessment of human rights conditions in every nation. The American Bar Association's reversal of its opposition to U.S. ratification of U.N. human rights treaties removed a significant psychological impediment to U.S. activism. Internationally, the signing of the Helsinki Final Act in 1975, entry in force of the U.N. human rights covenants a year later, and increased involvement by the U.N. Human Rights Commission in specific cases were important developments.

Human rights

Human rights considerations did not—at least in the aggregate—determine U.S. responses to violations in Brazil, Uganda, and the Soviet Union. Nor was there any correlation between the severity of those violations and American intercession. Indeed, Washington's response to Ugandan genocide was generally less forceful than its reaction to less egregious Soviet violations. Governments see opportunity in intercession to advance political and economic interests, with human rights at times being little more than a pretext or sideshow. It might even be argued that the stronger a response to human rights violations, the more likely factors *other* than human rights (e.g., domestic politics, war/peace issues) motivated it.

Certain aspects of a human rights violation or situation may affect intercession, however. Additional research would, of course, be necessary to test and verify a number of speculative hypotheses suggested by my own findings:

—U.S. intercession may be more forceful when the *victims* of human rights abuse are *admired* (e.g., Soviet dissidents and Jews) than when they are not (e.g., Brazilian leftists, Acholi tribesmen). [Considerations such as the victims' age, sex, race, religion, ethnicity, political affiliation, number, "guilt/innocence," and "helplessness" would differentially affect U.S. admiration—and, hence, U.S. intercession.]

—U.S. intercession may be more forceful when rights are violated that are especially *revered* or *central* in *American* law, history, and culture (e.g., free speech, free emigration) than when rights are violated that are not revered (e.g., economic and social rights) or that are universally acknowledged (e.g., no killing and no torture).

—U.S. intercession may be more frequent/forceful when a human rights *trend* is *worsening* (e.g., Carter-Soviet, 1977) than when it is improving (e.g., Carter-Soviet, late 1978), unless the absolute level of violation remains intolerably high.

—U.S. intercession may be more forceful when a target *government* is believed *responsible* for violations (e.g., Ford-Brazil) than when it is not seen as responsible (e.g., Nixon-Brazil). [Indeed, Washington may frequently offer assistance to governments perceived not in control of a human rights situation.]

—U.S. intercession may be more frequent/forceful when *victims* of abuse inside the target (e.g., Soviet Jews) *request* such assistance than when they do not seek American help (e.g., Brazilian leftists) —especially when those victims are admired.

—U.S. intercession may be more forceful when violations are *historically or culturally atypical* than when they conform to historical and cultural experience (e.g., Ugandan tribal killings) or stereotype.

Such conjectures—and they are just that—obviously require much refinement and qualification. While they suggest future avenues for research on intercession, one should remember that such human rights considerations may have only marginal influence on intercessionary decisions.

Thoughts on Unilateral Intercession

The "political" nature of unilateral intercession invites suspicion of an interceder's real motives. The Ugandan trade embargo crossed the line of "political interference" in an open effort to remove Idi Amin from power. American intercession in the Soviet case had propaganda value internationally and posed a genuine threat of destabilizing Soviet society. Intercession also had the potential to weaken the political authority of Brazil's military rulers. A prudent interceder will recognize that even if its motives are purely humanitarian, its action may bring changes which political forces not similarly motivated (e.g. Brazilian communists, Obote loyalists) may exploit for selfish ends.

Unilateral intercession may or may not be more "political" than multilateral action in a particular case—depending on context and the constellation of actors. A single government's action almost always will be faster and more flexible, however. Washington interceded quietly with Brazil while the Inter-American Commission on Human Rights remained stymied by procedural delays and political divisions. The United States imposed a trade embargo against Idi Amin while neither the United Nations nor the Organization of African Unity took any substantive action. Washington repeatedly raised the issue of Soviet dissidents and adopted stringent trade sanctions against emigration restrictions while Moscow quashed any hope of multilateral action. The effectiveness of these unilateral measures can be questioned. What deserves note is that they were made at all, while multilateral bodies were timid, proce- . durally slow, and/or politically paralyzed in responding.

Thoughts on "effectiveness"

This paper has focused on policy process and not policy "effectiveness." The latter is certainly an important measure in its own right, but also provides critical feedback for future policy decisions.

Effectiveness is extremely difficult to assess for a number of reasons. First, because an interceder's ability to bring about human rights change is extremely limited, "cause-and-effect" findings are difficult to prove. Target governments are essentially autonomous actors in treating their own people. Therefore, few interceders want to take credit—at least initially—for a target's improved human rights performance, and still fewer targets will concede an interceder's influence.

Second, "effectiveness" may have different meaning for different people. An intercession may be "effective" in releasing one prisoner, but "ineffective" in that it leads to harassment of others. It may be effective from a human rights standpoint, but not from a national security perspective.

Third, effectiveness must be judged both in the short and long term. Intercession may successfully achieve needed reforms today, but may also plant the seeds of a devastating revolution years hence.

Fourth, intercession may have important effects which are unintended or which go unobserved. It may fail to produce desired results in target X, but may have beneficial effects elsewhere.

Effectiveness may be easy to ascertain in certain specific cases, such as a senator gaining the immediate release of a political prisoner. Broader claims of effectiveness require careful analysis and considerable skepticism, given the limited power of intercession. Attributing the ebb and flow of Soviet emigration statistics to the policy of a U.S. administration may be just as difficult as demonstrating that a U.S. trade embargo brought about Idi Amin's overthrow. The evidence in these and related cases will often be conflicting and circumstantial.

The effectiveness of the Nixon and Ford administrations is harder to assess than that of the Carter administration. Because they interceded less often and more "quietly," there is less evidence upon which to base a conclusion. Their human rights goals and "policies" were also less well articulated, making it more difficult to judge success or failure.

Were the three administrations "effective" in dealing with the human rights violations in Brazil, Uganda, and the Soviet Union? Regrettably, they were not, in most instances. Clearly, the Nixon administration was not effective in the Ugandan case, as quiet diplomacy and diplomatic estrangement failed to affect a worsening human rights situation. Like Nixon's, Ford's administration did far too little in Uganda, and accomplished no human rights improvement. The Carter administration's reluctant trade embargo may well have set forces in motion that ultimately toppled Amin.

The Nixon and Ford administrations' effectiveness in the Brazilian case is hard to assess because of their quiet diplomatic approach. Congress, more than either administration, pressured Brazil's leaders to end torture, but Brazil's own internal dynamic probably had more to do with improved human rights conditions than either branch of the U.S. government. The Carter administration was, in one sense, extremely ineffective in the Brazilian case, alienating a government genuinely interested in reform. However, the administration was effective in reinforcing elements of Brazilian society even more determined than the military to achieve rapid human rights improvement.

The Nixon administration's détente diplomacy paid limited human rights dividends in the Soviet case, most notably in Jewish emigration. The Jackson-Vanik amendment undercut the Ford administration's effectiveness, but declining emigration and increased harassment of dissidents should not necessarily be blamed either on Congress or the administration. The Carter administration's approach proved ineffective, and often counterproductive, regarding Soviet dissidents. However, Jewish emigration rose dramatically to its highest level during the Carter years.

Thoughts on "consistency"

Given a choice between "effectiveness" and "consistency," most governments would prefer that their human rights policies and intercessions be effective. Yet interceders recognize the political value of consistency and aim to achieve it as well.

All three administrations were inconsistent from the standpoint of commensurate response, but then no government can afford such a policy in the real world. To the extent they had a "policy" on human rights, the Nixon and Ford administrations were consistent in eschewing all types of human rights intercession—unless domestic political pressure forced them to act. This reluctance to intercede was evident in the Brazil, Uganda, and Soviet cases.

The Carter administration, on the other hand, consistently injected human rights into its foreign policy decision making. It also attempted to achieve an overall "policy coherence," involving the consistent application of certain policy principles and decision criteria to all manner of human rights problems. Perhaps inevitably, mistakes were made, and such a policy was never perfected. Later, there was second-guessing as to whether a consistent case-by-case approach was really possible.

The Carter administration's most damaging "mistake" may have been its eagerness to make "human rights" an issue. By taking a number of controversial—and seemingly haphazard—actions early in 1977, the administration polarized the human rights issue to such an extent that each intercession thereafter brought criticism from one side of the political spectrum or the other. Even after a more coherent policy was established, critics judged U.S. actions less by the administration's own stated principles than by their own political standards of fairness and commensurability.

On Brazil, Uganda, and the Soviet Union, the Carter administration moved boldly long before this coherent policy was in place, and even before certain key policymakers knew their assignments. Certain policy adjustments (inconsistencies) were therefore to be expected. Inconsistencies also arose from the different bureaucratic treatment each case received. The Human Rights Bureau, for example, played a far more prominent role in the Brazil case than in the Soviet case. Of course, the Nixon and Ford administrations also handled the three cases differently from a bureaucratic standpoint—with only the Soviet case ever receiving presidential-level consideration.

A Final Thought on Human Rights Intercession

Political expediency and/or moral imperatives dictate most specific intercessions. Real political limitations and the enormous scope of global human rights problems dissuade most governments from undertaking a more comprehensive policy of intercession.

The Nixon and Ford administrations avoided such a policy for political and philosophical reasons. Yet, they also balked at a policy of selective indignation, believing it would invite trouble abroad and political division at home. Only when domestic political pressure for human rights action became threatening did these two administrations depart from their "live-and-let-live" posture.

The Carter administration, many observers feel, suffered from an exaggerated sense of moral burden, failing as a result to appreciate the need for moderation. Encouraged by Congress, the administration at first believed, unlike its predecessors, that the United States should speak or act whenever rights were violated. It also felt that even though intercession might fail to promote change in one country, it should still be tried in countries with similar problems where it might be effective. Half a loaf, the administration reasoned, was better than no loaf—even at the risk of appearing to be inconsistent.

The human rights "policies" of the Nixon and Ford administrations ultimately failed because they looked beyond human rights to a degree which unsettled Americans and challenged the American tradition of caring. They allowed human rights abuses to go unchecked, and created an international climate of silence favorable to new violation.

This silence was shattered by the Carter administration with mixed results for human rights. Thousands of individuals gained immediate relief and millions more found hope as a result of Carter's policies. However, some governments cracked down on human rights in a backlash against the new American "imperialism." There were, as Zbigniew Brzezinski concedes, "inherent contradictions" confronting the administration's policy.[23] Finally, as Professor Richard Falk correctly notes, "the Carter approach to human rights could not...be reconciled with a world of states or with the practical pursuit of U.S. interests in the world."[24]

Notes

1 For the purposes of this paper, I have defined "unilateral human rights intercession" as action by a single government (or its officials and agents) for the ostensible purpose of altering or maintaining human rights conditions of individuals under jurisdiction of another [the "target"] government. This action must *not* constitute "dictatorial interference" in the target's "internal affairs," including—but not limited to—use or threat of force. "Human rights" refers to rights enumerated in the Universal Declaration of Human Rights (1948) and the international Covenants on Human Rights (1966).

2 Based upon an extensive study by the author, "Unilateral Human Rights Intercession: The American Response to Human Rights Violations in Brazil, Uganda, and the Soviet Union, 1969–1978," (Ph. D. dissertation draft, Columbia University, 1985).

3 A 1972 memorandum issued by the assistant legal adviser for African affairs noted the "need"·for greater awareness by U.S. envoys of "current obligations of the U.S. Government in the area of human rights." The memo contained a strong message: Washington had a "legal obligation to promote respect for human rights," and this obligation had to be "taken into account in devising and executing policy." It also conceded that political expediency would inevitably temper government responses to human rights violations, but stressed that such expediency could not justify American actions that reinforced disregard for human rights. Memorandum of B. Keith Huffman, Assistant Legal Adviser for African Affairs, August 23, 1972, Washington, D.C., reprinted in Michael Bowen, Gary Freeman, and Kay Miller, *Passing By: The United States and Genocide in Burundi* (Washington: Carnegie Endowment for International Peace, 1973), pp. 31–33. While never repudiated by superiors, Huffman's memo apparently changed few minds at the State Department. B. Keith Huffman, interview, Washington, D.C., July 14, 1982.

4 "Secretary Kissinger Interviewed on 'Face the Nation,' " *Department of State Bulletin*, November 15, 1976, p. 608.

5 Section 502B, Foreign Assistance Act of 1961, as amended 1974, P.L. 93-559, December 30, 1974.

6 Kissinger decided that country reports would not be submitted to Congress. The Department "found no adequately objective way to make distinctions of degree between nations" and argued that

neither the U.S. security interest nor the human rights cause would be properly served by the public obloquy and impaired relations...that would follow the making of inherently subjective...determinations that 'gross' violations do or do not exist or that a 'consistent' pattern of such violations does or does not exist in such countries. "Report to the Congress on the Human Rights Situation in Countries Receiving U.S. Security Assistance" [reprinted in *Congressional Record*, February 18, 1976, p. S1896].

7 James Morrison Wilson, interview, Washington, D.C., October 14, 1982. Patt Derian said James Wilson, her predecessor as Coordinator for Human Rights and Humanitarian Affairs, had shown her Kissinger's replies to his memoranda to explain "why there wasn't more human rights activity." On all of Wilson's human rights initiatives, "Kissinger had checked the 'no' box. Great and small. And in some places...he had written 'no' in his own handwriting and underlined it! Put his initials." Patricia M. Derian, interview Washington, D.C. February 17, 1983.

8 Sandy Vogelgesang, "Domestic Politics behind Human Rights Diplomacy," in Tom Farer, ed., *Toward a Humanitarian Diplomacy: A Primer for Policy* (New York: N.Y.U. Press, 1980), p. 64.

9 Patrick Breslin, "Human Rights: Rhetoric or Action?" *Washington Post*, February 27, 1977.

10 Cyrus Vance. Address at the University of Georgia Law School, April 30, 1977. (Reprinted in *Congressional Record*, May 10, 1977, pp. E2862-64.) [See appendix B.—Ed.]

11 One official remarked that "a very ambiguous process determines what countries should be considered exempt from human rights pressures" and, likewise, focused upon. As an example of the "political" process by which countries were given attention by the administration, he cited "the conscious or unconscious need to have a Communist country receiving attention [as] a key determinant of the development of a focus on Cambodia." Interview not for attribution, September 28, 1978, Washington, D.C. [Interview conducted by Foreign Affairs and National Defense Division, Congressional Research Service.]

12 *U.S. News and World Report*, February 13, 1978, [Interview] pp. 28-32.

13 This was especially true at the presidential level. President Carter writes that whenever he "met with the leader of a government which had been accused of wronging its own people, the subject of human rights was near the top of my agenda." Jimmy Carter, *Keeping Faith: Memoirs of a President* (New York: Bantam Books, 1982), p. 150.

14 "Foreign Assistance and Related Agencies Appropriations for 1979," Hearings before a Subcommittee of the House Appropriations Committee, 95th Congress, 2nd Session (Washington: U.S. Govt. Printing Office, 1978), p. 429. Testimony of Mark Schneider, Deputy Assistant Secretary for Human Rights.

15 Carter, *Keeping Faith*, p. 151.

16 [See the author's case study of the Ford administration's human rights diplomacy with Brazil in chapter 10.—Ed.]

17 Sandy Vogelgesang, *American Dream, Global Nightmare: The Dilemma of U.S. Human Rights Policy* (New York: W.W. Norton and Co., 1980), p. 153.

18 Merritt, "Unilateral Human Rights Intercession" (dissertation draft).

19 Vogelgesang, *American Dream*, p. 153.

20 "Human Rights and American Foreign Policy: A Symposium," *Commentary* 72 (November 1981), p. 41.

21 Vogelgesang, *American Dream*, p. 151.

22 "Human Rights and American Foreign Policy," *Commentary*, p. 30.
23 Ibid.
24 Ibid., p. 35.

Sources Consulted

Brzezinski, Zbigniew. *Power and Principle: Memoirs of the National Security Adviser, 1977–1981*. New York: Farrar, Strauss, Giroux, 1983.
Carter, Jimmy. *Keeping Faith: Memoirs of a President*. New York: Bantam Books, 1982.
Drew, Elizabeth. "Human Rights." *New Yorker*, v. 53, July 18, 1977, pp. 36-38+.
Falk, Richard. *Human Rights and State Sovereignty*. New York: Holmes and Meier Publishers, 1981.
Kissinger, Henry A. *White House Years*. Boston: Little, Brown & Co., 1979.
_____. *Years of Upheaval*. Boston: Little, Brown & Co., 1982.
Merritt, Jeffrey D. "Unilateral Human Rights Intercession: The American Response to Human Rights Violations in Brazil, Uganda and the Soviet Union, 1969–1978" [Ph. D. dissertation draft, Columbia University, 1985].
Nixon, Richard M. *RN: The Memoirs of Richard Nixon*. 2 vols. New York: Warner Books, 1978.
Vance, Cyrus. *Hard Choices*. New York: Simon and Shuster, 1983.
Vogelgesang, Sandy. *American Dream, Global Nightmare: The Dilemma of U.S. Human Rights Policy*. New York: W.W. Norton and Co., 1980.
_____. "What Price Principle? U.S. Policy on Human Rights." *Foreign Affairs* 56 (July 1978): 819-41.
Weissbrodt, David. "Human Rights Legislation and U.S. Foreign Policy." *Georgia Journal of International and Comparative Law* 7 (Summer 1977): 287-313.
(Numerous other books and articles on human rights policy and U.S. policies toward Brazil, Uganda, and the U.S.S.R.)

Chapter 6

The Carter Administration and Human Rights

John P. Salzberg

While human rights abroad have long been an American concern, the Carter administration gave it a higher—and more controversial —profile. Since other writers in this volume are at times critical of the Carter policies, we present this view by one of the principal human rights advocates in that administration.

The Carter administration's human rights policy reflected a substantial, but not radical change from that of the Nixon and Ford administrations. Human rights were both in principle and practice a dominant goal of U.S. foreign policy. During the presidential campaign and in his inaugural address, Jimmy Carter emphasized the universal and absolute importance of freedom. From the very beginning of his term of office, his administration not only indicated the importance of human rights, but used various diplomatic tools to protect and implement these rights.

Quiet diplomacy, which critics of the previous administrations had thought often meant inaction, was given new meaning and significance. Officials at all levels of the government engaged in serious human rights negotiations for the release of political prisoners, accounting for disappeared persons and other concrete cases of persecution. Human rights was not just a subject for rhetoric in speeches but was a U.S. interest worthy of hard bargaining with tangible consequences linked to the outcome.

Public diplomacy was also heavily employed by the Carter administration, frequently after quiet diplomacy had failed to realize results. Opportunities for public comments included the noontime press briefing at the Department of State. Members of the press were likely to ask for comment on media reports that had appeared concerning such human rights abuses as torture, fraudulent elections or impositions of martial law. The fact that the press knew the Carter administration had an activist human rights policy and therefore was likely to comment on these developments led to greater press attention to human rights developments around the world.

The Carter administration breathed new life into human rights programs of international organizations. This was particularly true of the Organization of American States, where the U.S. has such an overriding influence. During the first year of his administration President Carter signed the Inter-American Convention on Human Rights and actively encouraged O.A.S. Member States to ratify the convention. Results were quick in coming: the convention went into force in July 1977—less than two months after the president signed the treaty. (Ironically the U.S. has yet to ratify this convention and most other international human rights instruments.) The State Department also played a preeminent role in revitalizing the Inter-American Commission on Human Rights—an independent expert body largely ignored by the Organization's Member States. The Commission had been limited to reviewing individual complaints through correspondence. Now the Commission would undertake visiting missions to states with human rights problems, and U.S. diplomacy played an active role in gaining access to these states for the Commission. Moreover, the responsiveness of the states to the Commission's findings often had a bearing on continued U.S. aid and other aspects of U.S. bilateral relations with those states.

The Carter administration also undertook a constructive role in strengthening the United Nations in the human rights field. The U.S. delegation to the Commission on Human Rights under the Carter administration made an important contribution in strengthening the UN's ability to investigate gross violations of human rights. During this period the United Nations broke away from the pattern of limiting its review of human rights violations to a few countries. The revised procedures for reviewing human rights complaints converted the UN commission into a vital forum with the active participation of non-governmental organizations (which often were the complainants), affected governments and governments with human rights concerns.

The last and perhaps most significant tool for human rights diplomacy—sanctions—took on new meaning. Under the previous two administrations sanctions were not used to advance human rights objectives. Under the Carter administration sanctions became a commonly accepted tool for promoting human rights, or at least for disassociating the U.S. from repressive actions by other governments. Military and economic aid programs were cut or eliminated to gross violators of human rights; the U.S. voted against or abstained on multilateral aid projects that would otherwise benefit human rights violators. Although the vote rarely prevented the project from being undertaken, some states withdrew a request before the vote to avoid embarrassment. Moreover, the mere threat of aid cut-offs became a powerful diplomatic tool in achieving results.

Finally, the policy was backed by a strengthened bureaucracy. Legislation transformed the Office of Human Rights to a Bureau of Human Rights and Humanitarian Affairs headed by an assistant secretary of state. There were now about a dozen professional staff in the bureau as compared with only several professionals in its predecessor. The administration appointed as assistant secretary for human rights Patt Derian, a long-time civil rights activist, whose commitment and ability meant that the bureau would play an advocacy role. As an assistant secretary, she had frequent access to the secretary of state.

Perhaps the most significant development in human rights diplomacy by the Carter administration was the willingness to apply human rights standards with respect to most governments regardless of their ideology or political alliances. The administration moved significantly towards an objective or universal human rights policy. This was particularly evident in Latin America where right-wing dictatorships had been traditional allies of past administrations, which tended to overlook human rights abuses in these countries because of their anti-communist stance. Repressive regimes in Chile, Argentina, Paraguay, Uruguay, Nicaragua, El Salvador and Guatemala found that the Carter administration expected more than friendliness to maintain close relations. The administration cut programs in such countries except when there were demonstrable signs of progress in human rights.

The Carter administration did not always give human rights sufficient priority. Several basic shortcomings will be cited: an excessive and short-sighted conception of national security; a lack of consensus within the administration about the priority that would be given to human rights; and, as a consequence, failure to give the Human Rights Bureau sufficient influence in the policymaking process.

Although the president and the secretary of state had enunciated the administration's view that human rights should be a priority factor in U.S. foreign policy, other senior administration officials were less than fully supportive of this position. With respect to certain regions and countries in particular, other considerations—especially national security—were given overriding consideration. President Carter had, of course, never promised that human rights would supersede all other foreign policy interests; but neither did he say that national security would supersede human rights. Moreover, these two apparently conflicting interests can be mutually supportive. Strong U.S. pressure upon a friendly but repressive regime to improve human rights enhances the U.S. national security. By promoting change, the U.S. identifies itself with the people who are likely someday to be in power. Even if U.S. pressure does not succeed in changing the repressive nature of the existing regime, we have disassociated ourselves from the repression and aligned ourselves with the people's aspirations for human rights and democratic process. To do otherwise is likely to alienate the people of that country from the United States.

The Carter administration's continued alliance with repressive regimes was particularly evident in East Asia. The strong military relationship with repressive and undemocratic regimes that had marked previous administrations continued under Carter. The Philippines, South Korea and Indonesia are the most obvious examples. When Carter took office the U.S. had substantial military aid relationships with these regimes. During the Carter administration, these relationships continued and in the case of the Philippines increased substantially. Marcos continued to rule by martial law without any serious justification; Suharto's forceful annexation of East Timor and General Chun's seizure of power in South Korea following the demise of President Park Chung Hee and the consequent human rights abuses following these events had no tangible effect on the U.S. alliance with these regimes.* Human rights policy was limited to quiet and occasional public diplomacy, but with sanctions effectively waived as a diplomatic tool for human rights.

The Carter administration was seen by some as having a double standard for its human rights policy. With respect to those countries not considered strategic to national security, the administration was willing to use sanctions; but for those countries considered strategic to national security, sanctions were virtually eliminated as a potential tool for human rights diplomacy. The credibility and moral legitimacy of the policy was impaired by this double standard. The administration lacked the vision to see that over the long run human rights and national security are inextricably linked.

The lack of consensus on human rights had a negative impact on the bureaucracy as well. The Human Rights Bureau, while equal in principle, was not in fact equal in influence with the other bureaus in the State Department. Regional bureaus had the upper hand in determining policy. They were the primary contact point in the department with the embassies. They were generally the bureaus responsible for drafting cables and often had sole responsibility for deciding which other bureaus would be authorized to clear on cables. Cables having significant human rights implications sometimes were sent without the Human Rights Bureau's clearance. There seemed to be no effective recourse to overriding higher authorities. Exclusion of the bureau from decision making was particularly a problem for the East Asian region, but certainly was not limited to that region. While administration officials were primarily to blame, the problem was also caused by the attitude of some career Foreign Service officers who refused to accept human rights as an important U.S. interest and resented the intrusion of this new bureau (with a high number of political appointees) onto the traditional "turf" of the regional bureaus.

---

* See Chapter 8 for an account by the U.S. Ambassador to the Republic of Korea. — Ed.

The fractured nature of the administration's human rights policy meant that Congress had continuing responsibility to monitor and legislate where necessary. During 1977 and 1978, for instance, the Fraser subcommittee continued hearings on individual country situations. In 1979 Congressman Don Bonker became chairman of the subcommittee. His approach differed from Fraser's in that he placed less emphasis on individual country hearings; instead, he focused on regional and general hearings. The emphasis was the same: to encourage the administration to give greater priority and consistency to its human rights policy.

In addition to hearings, Congress during the Carter administration continued to adopt specific country legislation—limiting or prohibiting military and/or economic aid to certain countries. This again was in the absence of sufficient pressure by the administration on the human rights front.

The congressional role has been and will be to monitor and if necessary legislate when an administration does not accord a priority to human rights that satisfies the prevailing congressional view. The tension between the two branches of government is inevitable but essential if human rights diplomacy is to remain a viable interest in U.S. foreign policy.

II

Implementing Human Rights Diplomacy

The Continuity of Methods

If we are determined to act, the means available range from quiet diplomacy in its many forms, through public pronouncements, to withholding of assistance. Whenever possible, we will use positive steps of encouragement and inducement. Our strong support will go to countries that are working to improve the human condition. We will always try to act in concert with other countries, through international bodies.

Secretary of State Cyrus R. Vance
April 30, 1977

Wherever feasible, we try to ameliorate abuses through the kind of frank diplomatic exchanges often referred to as 'quiet diplomacy.' But where our positive influence is minimal, or where other approaches are unavailing, we may have no choice but to use other, more concrete kinds of leverage with regimes whose practices we cannot accept.

We may deny economic and military assistance, withhold diplomatic support, vote against multilateral loans, refuse licenses for crime control equipment, or take other punitive steps. Where appropriate, we resort to public pressures and public statements....

Multilateral organizations are another instrument of our human rights policy.

Secretary of State George P. Shultz
February 22, 1984

Policy and Practice: Human Rights in the Shah's Iran

David C. McGaffey

Human rights concerns and actions were at the center of the debate on U.S. policies toward pre-revolutionary Iran. David McGaffey tells us how, as a U.S. consul in Iran, he helped implement the policies in the Carter years. Ambassador William Sullivan and Charles Naas, former counselor of embassy, add their comments.

While often identified with President Carter, 'human rights' have always been an important element of U.S. foreign policy. Americans see themselves as a moral people and believe that this gives them an obligation to promote certain moral standards in all of their dealings with other states. Since the concepts that formed the United States began with 'inalienable rights', not politically defined rights, we define as 'moral' those policies that support the protection and promotion of certain rights for individuals. We assert our right as a nation to promote these in our dealings with other states.

President Carter invented nothing new, but did upgrade and reemphasize our commitment to human rights internationally. He stated that we would seek through the exercise of our power to influence the behavior of all states, most importantly our allies. A naive statement of this policy would be that these allied states were inadvertently trampling on the rights of their citizens and that a reminder from the United States would be sufficient to modify their actions. A cynical view of the policy would be that we could look better in the eyes of the world by making statements, but that we would expect no change that interfered with the current state of relations between us and our allies. No one in the Foreign Service assumed that President Carter was politically naive, or totally cynical. Unfortunately, the human rights policy as enunciated did not give sufficient guidance or definition to determine exactly where between those extremes the real, desired policy would fall.

As a Foreign Service officer in Iran just prior to the revolution, it was part of my task to implement my government's human rights policies. This paper is an observation of the impact within Iran of some of the things I and others in the U.S. mission did to implement this policy. Since it is currently fashionable to state that Carter's human rights policy was a failure, this paper will also examine how the assertion and implementation of a policy basic to U.S. interests can come to be seen as a failure.

We should first examine whether we should have had a human rights policy focussed on Iran. Was Iran a country of appropriate concern to the U.S. in terms of human rights? Clearly, under the government of the Shah, there existed prisoners who must be considered political prisoners or prisoners of conscience. These were individuals jailed not for specific criminal actions, but for the advocacy of ideas in opposition to the Shah's regime. These ranged from Marxists to religious fundamentalists, from students to ex-government officials. There also existed, of course, classic criminals—murderers, bank robbers, etc. The problem class, in terms of U.S. policy action, consisted of those who were opposed to the Shah and took action against him, and who were imprisoned for specific criminal actions undertaken for political purposes. They were a problem because they made it impossible, or nearly so, to enumerate the strictly political prisoners, as the Iranian government asserted that all prisoners were in jail for specific criminal actions.

In the Shah's jails, especially but not exclusively those run by the political police, SAVAK, there were clearly acts of brutality, torture, and general mistreatment of prisoners. The Iranian government admitted to some extreme questioning of prisoners who were members of criminal or terrorist bands, in order to get information on the rest of the gangs, but denied any elements of purposeless, malign mistreatment.

Finally, there were numerous cases of 'disappearances'—individuals arrested, presumably by SAVAK, and carried off, with no information or access provided to family members. Prisoners of SAVAK were routinely denied trial, and the outside world often had no word of their location, their well-being, or even the charges against them for long periods.

On a different level, there were clearly broad restrictions on political participation and political freedom. The media were routinely censored, legal political parties were those sanctioned by the Shah and no others, political gatherings and public meetings were banned, and even certain writings of domestic and foreign authors were banned.

These facts would appear sufficient to warrant official U.S. concern. At the same time, there were mitigating circumstances. First, in Iran we were not dealing with large numbers nor with pervasive conduct. SAVAK was not a very secret 'secret police', in that its operations, personnel, even locations of its prisons were well-known among the populace. Moreover, a significant percentage of the population had regular and official contact with SAVAK. Their actions in general were considered legitimate, since Iranians generally and sincerely feared a subversive threat from the Soviet Union, with historical antecedents, and believed that SAVAK should take action against such subversive plots. There were indeed groups plotting the violent overthrow of the regime, as evidenced by numerous assassinations of both Iranian officials and U.S. government officials* for their presumed support of the Shah. It is difficult for the U.S. to roundly condemn actions taken against the killers of its own representatives. A most important basic freedom—the freedom from want and hunger—was clearly being provided by the Shah's program.

Most important, however, was the cultural context in which these actions occurred. Iran is and has been a violent society—often cruel by U.S. standards. Every regime has had its political police. (In fact, one of the first actions of the current revolutionary regime was to rename SAVAK and rebuild it into its own political police.) By the standards of Iran, the abuses against political opponents were relatively rare and mild. Few people were arrested; most of those arrested were eventually released in relatively healthy condition. The differences between treatment of ordinary criminals in ordinary prisons and political prisoners in SAVAK prisons were not extreme. Americans in ordinary prisons regularly reported the beatings by guards of Iranian prisoners without even the SAVAK justification of seeking information. Even outside of the prisons, cruel behavior, by U.S. standards, was fairly routine. Teachers all carried wands or rods, and I could see among the students passing my office each day some limping with bloodstains on their backs. Parents chastised their children with a physical directness shocking to American eyes. If physical violence against those in your charge is a norm in the culture, how could we judge when physical violence against prisoners exceeded the norms and became a violation of human rights in Iranian terms?

Moreover, Iran was an important ally in security, economic, and even democratic terms. Not only were we committed to Iran as a bulwark against Soviet expansion and as the 'policeman of the Gulf'; not only was Iran a major supplier of oil to our allies and a major purchaser of U.S. exports; the Shah was also a modern leader publicly committed to the economic and political develop-

---

* Examples of anti-U.S. actions included the kidnapping attempt against Ambassador MacArthur, the maiming by bomb of General Price, the killing of two members of the Military Assistance Advisory Group, the killing of three officials from the Rockwell Company, the assassination of a local employee near the embassy who was mistaken for an embassy officer who usually made "the run" from the embassy to the consulate. In addition, Ambassador Helms (later Ambassador Sullivan) and most top officials in the embassy (up until 1976 when terrorist policy changed) were reportedly on a target list for assassination by the Mujahidin-e-Khalq.—Ed.

ment of his country, and was pledged to move his nation from a feudal status to a modern democratic state.

Could we, as outsiders, know enough to tell this government that its methods of dealing with its own people were incorrect? On balance, the U.S. judged that there was sufficient basis for concern, and that it was appropriate for us to attempt to move the Shah and his government toward a greater concern for human rights. The questions raised above, however, remained unanswered and contributed to some uncertainty about how precisely to implement our policy.

Roughly speaking, U.S. human rights policies were implemented in Iran through three approaches: direct, specific requests to prevent, halt, or mitigate certain egregious acts of human rights abuse against known individuals; general discussions of human rights with political and security leaders designed to change their basic concepts and perceptions of the human rights issue, so as to influence their future decisions; and worldwide media attention to public pronouncements, policy statements, documents and hearings, interpreted within Iran through the international and local media. These all had some impact. Most important, perhaps, was the impact of our human rights policies within the general population through the international media, reporting not only U.S. efforts in Iran but our policies and actions worldwide.

Let us first examine the impact of specific requests and general conversations. I will use for examples only events I was personally involved in, although I understand that the experience of others, including our ambassadors, was essentially the same.

Specific Requests

As the Principal Officer at the U.S. posts in Tabriz and Isfahan, Iran, from 1976 to 1979, I had occasion to deal regularly and directly with a number of SAVAK provincial chiefs. They saw me as representing an ally, with a shared perception of the Communist threat, and a shared interest in preserving the stability of Iran. They were in general candid and forthcoming, if not often cooperative.

On twenty-four occasions, I was requested to intervene with these officials on behalf of some individual, reported to be an incommunicado prisoner, to be unjustly imprisoned, or to be undergoing torture. Of those twenty-four, most came to my attention through the U.S. Congress, when some individual in the U.S. asked his congressman for assistance. Some came to me in the form of direct requests for assistance from U.S. citizens, and one was brought to me by local Iranian contacts, since the prisoner was reportedly married to an American. In every one of the instances, the SAVAK chief was willing to take action—resulting in the release within Iran of four individuals, the release and deportation to the U.S. of five individuals, and information about (and at least short-term better treatment and perhaps earlier release of) fifteen individuals. These were all cases where the person was identified by name and location.

In numerous other cases, where I was sent on a fishing expedition to determine names and/or locations of prisoners reportedly being abused, there was often some movement, but never directly tied to my intervention. I would merely hear, some months later, that a prisoner had been released or a family had gotten a letter. Since SAVAK at its own initiative did regularly release prisoners or change their status, I cannot say that U.S. intervention had a direct positive effect.

Intervention on name cases normally results from some direct U.S. connection. The prisoners are married to or related to U.S. citizens, are employed by a U.S. firm, or otherwise have some strong U.S. tie before their names come to the attention of the U.S. government. That attention is typically through an appeal to a congressman from a constituent with a personal tie to the prisoner. The congressman in turn requests assistance from the Department of State, which in my territory meant me. My experience, apparently typical, indicates that the U.S. does have the power to improve the situation of such individuals.

Even at the time, however, I had doubts whether such assistance did anything to promote the U.S. human rights policy. Those SAVAK regional chiefs appeared to consider each request as an appeal for a personal favor, easily granted to a relatively powerful individual; and I grew to expect return requests for favors—for visa services, for introductions, for intervening with U.S. school authorities on behalf of Iranian students, etc. As long as no such return request was either illegal or repugnant, I complied, understanding that this was the way the game was played. My intervention was so vital to the individuals rescued, and to their families, that I would play the local game in order to be able to assist. But I conclude that I was not, in fact, advancing U.S. human rights policy, and in fact may have been working against it.

The key to U.S. policy was to promote a system of fair law, with equality of treatment under the law. Secondarily, it was to deter certain practices that are seen as, in essence, morally offensive—torture, etc. But our primary aim, it appears to me, in campaigning against arbitrary arrest, incarceration without trial, failure to publish charges and the like, was to ensure that individuals could expect equal treatment, without prejudice, under the law. My practice (and the general practice of U.S. intervention on behalf of individuals) instead reinforced the concept that certain persons—those having family connections, wealth, *or important friends* (such as the USG)—were sacrosanct, while those without such protections, acting in an identical manner, are fair game. On numerous occasions, SAVAK chiefs apologized to me, on releasing some person, in phrases asserting that, if they had known that this person was a friend of the consul, of course he would never have been arrested.

An underlying concept to our human rights policy is that those guilty of crimes should be punished, while those innocent should be free. Since the system of SAVAK prisons did not include trials or any such formalities, I have no way of knowing whether all of the persons I intervened for were in fact innocent. This was usually a valid assumption, since relatively few individuals were jailed for specific enumerated crimes and those names were usually known. However, it is perfectly possible that I assisted in the freeing of guilty individuals while innocents sharing cells with them were punished. This is an almost inevitable consequence of intervention on behalf of individuals, since the U.S. has effectively no facilities for independently determining guilt or innocence. We seldom intervene in situations where we feel the court system is dependable, and we normally hear of cases through obviously biased sources—members of the person's family.

Regardless of the guilt or innocence in any one case, however, we do damage to the promotion of our own policies if our intervention serves to reinforce attitudes that it doesn't matter what you have done, only whom you know. Thus it appears to me that the first category of implementation was effective, but limited, and possibly severely flawed.

Direct Persuasion

The second major set of actions involves attempts by U.S. officials, speaking directly to involved foreign officials, to persuade them that their human rights–related policies or practices currently in effect are either inherently wrong or counterproductive. The latter argument—that their policies or practices are counterproductive—can only be applied to an allied state, where the foreign official can believe that the U.S. has shared interests with the target country. These discussions are almost always discussions of means, following a statement of sympathy for the presumed goals of the foreign government. The argument that policies or practices are inherently wrong falls into the category of preaching, and while it may be soul-satisfying (as when castigating the USSR's treatment of its populace), it is unlikely to be effective in changing policy. At best, it is a tactic used to convey the implicit threat of a possible alteration of U.S. relations with the transgressor, but like most veiled threats, it will usually be ignored until made explicit.

In the case of Iran, the Carter administration made extensive use of the persuasive tactic at all levels. President Carter in his private meetings with the Shah attempted to show him that repression of disaffected citizens is likely to strengthen opposition. He counseled liberalization, attention to the real grievances of interest groups, and a campaign for personal popularity. In these conversations, the Shah listened politely and made no commitments. Similarly, high-ranking U.S. officials, during numerous visits to the country, spoke of torture and arbitary imprisonment as ineffective in building a modern, democratic state.

The Shah was equally noncommittal. The various American ambassadors had regular meetings with the Shah and his senior officials and, again, attempted persuasion. Finally, I and my lower-level colleagues were enlisted to convey similar messages to local authorities, such as governors and SAVAK chiefs.

To my knowledge, neither the Shah nor other officials ever explicitly stated that they would follow or were following American advice. In my own experience, I most often met with a lecture stating that I clearly did not understand the local situation sufficiently. Current methods were the only safeguard of the regime against hotheads, subversives, and foreign agents.

However, both nationally and locally, there were definite and major changes in specific policies along lines that accorded with U.S. advice. The Shah publicly ordered an end to torture, allowed certain SAVAK officials to be charged with criminal excess and punished, began increasingly to permit freedom of expression in the press and freedom of assembly for opposition political groups, and ordered large numbers of prisoners either freed or remanded for trial with defense lawyers provided. In both Tabriz and Isfahan, local SAVAK offices reduced, at least in visibility, their more egregious offenses—resorting more often, for example, to formal arrest in lieu of the midnight knock on the door.

Two reactions made themselves immediately apparent. First, the population of Iran relied more on the prior reputation of the regime and SAVAK than on current actions in determining their attitude. The policy changes were viewed with deep suspicion. Iranians believed either that the same old policies were being carried out in a more covert fashion (and the rumors were flying), or that the regime had somehow lost the strength to continue to carry out its preferred policies. Iranian officials at every level expressed a perhaps naive disappointment that the popular response was other than gratitude.

Second, the U.S. failed to win points for this advice. The general populace seemed divided into two groups—those who believed the U.S. was responsible, and was therefore an invidious puppet-master illegitimately intervening in the affairs of the country for unknown but probably bad reasons; and those who believed that the U.S. was not responsible, and had therefore demonstrated itself a 'paper tiger', unable to influence even its ally. This latter group, usually unaware that such conversations had taken place, ascribed the policy changes primarily to the internal pressures generated by opposition groups, or to reasons internal to the Shah.

In fact, there remains a serious question as to whether these private pressures did or did not affect the observed policy changes. While the similarity of trend makes it easy to assume that the Shah was acceding to our advice, it is also true that on many more issues, the Shah ignored or acted contrary to U.S. advice. It was a common plaint of U.S. ambassadors that the supposed puppet-Shah was a deeply self-motivated monarch, who ended up doing as he pleased regardless of the courtesy he showed to American advisors. The policy changes instituted by the Shah were, in fact, consonant with his broad scheme for transforming Iran, eventually, into a "Western, industrialized, democratic state." At best, U.S. advice may have affected the timing of certain moves and probably did reinforce existing preferences and tendencies in the Shah; but it may not have had any significant impact. At worst, our advice may have caused the uneven application of specific measures at times when they were counterproductive, since they lacked an integrated structure of policy to give them political meaning in Iranian eyes.

The second set of tactics, then, were certainly coincident with measurable policy changes that had a measurable political impact on Iran. The extent to which these tactics actually caused any changes remains uncertain, however, and the political impact was certainly not that which the U.S. government either expected or wished.

Public Statements

The third area of action on human rights was more diffuse in its application to Iran, but appears to have had the greatest impact on Iranian affairs. This area involves the impression the Iranian population in general gained of what U.S. human rights policies were, and their interpretation of what that meant in terms of their own political actions and choices. This impression was gained from a plethora of sources, primarily the international media reporting statements made by President Carter and other U.S. officials on human rights, regardless of the context of those statements. It was gained from statements made about U.S. policy by Iranian opposition figures and by the Shah's regime, as well as from statements made by Americans in Iran (from the carefully crafted words of the ambassador to the casual joke of a helicopter pilot in Isfahan) and by Iranians living in the U.S. Much of it was derived from the wishful thinking of individuals, which was then spread as gospel to others.

The U.S. government never undertook a planned, coordinated or integrated program to convey precisely what our policy was, and how we saw it applied to their country. Our efforts were directed at the Government of Iran, who we presumed controlled both their own policies and the political dynamics of the country. This second assumption, in Iran as elsewhere, was proven false. Despite our failure to focus the implementation of our human rights policy on the education of the general population, it did have an impact, which some authorities consider decisive in influencing the flow of events.

First, while our persuasive efforts toward the regime were private and involved a discussion of means to common ends, the media reports of our policy worldwide focussed on the more dramatic examples of condemnation and preaching. While not specifically directed at Iran, such statements were widely heard in Iran as a condemnation by the U.S. of all human rights violators, specifically including the Shah. We did publicly attest to violations in Iran, in the State Department annual report to Congress if not elsewhere, and the potential opposition to the Shah read this as a U.S. abhorrence of the Shah and his regime.

Since the U.S. was seen as simultaneously all-powerful (at least vis-a-vis Iran) and as a deeply moral country, Iranians assumed that the U.S. could not continue to support a regime guilty of crimes against such deeply held American values. On several occasions during and immediately following the revolution, I received petitions directed to President Carter personally or to the U.S. government. They came from groups—university professors, U.S.-educated professionals, even religious groups—and the gist was the same in all of them. In effect, the petitioners said, "We have done what you wanted in getting rid of the Shah, so..." Some of them wanted merely advice as to what they should do next. Others, upset over the path of the revolution, wanted the U.S. to step in and correct things.

The important element is that significant numbers of well-educated, politically potent Iranians read the Carter human rights policy, as enunciated through public speeches and the media, to be a specific condemnation of the Shah and a call to action by a powerful sponsor. The Iranian political lexicon does not permit distinctions between the sin and the sinner and read U.S. condemnation of certain actions as the denunciation and abandonment of the Shah and his regime. To date, I find many Iranians who believe that the revolution, and the rise of Khomeini, were the result of direct U.S. plans and wishes. The public image presented of our human rights policy was a major contributor to this belief.

Conclusions

To sum up, there were at least three categories of implementation of our human rights policy that had an impact in Iran: Direct intervention on behalf of individuals; direct intercession on behalf of principles; and indirect education through public pronouncements and the worldwide media treatment of the policy. All three were effective. The effects, however, were not necessarily what the U.S. needed to serve its interests. Direct intervention resulted in the release of individuals regardless of guilt or innocence, but contributed to an unfortunate misimpression of the proper relationship between Iranian officials and U.S. officials. Direct intercession on principles apparently resulted in specific Iranian actions and/or policy changes, but those changes had longer-term political effects which contributed to the course of the revolution. Public education was perhaps the most effective, but instead of being seen as a guide to action by persons or regimes, it was read in Iran as a call to action against a specific regime. This certainly had no effect on the human rights behavior of the successor regime, but may have contributed significantly to its coming into existence.

What explanation can we provide for this unfortunate result of attempts to implement a worthwhile policy? The first and most important is the confusion of ends and means. Because the human rights situation of any country was evaluated through an enumeration of such elements as numbers of prisoners held without trial, or charged with 'political' crimes, we came to feel that the numbers represented the reality. Our implementation efforts were then, at one level, aimed at the release of specific prisoners, as if the release of one individual signaled an improvement in the human rights environment in a country. Since that was our goal, we sought the most efficient means to achieve it, and succeeded, while releasing prisoners, in reinforcing an attitude that prisoners are to be taken and released according to the likes and dislikes of powerful sponsors. This was directly contrary to the interest of our policy—we subverted the larger end through effective but narrowly focussed means.

Similarly, where our goal was increasing political freedom in Iran, at times we fell into suggesting specific political actions related to freedom within the American political culture. Where our recommendations resulted in actions that hastened the revolution, it appears that we contributed to decreasing the political freedom available to Iranians, now under the current, more restrictive regime. As strangers in a strange land, it is an act of incredible arrogance for us to pretend to understand the full impact of specific political actions within an alien political culture. We can and should urge goals, but the determination of means should be left to the political experts of that country—whose mistakes, while as numerous as our own in the U.S., will at least fit into their system and be less susceptible to misinterpretation.

A second lesson may be the importance of local application and focus. As we enter the era of instantaneous global communication, it will be easy to fall into the trap of believing that, since the same words are heard by everyone, the same meaning is conveyed to everyone. This is not even true within the U.S., and should not be expected internationally. A major task of U.S. officials overseas must be to test the local waters constantly for the interpretations, understandings, and misunderstandings of the U.S. engendered by public media. They must then not only make known to U.S. officials how their words are being heard in various countries, but must also interject themselves as interpreters, challenging misunderstandings, reinforcing concepts, and correcting misinterpretations. They must be officially sanctioned as the authorities, within that country, on the meaning of U.S. policy statements. If not, it will appear as though the U.S. government is speaking with many voices. But that danger is minimal compared to the current problem of a single voice with meaning assigned according to the biases and perceptions of multiple cultures.

This means that policy statements should focus strictly on ends and goals, not means. Implementation will differ from country to country, and specific actions in one country will be accepted while the same actions are condemned in another. The necessity of explaining these differences to a possibly aroused population in the U.S. may add immeasurably to the understanding of foreign cultures by Americans. If the U.S. government is not prepared to shoulder this burden, it should consider the alternative of abandoning attempts to extend its influence overseas.

Finally, the lesson that must be learned and constantly relearned is that the U.S. is and remains a tremendously powerful country, able to deeply affect occurrences in other countries. Despite the laments of political scientists about the growing weakness of the U.S. in international relations, it is apparent that U.S. actions produce immediate and long-term international reactions. The weakness cited by theorists is probably more a weakness of their theory in describing the changes in the *ways* the U.S. influences events than a lessening of that influence. U.S. strength rests on a number of pillars, and an important one is our commitment to human rights. Since others will take action on the basis of their understanding of our human rights policies, we must take pains to reflect, observe, and understand how our policies are heard differently in different cultures.

Some Comments from the Ambassador's Perspective

William H. Sullivan

There has been much speculation that the human rights policies of the Carter administration undermined the authority of the Shah and led to the revolution that installed the Ayatollah Khomeini. In my judgment, this speculation is unfounded and the causes of the revolution ran much deeper.

However, as David McGaffey indicates in his article, the human rights activities of the administration—and especially the wide publicity that Washington gave to them—did cause a great deal of confusion in Iran and may, in some instances, have been counterproductive.

As far as the Shah personally was concerned, two factors have to be borne in mind. He desperately wanted to be perceived as showing a "decent respect to the opinions of mankind," especially the Western "civilized" elements of mankind. He used to say that he would like to be like the King of Sweden, if only he had a nation full of Swedes. The second factor was his sense of imminent mortality. He said he had about six years to make his country governable by his young son, who would have to function in a more restricted constitutional form.

Both of these factors impelled him to try to move toward a less autocratic regime, but he was uncertain how rapid such movement could be. McGaffey illustrates that the rate of movement might have been impeded rather than accelerated by the way the Carter administration conducted its human rights policies. Although the Shah never complained explicitly about statements from Washington, he used to rail about the hectoring he got from the BBC and, by inference, suggested he could do without similar statements from American sources.

These observations are a coda to McGaffey's thoughtful assessments, and are intended merely to suggest that, from top to bottom, Iran was and is a far more complex society than many of our policymakers have understood. In the absence of such understanding, simplistic policies, no matter how nobly motivated, may often go awry. David McGaffey, who was in the trenches during those convulsive years in Iran, has written an article that deserves serious attention.

Further Comments on Iran

Charles Naas

David McGaffey has done an excellent job in outlining the various strands of our foreign policy on human rights, pointing out that they were at times contradictory and showed a naive absence of knowledge of what the impact and the results would be. This is a natural consequence of the failure by the Carter administration to define with clarity and precision, first, what we meant by the rhetoric; secondly, what we expected the Iranians to do, and, thirdly, what we were prepared to do, or not to do, if the Iranians did not take our ideas to their bosom. I say this despite the efforts of Deputy Secretary of State Warren Christopher to provide such precision.

That effort was bound to be a failure, for "human rights" means so many different things to different people. The Department of State had little or no influence over the myriad American organizations that picked one feature—freedom of speech for writers and poets, or political prisoners, or torture, or elections, etc.—and bore in heavily with testimony on the Hill, letters and petitions, visits to Iran to see life in the raw, and feeding Amnesty International files with rumors, hearsay, propaganda, and some truth. To add to the cacophony of voices, our own Human Rights Bureau was ill-disciplined, filled with the belief that its members knew directly from God, or Carter, or Thoreau, or Locke, what was necessary. The point is that the Iranians were hearing these voices, too, and were picking and choosing what they liked or did not like from the confusion.

McGaffey's first point concerning specific appeals for the release of individual prisoners is pertinent. I myself went to considerable effort both from Washington and, later, Tehran to gain the release of a man that I had pretty good reason to believe was guilty as charged. The pressures of a certain congresswoman in the long run simply could not be denied. And here is a point McGaffey does not make—and perhaps should not be in print! It was my hope (and others' in Tehran) that such actions in response to congressional pressure *might* alleviate more general, ill-defined pressures on human rights and possibly add a vote here and there for other purposes.

McGaffey correctly states that prisoners were routinely denied trial. In fact, many were tried, but in the military court as prescribed by the law. The trials were not open to the public, and most often the public (and the embassy or consulate) were unaware the trial had taken place.

Perhaps the only aspect of our human rights initiatives that I felt comfortable with was in this area of the military court's procedures. William Butler of the International Commission of Jurists visited Iran at least twice with our backing and help. Butler is a highly intelligent and sensitive person who understood that a human rights policy could be effective—and helpful—only to the extent that it was specific, reasonable in its scope to the Iranians, and low-key. Butler did not start out alleging that there were so many thousands of innocents being held as political prisoners. He recognized that a state has the right to protect itself against internal subversion and that special courts might be necessary for the protection of evidence, etc. He therefore concentrated on the procedural aspects of the military court system to assure that anyone caught up in the system received fair due process—independent lawyers, for one—and that all prisoners would be treated the same. His proposed revisions to the law were well-received by the Shah and most were incorporated in the law before the deluge.

One of the ironies, recognized by most individuals who analyze human rights policies, is that it is our allies who bear the brunt of U.S. do-goodism. You will recall that on the Hill it was usually Korea, the Philippines and Iran that drew attention—nations with which we had developed close relations for significant strategic reasons. I guess the attitude was that if we cannot make progress with our adversaries, do in our friends.

In addition to those signs of change in the Shah's policies cited by McGaffey, one might also mention visits to prisons by the International Red Cross, the work of Bill Butler, and the "informal" audience the Shah had with Martin Ennals of Amnesty International. Unhappily, as McGaffey and other authors looking back at the revolution point out, all these "progressive steps" were distorted as to their meaning in one way or another by Iranians. I know that Prime Minister Mehdi Bazargan and other so-called moderates saw these actions as indicating a step back from the Shah by the U.S., a weakening of the Shah's control, and the opportunity to pursue their long-suppressed opposition. In sum, the Iranian perceptions of our policies and rhetoric were the significant factor—not what we may have intended, if in fact we knew ourselves.

I would say that the Shah's motivations for policy changes were more complex than McGaffey indicates. In the summer of 1976, well before the elections, he commissioned a leading U.S. public opinion pollster to survey American attitudes towards him and Iran. The survey was in depth and was generally limited to knowledgeable bureaucrats, Hill folk, and "leaders of public opinion." He was shocked and distressed by the results—which by the way he did not bury but made available to his palace staff. He realized that if he was to be successful in pursuing other objectives—arms sales and continued recognition by us of his preeminent role in the Gulf—some changes were necessary to gain support of the U.S. public and Congress and an evangelical president. Secondly, he was a very proud man who in a somewhat mystical fashion saw himself as the embodiment of the nation and an ancient civilization. The poll results hurt this *amour propre*.

Also, and this may not be the place for this comment, the Shah could not fully comprehend why we ignored his enormous efforts in the areas of social and economic human rights. Taken together, the Iranian performance was excellent, but the human rights advocates wanted to concentrate in imprecise and vague ways on political issues. It is ironic that most authors now trace the roots of the eventual revolution to these early reforms—women's rights, land reform etc.—since they roused the ire of vested interests, particularly the clergy led by the Ayatollah Khomeini.

I would like to make an additional point, one which has not been often noted. At the very time that the revolution was building up (September–November 1978), we as a government were still urging the Shah to release more prisoners. And he did. And they immediately went underground to add to the revolutionary tide. At the same time, the Human Rights Bureau fought tooth and nail to prevent the sale to Iran of tear gas. My God!

I do not wish to leave the impression that I join the Iranian exiles in blaming the human rights policies alone for the fall of the Shah. Tomes have been written analyzing the complex economic, social and political factors. But, at the same time, we cannot ignore the fact that we contributed importantly by pushing our domestic values into a society we only vaguely, if at all, understood. Is Iran or Nicaragua better today for all our efforts? It should give us pause.

Chapter 8 KOREA

A Special Target of American Concern

William H. Gleysteen, Jr.

Because of Korea's significant security position, a conflict has long existed between security concerns and U.S. expressions and actions on human rights in that country. Ambassador Gleysteen recounts this conflict as seen from both the operating level in the State Department and the U.S. Embassy in Seoul.

In a sense it is not surprising that Americans have made the Republic of Korea a target of special human rights concern, because South Korea has been deeply entangled in our Asian experience and has also suffered considerable notoriety for its record of strongman rule, violent political transitions, and periodic repression. Yet our concentration on Korea is a bit puzzling, since its political record is not bad by world standards while its social and economic achievements are outstanding.

The most basic reason for special concern is undoubtedly our security involvement in a hostilely divided country, generating anxiety that "bad government" in Korea could leave us in an untenable position. The legacy of the postwar occupation and aid program era may help explain our tendency to lecture to Koreans and intervene so freely in their internal affairs. The confrontational quality of Korean behavior and media drama have sharpened the American focus, as has the deep involvement of our Christian missionaries, who are on the leading edge of the Korean human rights movement. Whatever the reasons, the U.S. is thoroughly entangled in the Korean human rights situation—Korean activists constantly seek our intervention, while Korean governments have become so accustomed to it that our failure to react vigorously risks being misconstrued as indifference to repressive measures.

The views expressed in this article do not necessarily reflect those of the U.S. Department of State.

The focus of attention has been essentially political, as might be expected in a society which is politically authoritarian yet remarkably free of social, economic, or religious restrictions. Over the years Americans have worried over: 1) repression of opposition activity in the political arena and labor movement; 2) detention and harsh treatment of political prisoners; and 3) freedom of expression. At various junctures, particularly during political transitions, our concern has stretched beyond these issues to embrace the broader institutional problems of "democratization" and "openness." American human rights advocates share the view of their Korean counterparts that these broad developments ultimately determine the way Korean governments deal with individual human rights problems. For the most part, American administrations have also been responsive to this view because of conviction that our military presence requires political stability and that political stability in Korea requires some sense of progress toward a more pluralistic political system.

The State of U.S.-Korean Relations in 1977

U.S. relations with Korea were severely strained during the Carter administration, partly as a result of events in Korea but to a considerable extent through deliberate actions of the president himself. In 1977 the Congress and Department of Justice were in full pursuit of their investigations of the "Koreagate" scandal.* Americans were appalled by the extent and brazenness of Korean efforts to bribe Americans of influence. Koreans, including many who strongly disapproved of their government's behavior, were angered by high-handed American demands as well as by the deluge of American ridicule obfuscating the fact that the majority of the guilty were American, not Korean. In any event this affair, which began as an ill-advised effort to shore up Korean security, severely bruised relationships during the formative months of the Carter period.

Intensifying the strain, President Carter publicly reaffirmed his campaign promise to withdraw U.S. ground forces from Korea. He did so, moreover, without consulting the Koreans or offering a clear explanation of what he hoped to accomplish. Although President Park Chung Hee decided to limit the damage by going along with Carter's move, he was deeply disturbed by its implicit

---

* From 1970 to 1976, Korean government officials reportedly participated in detailed plans to influence the foreign policy of the government of the United States. The scandal involving the alleged bribery of U.S. congressmen by South Korean businessman and socialite Tongsun Park, identified as an agent of the Korean Central Intelligence Agency (KCIA), and by former Ambassador Kim Dong Jo was widely reported and dubbed "Koreagate" by the media. Investigations led the House of Representatives to censure one member and reprimand two others.—Ed.

message of a weakened security commitment. Almost all other Koreans—
dissidents as well as loyalists—displayed bitter disappointment, confusion, and
frustration.

Further complicating the situation within Korea and between the U.S. and
Korea, the Korean people were demonstrating weariness with President Park's
long rule, while Park himself was becoming erratic as well as authoritarian.
Human rights were a casualty—large numbers of students, dissidents, and
opposition figures, including Kim Dae Jung, were in jail; the government was
harassing its critics in the National Assembly and media; prisoners were often
treated harshly; innocent people were branded pro-Communist; and strains
were beginning to show within the control structure. In short, the situation
could not have been less auspicious for the human rights effort to which Carter
had committed us.

The High Human Rights Profile of the Carter Administration

Historians may conclude that the Carter administration was, if anything, only
marginally more successful than previous administrations in promoting human
rights in Korea. But no one can dispute that Carter adopted a far higher profile
than his predecessors and gave greater weight to human rights in relation to
other interests. Moreover, the president emphasized his own personal involvement, created new bureaucratic machinery, and in effect suggested that
concern for human rights would be an important criterion for judging the
performance of his officials. Together with the Philippines and Indonesia,
Korea was almost automatically placed on East Asia's list of most prominent
human rights offenders. Dissidents and opposition leaders in Korea were
delighted with the new American posture; Park and his regime braced
themselves to cope with American pressure.

Along with this new high profile, some of the past strain and argument
between officials and special advocates of human rights moved from the outside
to the inside of the administration. The new Bureau of Humanitarian Affairs
within the Department of State and parallel structures in the National Security
Council and congressional committees almost immediately took issue with the
judgments, methods, and even dedication of our embassy in Seoul and those of
us in the more established parts of the Washington bureaucracy. They wanted a
higher priority for gathering intelligence on human rights cases and insertion of
human rights into almost all U.S. representations made to Korean officials.
They seemed to overrate the value of hortatory measures and symbolic
sanctions and did not hesitate to advocate quite direct intervention in Korea.
They favored experiment with relatively strong sanctions, and at least some of
them questioned the overriding nature of our security concerns in Korea. They
were responsible for a great increase in the volume and condemnatory tone of

critical public statements by the U.S. government.

Within the government, no significant element sought to defend Korea's human rights performance, but it fell to the embassy in Seoul and operating bureaus in State and elsewhere to moderate demands, explain the context, and question the wisdom of some measures proposed. Arguments were frequent and often heated. Although both sides displayed exasperation, few battles were really bitter, and they diminished over time with commonly shared experience—as well as events in Korea.

Issues in Dispute

Arguments advanced in the American human rights debate rarely challenged the premise that the United States had a significant national interest in Korea's military security, political stability, and continued economic development. Officials preoccupied with human rights did not, for example urge a faster pace of U.S. troop withdrawals, while those of us with operating responsibility in Korea agreed that long-term political stability in Korea required progress on human rights issues. To the extent there was any problem, it was a feeling that strong human rights advocates failed to appreciate the dangers to these basic interests from various steps they recommended, and an opposite feeling in human rights circles that these interests were trotted out too frequently as rationalization against experiment. This apparent consensus on major interests and objectives did not extend to many other areas.

Fairness

Fairness was frequently an issue, not that anyone condoned Korea's human rights abuses but that many of us felt Korea was being assessed, singled out, and criticized for its sins without regard for its virtues. It often fell to me to explain that Americans should keep in mind that the Korean government had done well by its citizens in fostering security, economic progress, and equitable distribution and that these were more important to Korean farmers and workers than the individual political rights sought by elements of Korea's small, though growing, middle class. And, in assessing the degree of moral outrage, we pointed out that Koreans were far more tolerant than Americans of authoritarian rule because of tradition, as well as the difficulty of governing a fractious people in a divided country.

Ultimately this perspective gained ground and reinforced the realism of higher-level decisions. Initially, however, it was dismissed rather summarily by human rights activists who logically enough wanted to place Korea in the "gross violator" category of countries. Lumping it with South Africa or Chile would reinforce Korea's guilt by association and make easier the application of sanctions called for in legislative amendments.

Efficacy

In theory, the Carter administration had a large assortment of tools for the enhancement of human rights in Korea; i.e., a security treaty; a large American military presence; foreign military sales credits; government and private loans; markets for Korea's exports; high-level visitors; supply of police equipment; the U.S. voting pattern on Korean issues in international financial institutions; public criticism; and diplomatic representations. The inability to apply this array of apparently massive influence created great frustration in American human rights circles and among opposition/dissident elements abroad who exaggerated both the extent of our usable leverage and the efficacy of any leverage for human rights purposes. They generally agreed we could not threaten to pull out militarily or to cut access to our markets and private financing. But short of such drastic measures, they pressed for sanctions and downplayed the prospect that the Korean government would see these as threatening its survival and react with nationalistic defiance. The embassy and many of us in Washington considered such views dangerously naive.

Despite battles of words and memos at lower levels, senior leaders never experimented with major sanctions. Apart from the apparent danger to our security and economic interests, the president had already played his security card and could not talk of accelerating military withdrawals when these were proving highly controversial in Congress and objectionable even to human rights workers in Korea. Nor could he limit market access or governmental loans without heavy cost to the well-being of the Korean people. After some essentially unsuccessful experiment with symbolic actions, the U.S. resorted to traditional instruments of pressure, i.e., diplomatic representation and public criticism of Korea, making much greater use, however, of these than previous administrations. With the partial exception of President Carter's visit to Korea, positive incentives were not used.

In addition, operating officials sought—for the most part unsuccessfully—to avoid overloading the circuit to President Park. Despite warnings that we were dealing with a man under siege, we leaned heavily on Park for human rights progress precisely when we were punishing Korea for the sins of "Koreagate" and pushing ahead with a phased withdrawal of U.S. ground forces. Given such ill-considered timing, it is not surprising that nothing significant was achieved. Later, in the context of shelving the scheme for troop withdrawals and engaging in a Carter/Park summit meeting, we were able to achieve a substantial release of political prisoners, although the gain was shortlived. In the changed context after Park's assassination, the U.S. was able to devote a major effort toward political moderation and concern for human rights without having to worry too much about overloading the circuit.

Consequences

Granting that our colleagues in the human rights bureaucracy understood, or came to understand, the dangers of using bludgeon weapons for human rights purposes, there were many instances where the consequences of proposed actions were not so readily obvious even though the costs were still substantial. The most common was making so many representations to the Korean government that our coin was debased. Korean authorities assumed we were simply going through the motions and hence dismissed our efforts. The most dangerous problem was a periodic suggestion that we criticize Korean leaders personally or signal in other ways that we were dissatisfied with their conduct. Proponents of this idea failed to appreciate that American official comments were studied with minute care and frequently misconstrued in Korea. Thus, if we were to hint that we were even toying with lifting the mantle of legitimacy accorded the Korean leader, the consequences could be extremely serious—very likely encouraging others to topple him. This prospect, which appeared so dangerous to officers who had experienced coups and their aftermaths, did not faze some of the more passionate human rights workers. Although, fortunately, such dangerous proposals were squelched before they reached senior leaders, who would certainly have vetoed them, the sum total of lesser U.S. actions on the human rights front may have unwittingly contributed to President Park's fall and the unhappy chain of subsequent events.

The most benighted practice—at least in terms of foreign policy effect —was the resort to almost constant public criticism of Korea by official spokesmen. Understandably, it was necessary for the Department of State to deplore egregious cases of repression as a way of reaffirming U.S. policy and reassuring human rights constituencies in Korea, as well as in this country. A steady stream of public complaint, however, not only failed to accomplish anything in Korea, but also undercut the effectiveness of unpublicized diplomatic representations. Never did any Korean president during this period take any helpful action in response to our public complaints. In a number of instances, one of which is discussed below, the leaders refused to consider our request unless we first ceased fire in the daily briefings in Washington.

And, finally, our high human rights profile emboldened opposition and dissident elements in Korea—encouraging them to climb out on a limb from which we could not rescue them. These groups sought U.S. help—sometimes for the crudest kind of intervention in Korean domestic affairs—to compensate for their political weakness. They welcomed our public criticism, the more the better, but if we were unable to protect them from their own authorities, as was often the case, they had some reason to complain bitterly.

Case History #1: The Last Stages of the Park Era

Although human rights conditions shifted with the vagaries of Korean politics, the pattern of essentially intolerant, arbitrary, and sometimes brutal behavior did not vary much during the 1970s. Largely through unpublicized representations, officials of the Nixon and Ford administrations had done their best to moderate some of the extremes. The process continued without radical change under Carter. The president's personal dedication and the omnipresence of his human rights lieutenants raised expectations. But even though the professionals were spurred to new efforts, they remained skeptical. Whereas they shared the general American hope that relaxation of controls would ease animosities and enhance political stability, they knew that Park Chung Hee saw the situation quite differently; i.e., he was firmly convinced that greater liberality would only embolden his opponents to challenge him more strongly. The threat to his survival was made worse by other problems in the U.S.-Korean relationship.

Nevertheless, the embassy and the State Department did not dispute the need to pressure the Korean government; and they did so, trying—rather unsuccessfully—to limit public criticism and—more successfully—to be selective about targets. Serious representations were made with great care to key officials, such as the foreign minister, the KCIA director, the Blue House secretary general, and occasionally President Park himself. Lesser issues were relegated to normal diplomatic channels. The ambassador and his staff were the yeomen, but in almost every contact with senior Koreans, key U.S. cabinet-level officials raised human rights concerns. In fact, President Carter spoke of little else during his first meeting with the Korean foreign minister. A few congressmen and senators occasionally spoke differently, but generally helped reinforce the human rights message, which was particularly helpful from those identified as special friends of Korea.

Park's response was tactical. He released some prisoners; his ministers decried reports of torture, which seemed to diminish; yet "Emergency Measure 9," under which Park could detain virtually anyone for the most minor slur, remained in force, and people were jailed for political crimes. The effect on Americans was frustrating, leading to a higher level of critical public comment from U.S. spokesmen and stronger demands for sanctions.

Sanctions proposed included U.S. abstentions or even negative votes in international financial institutions for loans to Korea that did not directly "benefit basic human needs"; reducing foreign military sales credits and concessionary grain sales (to which we were committed by a formal agreement); barring Export-Import Bank funding of Korean projects; refusing sale of equipment to the Korean police; and further escalating public criticism of Korea. Economic and security considerations ultimately overwhelmed efforts to engage all but a few of these sanctions. Denial of police equipment was generally approved without much argument, forcing the Koreans to purchase it elsewhere.

Most of the bureaucratic skirmishes and battles were fought over application of symbolic sanctions, the degree of public criticism considered proper, and occasionally the granting or denial of high-level recognition, particularly the treatment of senior visitors and the holding of summit meetings. The United States continued to vote in favor of most loans to Korea in international financial institutions on the grounds that they benefitted the Korean people. But great energy went into proving this benefit, and in late 1977 human rights frustrations finally resulted in two U.S. abstentions. These public rebukes, which did not prevent the loans from being approved, angered Korean officials and pleased their opponents. Although there was no observable effect on human rights, advocates of sanctions intermittently pushed for more abstentions or even negative votes. By late 1978, however, attention shifted to high-level diplomacy.

The idea of a Carter-Park summit meeting was broached to Park by me in the fall of 1978, and the meeting took place in Seoul at the end of June 1979. Our hope was that this long-delayed meeting would symbolically clear the air and signify the beginning of a less strained, more fruitful era in U.S.-Korea relations. The "Koreagate" investigations were nearing completion and due to pass into political oblivion after the November U.S. congressional elections. Moreover, developments in Congress as well as a reexamination of North Korean troop strength seemed likely to slow or reverse Carter's earlier decision on troop withdrawals.

It was clear to me as ambassador and to my seniors in the State Department that such a meeting could not take place unless it were to improve the human rights situation. I was convinced it could, because I knew President Park wanted such a visit and saw it as very beneficial to him as well as to Korea. Throughout the preparations and during the course of the visit, we used every possible direct and indirect channel to convey to Park the importance of the human rights aspect. Park indicated his understanding without making any promises. Although other considerations were obviously at work, the Korean government's behavior began to show a new sensitivity to American reactions. Park handled the setback in the December National Assembly elections with moderation, and most prominent political prisoners were released at year's end. Even though Kim Dae Jung remained under virtual house arrest and periodic new arrests occurred, human rights conditions clearly improved.

During Carter's brief stay in Seoul, concern for human rights and political liberalization were prominent in the rhetoric and symbols of the visit as well as in behind-the-scenes negotiations. In addition to his private comments to President Park, President Carter spoke bluntly about human rights in his speech at the state dinner, and he went out of his way to meet with political opposition and human rights leaders. More important perhaps, he requested through me demonstrable results in the human rights field. Park agreed without much argument, surely influenced by expectation that Carter would shelve his troop withdrawal policy—and by a desperate desire to have the summit appear successful. His specific response was a large scale release of most so-called "EM 9" prisoners.

At the time, Carter's visit seemed to have been well designed and more effective than any other measure tried by the administration. Park's critics—both American and Korean—acknowledged a considerable achievement while professional officers such as I felt vindicated in our view that while Park could not be pressured into concessions, he might ease political restraints, if there were sufficient incentives.

But the period of relaxation was brief. Within months, political, labor and student problems boiled up, and President Park lost his grip to the point that his confidant, KCIA Director Kim Jae Kyu, seemed convinced—quite wrongly—the nation would welcome his bloody assassination of Park on October 26. At a minimum, the apparent gains we achieved were short-lived. Debatably, we also helped set the scenario Park always feared. Partly because of their conviction that a new era of U.S. support had dawned under Carter, opposition political leaders, labor unionists, religious dissidents, and students adopted more confrontational tactics on the assumption that they would have U.S. support. Fed by confrontation and other volatile factors, events spiralled tragically out of control.

Case History #2: Strategy toward Choi and Chun Governments

With President Park's death, the issues of human rights and political liberalization took on greater complexity. Arguments among Americans lost their aura of positional warfare fought in Washington. The importance of local context became obvious, and people in Washington tended to defer more to those of us participating in events in Korea. In the reformist atmosphere at the beginning of President Choi Kyu Ha's interim regime, the human rights situation was relatively good and overshadowed by our preoccupation with efforts to broaden the base of the Korean government. Almost everybody was out of jail, Kim Dae Jung had his full political rights restored, and media controls were minimized. Human rights activists tended to shift their attention to issues such as constitutional reform and direct presidential elections. Some pressed for the U.S. to offer constitutional guidelines; many wanted U.S. intervention with the Korean Army and security authorities to permit a direct presidential election in which Kim Dae Jung could compete freely.

Although we refrained from such crude interventionism, the suddenly created vacuum at the center of Korean politics sucked us into a very activist phase of diplomacy. Publicly we urged that Korea establish a "broader based, more pluralistic government." Privately we pressed the same message vigorously, calling on the authorities to be open-minded and on opposition elements to be measured in their demands. The atmosphere was optimistic, almost inebriated. Even the embassy's initial caution gave way to excessive hope. The seizure of power within the Korean Army on the night of December 12, 1979 by General Chun Doo Hwan (then Defense Security Commander) dampened our spirits; but among the Korean people, especially the middle class reformers, the "Seoul spring" continued. They did not adequately comprehend that the new governors of Korea were if anything more law-and-order oriented than Park. In the best of circumstances, these men had in mind Confucian or "guided" democracy.

Faced with escalating demands from opposition politicians, mounting student ferment under radical leaders, and growing labor troubles, the general's discomfort with a political free-for-all began to turn into paranoia. Problems culminated with massive student demonstrations in Seoul, a harsh political clampdown on May 17, and the Kwangju uprising a few days later. Korea's three most prominent political leaders were jailed; law and order were enforced repressively; political activity and the media were tamed by a radical "re-structuring"; arrests multiplied; and allegations of harsh treatment reappeared. Fairly or not, people compared conditions unfavorably with the arbitrary authoritarianism of Park's last years. A fair number of Koreans, particularly dissidents and human rights activists, held the United States partly responsible for the unhappy mess.

Sobered by the December 12 incident, which we did not have the power to reverse, the United States shifted its emphasis back to the classic objectives of political moderation and humane behavior while still trying to hold open the door for at least some progress toward more liberal institutions. Toward these ends we made repeated, blunt representations at the highest levels to the dual authority structure—the formal one headed by the president and the effective one headed by General Chun. Our efforts to preserve constitutional govern-ment, as well as some scope for politicians, journalists, religious leaders, and students, had some observedly helpful effect, if only because the newly emerging leadership, in its search for legitimacy, could not afford to alienate the U.S. On the other side, we balanced these efforts by using every possible means to warn the beneficiaries of eased controls about the danger of escalating confrontation. Our approach seemed resonant with the general mood in Seoul, but the vigor of our efforts, including my personal appeals to political leaders, was not matched by accomplishment. In particular, the students were mesmerized into the direct challenge that wiped out all the bits and pieces of progress made during the half-year interlude after Park's demise.

As General Chun and his colleagues progressively took over formal as well as de facto control of Korea, we faced a very difficult political and human rights dilemma. On the one hand. we did not have the power to prevent their rise, and once they were in formal control, we could not perpetually treat them as pariahs if we were to have effective relations with Korea, including influence on human rights issues. On the other hand, at least until the Korean populace demonstrated acceptance or tolerance, premature U.S. acquiescence could be costly. Our strategy was to keep some distance. By the very act of my meeting with General Chun on the day after his coup, we signified our willingness to deal with him, but we let it be known what we were trying to do to preserve constitutional authority and political moderation. To register our objection to repressive developments, moreover, we refused to hold certain formal—as opposed to working—meetings or visits, and we held down social contacts. Too subtle for some people and too interventionist for others, this approach may have had some useful effect at the beginning. Eventually, contacts crept back toward normal levels, and our concentration on Kim Dae Jung's case led us into steps signifying complete regularization of relations. In the meantime, we could not really measure public support or tolerance of the new regime. An uncharacteristic tameness had settled into Korean politics from fear of being hurt by the government's tough-fisted controls, as well as from a conservative reaction among people who feared that further upheaval would jeopardize accomplishments of their generation.

During this period relatively few people challenged the tough rules, and those who were jailed or barred were generally treated without brutality. U.S. policy played a marginally useful role, but in human rights circles resentment toward the regime began to spill over onto the U.S. Just as our influence was seen in terms larger than life, our inability to reverse the course of events was sometimes branded as conspiratorial collaboration with a harsh regime.

Case History #3: The Kwangju Uprising

The ten days of chaos in Kwangju in May 1980, which may have scarred Korea far into the future, damaged the U.S. human rights image more than any other development in recent times, although the extent was not immediately apparent. The cause was misunderstanding, misinformation, and disinformation about U.S. behavior which was not disputed by those aware of the facts.

Failing to appreciate adequately the historical regional animosity that helped kindle the explosion, the U.S. did not anticipate that the people of the Cholla provinces in which Kwangju is located would react so vehemently to the re-arrest of Kim Dae Jung, their fellow provincial, whose brutal harassment by the Park regime had made him a martyr. Ironically, we were distracted at the time in Seoul with a very strong protest against Kim's arrest.

Both the embassy and the U.S. military command learned of the affair after the crucial damage was already done. Without our knowledge, the Korean authorities decided to cope with tumultuous, but not particularly violent, demonstrations in Kwangju by reinforcing police with Army Special Warfare units, which were not and have never been under U.S. (U.N.) command. The Special Forces used highly provocative tactics which infuriated the people of Kwangju, causing a rapid escalation of violence and killing, forcing government forces to withdraw for several days to a security perimeter around the city.

Frustrated by our limited influence and ignorant of what was going on, the U.S. government in Seoul and Washington immediately deplored the violence and encouraged a peaceful settlement. We strongly endorsed efforts by the Catholic Archbishop to mediate a settlement, which until the last two days held some hope of success. We leaned as hard as we could on the Korean Army to keep talking and minimize any further violence. And we issued a number of public statements, including a carefully crafted one calling on both sides to settle the issue peacefully and warning North Korea not to meddle. The Korean authorities agreed to broadcast and airdrop the statement, which was well publicized in U.S. media. However, few if any Kwangju residents heard or read our statement, while many of them heard disinformation that the U.S. facilitated and supported the repression. I can only speculate as to who was responsible for this nasty twist.

This development may have confused local reactions to the denouement. In making contingency arrangements to reassert government authority in Kwangju if negotiations failed, Korean military authorities requested permission to move the 20th Infantry Division from the Seoul area to Kwangju. They wanted to do so because the unit had been on martial law duty in Seoul and was well trained to avoid needless casualties. The U.S. Commander concurred after checking with me (and I reported our decision to Washington), not so much because we had poor technical grounds to object, but because we accepted the need to reestablish governmental authority if negotiations failed and we wanted to prevent reuse of the Special Forces for this purpose.

Ultimately negotiations broke down, apparently over the refusal of militants to turn over weapons seized from government arsenals. We were notified in advance of the 20th Division's entry into the city, which took place with hardly any casualties until the forces reached the center of the city, where about thirty militants refused to surrender and were killed. Almost immediately, and acting without instructions, I urged the government at a high level to apologize or at least express deep regret for what happened at Kwangju. It did not do so, presumably for fear that the slightest acknowledgement of error would unravel its web of authority.

Not much was said praising or criticizing the U.S. at the time. Within a few months, however, a myth sprang up in Kwangju that the U.S. was partly responsible for the incident. The timing postdated the Reagan-Chun summit meeting, suggesting that act may have provoked someone to maliciously disseminate false charges against the U.S.

Case History #4: Kim Dae Jung

The Carter administration's human rights policy in Korea focussed to an extraordinary degree on the fate of one man, Kim Dae Jung, the courageous, ambitious, and supremely self-assured politician—idol of human rights activists and almost treasonous devil in the eyes of law-and-order men. Kim had become such a symbol for Americans that for the first three and a half years of the Carter administration we were concerned with his treatment in prison, his release, his return to politics, and his protection from distrustful army officers. In the massive crackdown on May 17, 1980, Kim was clearly the main target, although the Army decided to immobilize both oppositionist Kim Young Sam and loyalist Kim Chong Pil at the same time.

On Sunday morning, May 18, I called on President Choi and "Emergency Martial Law" Commander Yi Hee Sung to protest the events of the night before, to request the release of the "three Kims," and to urge the promptest possible ending of the emergency as well as continued pursuit of liberalized constitutional arrangements. We did not expect Army authorities to reverse their carefully planned move, but we felt it essential to warn them of limits in their dealings with us and to maintain our credibility with a very despondent Korean public. Kim Dae Jung was eventually court martialed and sentenced to death under farfetched charges of instigating the Kwangju uprising and subverting the interests of the state. The U.S. publicly denounced the move in strong language and made clear to General Chun and his new control structure that the U.S. government's attitude would be importantly affected by disposition of the Kim affair. Nothing happened, first, because of the drawn-out appeals procedure, and then because of a reported debate in which hard-line officers allegedly argued that Korea should not knuckle under to colonial-style pressure from the U.S. and should instead end the threat once and for all by executing Kim.

In the summer of 1980 the U.S. decided at a high level to make a major effort to save Kim Dae Jung's life. I did not object but I did express reservations. I felt Kim's life would probably be spared anyway, and I feared that too much concentration on Kim might force us to sacrifice other human rights cases and political objectives. During the next six months Kim's fate consumed more of our time than any other matter. I made repeated representations to the president and his key colleagues. From these I concluded cautiously that the odds were fair that Kim's sentence would be commuted. In Washington and Tokyo, however, fears continued, and the embassy was subjected to considerable backseat driving and, worse, public comments that were clearly angering President Chun. Eventually, under a rather blunt threat from a senior official that we were severely complicating reconsideration on the Korean side, we managed to silence ourselves, but only with great difficulty. Even after the election defeat in November, certain human rights activists argued so strongly for condemnatory public statements that I charged on one angry occasion in

Washington that they seemed to feel loyalty to the human rights community was more important than Kim's life.

The November election introduced a new complication because some Koreans assumed that a Reagan administration would be less concerned about Kim. They were reinforced in their view by some ill-considered private remarks of persons being considered for cabinet positions. Fortunately, whether because of frantic efforts by the outgoing administration or simply common sense, President-elect Reagan let it be known publicly that he wanted Kim spared.

The election also accelerated the conclusion of a tacit bargain between the two governments. Even if President Chun had always intended to commute Kim's sentence, he would have wanted to extract some benefit to his regime, and on the U.S. side most of us understood fairly clearly that our massive concentration on the Kim issue opened us to paying a price in return. By early fall 1980, it was apparent that President Chun wished to be invited to Washington, not only to signify full regularization of U.S.-South Korea relations but to give an aura of legitimacy to his new government. Quite clearly, he could not visit Washington if he were to carry out Kim's death sentence. As discussion proceeded, the logic of this process resulted in an implicit trade-off. Many other considerations were involved on both sides, but there is no question that President-elect Reagan could not have invited Chun without its being understood in advance that Kim's sentence would be commuted. Equally clearly, the invitation meant U.S. relations with Korea were fully normalized and that the distance maintained by the Carter administration was eliminated. Officials of both the outgoing and incoming administrations were willingly involved in the process that led to the implicit bargain. Only the new president's confidants were involved in his decision to make President Chun his first state visitor. The Carter administration probably would have let a few more months go by.

In any event, the affair ended with an ironic twist. Strong human rights advocacy prompted the U.S. into a major effort on behalf of Kim Dae Jung, who was freed by a process that appeared to many to convey premature U.S. support for the Chun government. Among the most outspoken critics were Kim Dae Jung's supporters.

Conclusion

Although I was usually arguing the conservative case from my initial Washington perch and later in Seoul, I believe the Carter administration was right to make an issue of human rights in Korea. One can argue that conditions in Korea did not improve very much, even that they worsened. But if we had not made a considerable effort in Korea, I am convinced things would have been considerably worse and that America's reputation among the Koreans could have been severely damaged. My argument with what we did was largely over issues such as fairness, the instruments we chose, and the excessive expectations of many involved.

This brief review suggests a number of conclusions, many of which are applicable beyond Korea. First, even with friendly or allied countries, U.S. power to influence human rights developments is severely limited. Many sanctions are inherently unusable, while other forms of pressure do not work in conditions where a foreign leader is convinced liberalization threatens his survival. Incentives such as state visits are effective but the results may not last. One of the most tempting but most counterproductive instruments is that of condemnatory public statements from Washington.

Second, the Carter administration and especially the president himself failed to appreciate that we could not expect significant relaxation in the human rights area from a regime that was under siege from U.S. policy on "Koreagate" and troop withdrawals. Third, excessive U.S. pressure or signs of U.S. dissatisfaction affect the "legitimacy" and survival of a Korean leader. In the case of Park Chung Hee, our actions and words may have contributed indirectly to his demise. Fourth, in Korea authoritarian leaders removed by violence are likely to be replaced by other authoritarian leaders. And, fifth, the Korean case demonstrates that one of the most difficult issues for the U.S. is how to stay close enough to the authoritarian leader of an important ally without losing stature with other elements of the population, especially a relatively liberal middle class. Sometimes it is impossible.

Release in Indonesia

David D. Newsom

Thirty-five thousand detainees left over from a national upheaval became an issue in U.S.-Indonesian relations. The resolution of that issue represented a successful use of diplomacy on a human rights problem.

The year 1965 was a year of upheaval in Indonesia. As the recent film termed it, it was "the year of living dangerously."

At the end of September of that year, a group of air force officers in apparent collusion with members of Indonesia's Communist party staged an effort to eliminate the leadership of the Indonesian army. Most observers conclude that, as President Sukarno grew increasingly old and ill, the Communist party saw the army as its only obstacle to ultimate leadership in Indonesia. So, on the night of September 30 and October 1 of 1965, seven of the top generals of the Indonesian army were rounded up, taken to an air force base outside of Jakarta and killed, their bodies thrown into a pit.

The Communist party in Indonesia at that time had a strength estimated at three million, making it the largest Communist party in Asia outside of China. It had numerous organizations for youth, for workers, for farmers, for artists, for poets. It had close ties with the party in the Chinese People's Republic. Sukarno, the dynamic leader who brought Indonesia to independence, had increasingly leaned toward support of the Soviet Union and China. The leadership of the Communist party undoubtedly felt that, with senior officers of the army opposed to them out of the way, they would find it easy to cooperate with and ultimately set aside Sukarno in the declining years of his life.

On October 1 the tide of events reversed. General Suharto, commander of the coast defense forces, moved on the air base, permitted Sukarno to flee and captured the officers and party officials who had staged the coup. Throughout Indonesia there was an uprising against the members of the Communist party, those suspected of membership and, in many cases, against Chinese Indonesians in general, a manifestation of age-old tensions. Estimates ranged from 300,000 to 500,000 killed on Java and on other islands during the period immediately following these events.

The army moved to take control, and a very large number of persons suspected of affiliation with the Communist party and Communist front organizations were arrested. Many were eventually released; but, as the 1970s approached, some 35,000* remained in detention and without trial.

Western opinion toward the changes in Indonesia was generally favorable in the years immediately following 1965. Substantial economic assistance programs were arranged by a group of Western nations led by the Dutch and cooperating closely with the World Bank. The United States was an active participant in what came to be known as the IGGI (Inter Governmental Group on Indonesia).

The continued detention of persons suspected of Communist affiliation was not forgotten. It was kept alive by relatives of those that had been detained and, particularly, by Amnesty International.[1] Carmel Budiardjo, the English-born wife of one of the detainees and a former member of the British Communist party, was particularly active in Europe and the United States in calling attention to this group of prisoners. She appeared on one occasion before a committee of the U.S. Congress.[2]

As relations with the new Indonesian regime grew closer, there was increasing unease in friendly countries, especially The Netherlands and the United States, over the human rights situation in Indonesia, with particular focus on this group of prisoners. The Indonesian regime was seen by many abroad as a traditional military regime, with a security apparatus often operating in an arbitrary fashion. Critics suspected that the regime had no intention either of bringing the detainees to trial or, ultimately, of releasing them.

The attention to the prisoner problem in Indonesia came at a time of growing attention in the United States to human rights conditions in other countries. It was in the period of the greatest controversy over Vietnam. The U.S. House of Representatives, stimulated by the work of a subcommittee of the House Foreign Affairs Committee, was seeking through legislation to attach conditions to foreign assistance. In the period from 1972 until the Carter administration was inaugurated in 1977, some eleven different amendments were attached requiring a consideration of human rights conditions in countries where the United States provided economic, military and commercial credit assistance.

The war in Vietnam and the concern in the United States over the security of countries on the periphery of Asia led to offers of military assistance to the Indonesian government. Discussions on military aid to Indonesia came at a time of debate within the United States over the support of any military regime con-

---

* Some estimates by human rights groups were higher. This is based on my best estimate from conversations with both official and nonofficial sources in Indonesia.

sidered oppressive.[3] At one point in 1977, a Senate subcommittee voted to stop military aid grants to both Thailand and Indonesia.[4] The action, however, was not supported by the full Senate.

In January 1974, Prime Minister Tanaka of Japan visited Jakarta. His visit provoked serious rioting in the Indonesian capital. The reaction of the regime to this rioting was a series of further arrests and the placing of restrictions on intellectuals and students suspected of socialist orientation. Following the arrests there was a series of trials, one of which, the trial of a student, Hariman Siregar, received international attention.[5] One prominent Indonesian intellectual, Soedjatmoko, was prevented from leaving the country. These actions increased attention to Indonesia in the United States both in the Congress and in the intellectual community. They were reminders of the continued detention of those from 1965.

I went to Indonesia in February 1974. It was clear to me that, if smooth relationships were to continue between the United States and Indonesia, some steps would have to be taken to deal with the human rights problem. While the U.S. administration under President Ford clearly favored continuing military and economic assistance to Indonesia, there was strong sentiment in both the Senate and the House for restricting such aid as long as there were "gross violations of internationally recognized human rights." While I did not have any specific instructions, it seemed clear to me that the continuation of normal relationships would be more readily guaranteed if I could find a way to encourage the Indonesian government to release the detainees from 1965.

Outside diplomatic involvement in as sensitive an internal matter as the prisoners of Indonesia is not normally welcome. If there is the least hint of a threat by another country, however friendly, national pride is aroused. A country is more likely, under such circumstances, to renounce foreign assistance than it is to appear to give way under foreign pressures.

There were clearly different viewpoints within the Indonesian ruling circles about what should be done with the detainees. I had no desire to appear to be involved in an internal debate within the Indonesian government. At the same time, there seemed to me to be within that government a certain indifference to the problem and bureaucratic inertia in dealing with it. My conversations with officials, however, increasingly revealed a degree of concern over the continuation of this problem and a feeling that some way possibly should be found to resolve the issue.

In the minds of some officials there were very real questions regarding the wisdom of releasing these remnants from a Communist past. Within an army that had been decapitated by a Communist coup, there was understandably a strong reluctance to take any measures which might bring about a revival of the Indonesian Communist party. There was a genuine fear that the return to their villages and regions of those who had been associated with the Communist party might stimulate once more some of the unrest that had marked that period.

Officials worried about the availability of jobs for former detainees released
into a society where there was already a high measure of unemployment and
underemployment.[6] The Tanaka riots of 1974 reminded the regime strongly of
the continued existence of opposition.

In 1974, therefore, while one could find some hints of a desire to resolve the
problem of the detainees, most of the evidence suggested that there would be
strong resistance to any mass release of these people.

Indonesian authorities were sensitive to the attention being given to the
prisoner question by the press in Europe and in the United States. An effort was
made to deny the charges of harsh treatment of these people by a publicity
campaign aimed at demonstrating the humane policies of the detention. Some
of this centered around the detainees who were held on Buru Island, an island in
Central Indonesia to which approximately 10,000 of the prisoners and their
families[7] had been taken and placed on small farms.[8] There were some visits by
journalists to Buru Island. The general conditions were not impressive and the
effort to publicize the beneficial treatment backfired.

As a diplomat in this situation it seemed to me that I had four objectives.

First, I needed to establish for the Department of State in Washington, as
accurately as I could, the facts regarding the problem. It might be asked why the
United States government would need to undertake the responsibility for knowing the facts in such a situation in a foreign country. The Congress and the
public debate already established a U.S. interest in the problem; the Executive
was expected to make the best effort possible to ascertain the facts. Amnesty
International claimed there were 100,000 detainees in Indonesia.[9] The Indonesian government used a figure of 35,000. What was the correct figure?
There were reports of detainees being held in various parts of the country.
Where were they being held? There were also reports of maltreatment and of
bad conditions. Some reports talked of various categories of prisoners—A, B,
and C. What were these categories and what was their significance?[10]

The second objective was to legitimize the interest of the United States in the
human rights situation in Indonesia, to a point where our inquiries to the Indonesian authorities would be accepted as appropriate. Governments generally
consider probing by diplomats into a sensitive internal matter such as this quite
inappropriate. Advocates of an active human rights policy in the United States
advised me that American diplomats could base their concern upon the United
States' broad interest in international human rights. This was not a satisfactory
rationale in Indonesia; perhaps it was not in other lands either. I had more than
once been reminded that the United States was one of the nations, for example,
that had not ratified the universal convention on human rights. A basis had to be
found that placed our official interest in this question within the context of the
relations between the two countries. The legislation passed by the Congress
placing conditions upon the delivery of military assistance was an obvious

factor in the relationship. That factor needed to be conveyed in a way that did not sound like a threat.

The third objective was to seek a form of leverage or persuasion that might lead the Indonesians to decide on their own to take the measures necessary to remove this problem. Foreign countries do not react well to public pressures. Events, however, which may well bring an issue like this into focus, can lead a country to concentrate on the problem and to determine, on their own, whether some solution is possible. While it is difficult to document, it is possible, for example, that the visit by President Ford to Indonesia in December of 1975 raised the issue in the councils of the Indonesian government along with other subjects that they expected either to discuss or to be asked about in the visit by the president.

Finally, in a situation such as this, the American ambassador needs to keep in mind the desirability of avoiding a close identification with the policies of the host government, but without offending that government. Credibility with the critics at home is important both for the Department of State and for the ambassador if the steps that are taken by a foreign government are to be seen as progress. Therefore, occasions need to be found—through meetings with opposition figures, carefully worded statements or specific actions—which suggest that the American ambassador does not accept the conditions that prevail and is working to improve them.

With these objectives in mind, my colleagues in the embassy and I set on a plan to accomplish our task. First, we sought those who had similar concerns in the diplomatic community. It was useful to confer with them, to exchange information and to determine whether among the various interested countries there were one or more that had a greater opportunity to influence the situation than others. Joint approaches are not usually welcomed by a foreign government, but individual diplomats coordinating and working in parallel can often be effective. I found especially helpful colleagues in the ambassador of The Netherlands and in the papal nuncio. When the Indonesian government did proceed to release the prisoners, they invited to the opening ceremony the diplomats of those countries that had been working together and separately on the problem. I was to learn later, for example, that the Japanese had also been concerned and had been making their views known because of strong interests they had in the stability of Indonesia.

Having established an informal network of diplomatic colleagues, my next task was to find those within the Indonesian establishment who would understand and accept the American interest in this problem and who perhaps also could interpret the American concern to those in the Indonesian government to whom this was a particularly sensitive problem.

I was fortunate to find in a semi-official think tank, the Centre for Strategic and International Studies, a group that had close ties with the Indonesian leadership and yet also understood much about the American political situation.

Through them I was able to meet and establish a friendly relationship with a senior Indonesian general. I was also to make the acquaintance of another general who was one of President Suharto's political advisors. Once I felt that a satisfactory relationship had been established, I approached both generals. In keeping with my responsibility for maintaining a cordial relationship between the Indonesians and the United States, I explained, I felt it my duty from time to time to acquaint them with developments in the United States that might affect that relationship. One of the developments was the enactment of recent legislation* requiring that human rights conditions in a country be considered when the United States provides military assistance. I said I was making no suggestion that this law would be applied against Indonesia, but I felt that the Indonesian authorities should be familar with the legislation. I gave to each a copy of the legislation.

At the same time, it became increasingly clear that the Executive was under pressure to prepare human rights reports—subsequently mandated by a revision of 502B in 1976.[11] These reports were to comment as candidly as the situation would allow on conditions in countries receiving American assistance. Clearly, this would be a sensitive matter in many countries. It was important therefore to prepare the groundwork so that there would be some understanding within the Indonesian government of the background and the content of these reports. That was the second part of my agenda with Indonesian officials.

A third was to encourage, wherever I could, as much openness as possible on conditions within the detention facilities. Here, in collaboration with other diplomatic colleagues, I stressed the value of turning to an organization such as the International Committee of the Red Cross. The International Committee of the Red Cross, unlike some other human rights organizations, does not work publicly, but provides on a confidential basis to the highest authorities of a country its evaluation of that country's detention facilities. The fact that a country's leaders have turned to the International Committee of the Red Cross is to many reasonable critics an indication of intentions to improve conditions, if not necessarily to release the prisoners.

Finally, to emphasize to a wider audience the concern of the United States over human rights conditions, I found occasional opportunities to work into public speeches reference to some of the activities relating to human rights in the United States Congress and in the Executive.

Sometime late in 1975 the Indonesians made a decision to begin releasing the 1965 detainees. It is not possible to state with any certainty what led the Indonesian government to that decision. Clearly the attitude of the United States and the existence of the U.S. legislation were factors.

Not long after I had given copies of the legislation to the two Indonesian generals, I was approached by one of them. He explained that he understood the

---

* Section 502B of the Foreign Assistance Act of 1961, as amended in December 1974.

nature of the problem that I had brought to their attention, but that it would not be possible for him to take this legislation to the president and explain that it had been given to him by the American ambassador. The president would almost certainly regard this as a threat, and his reaction might be adverse. Instead the general suggested that I help arrange a visit by an Indonesian group to the United States to confer with persons in Congress, in the Executive and in the private sector about relations with Indonesia. Such a group could then come back and report to the president on the basis of their own investigations. If their visit confirmed that the human rights question was a problem, the Indonesians, themselves, could consider ways to meet it. This is what happened. I can only conclude that when the group returned and gave its report to the president, it brought home to the Indonesian leadership the need to respond in some measure to this outside concern.

So, in 1975, a small group of prisoners was released, and annual ceremonies followed in 1976, 1977 and 1978.[12] By 1978 all but approximately 200 had been released and returned to their villages. The 200 represented Class A prisoners who would face trial for actions against the state.

The release of the prisoners brought its own problems for the foreign diplomats in that country. The diplomats in their reporting and in their reaction to events needed to determine how genuine the Indonesian intentions were.

I recall one of the release ceremonies in a military camp outside Jakarta. The diplomatic representatives of countries that had shown an interest in the problem were assembled, together with a few selected Indonesian officials and journalists. The prisoners were driven up in trucks, filed into the hall and sat down. There was speech by an Indonesian general about the need for loyalty to the state, and then all the prisoners were required to stand and give an oath of allegiance to the national philosophy of Indonesia. The prisoners then filed back outside into the trucks and were driven away. There was no opportunity to talk with the prisoners or to determine where they were going after the "release" ceremony.[13]

The effort was obviously greeted with considerable skepticism and in the weeks that followed such organizations as Amnesty International kept up the pressure on Indonesia, questioning whether any releases had actually been made.[14] In such a case the diplomat is faced with a dilemma. If he or she should comment favorably on such a ceremony, there is a risk, in the absence of other information, that the diplomat is identifying with an unsatisfactory solution. If, on the other hand, a step which may have been taken following a very considerable debate within the Indonesian government receives no international acknowledgment, hard-liners can be expected to argue that there is no benefit to the Indonesians in such releases.

What I did do was to point out to some friendly contacts in the Indonesian government how this was perceived by those who saw it. In doing so I expressed no doubt that this was a genuine release, but stressed the desirability of adding features to such a ceremony to give it greater credibility.

The Indonesians did proceed with release ceremonies in succeeding years, and the international community generally came to accept the genuineness of the effort.

One problem remained for the United States government in Washington. Given the emergence of the East Timor question as another human rights issue and the fact that there were still prisoners in Indonesia who had not yet been tried, should the administration acknowledge the progress made in prisoner release? Clearly there were advantages in terms of relations with the Indonesians. But it was not until May of 1978 that Vice President Mondale made a statement acknowledging the Indonesian progress in this area.[15]

The decision to release the prisoners in Indonesia was one made by Indonesians. It is perhaps one that they would have made in the course of time as pressures within their own society mounted. There can be little doubt, however, that concern in the United States, the legislation that reflected that concern, and the efforts of diplomacy by several nations hastened that process; and people are free today because of diplomacy on behalf of human rights.

NOTES

1 Lexie Verdon, "Amnesty Finds Indonesians Worst on Prisoner Rights," *Washington Post*, October 19, 1977, A10.

2 Rowland Evans and Robert Novak, "Aid vs. Human Rights," *Washington Post*, January 15, 1976, A19; "Human Rights Violations in Indonesia," a Letter to the Editor by Carmel Budiardjo, *Washington Post*, February 11, 1976, A12.

3 David A. Andelman, "Jakarta Strives to Keep Foreign Aid; More U.S. Arms and Other Help Due," *New York Times*, November 26, 1975, p. 8; Don Oberdorfer, "12 Groups Press Carter on Human Rights Overseas," *Washington Post*, January 17, 1977, A2.

4 "US Military Aid Is Barred to Thailand, Indonesia," *New York Times*, May 4, 1977, p. 17.

5 H.D.S. Greenway, "Indonesia: Another Round of Political Trials," *Washington Post*, August 14, 1974, A15.

6 Jusuf Wanandi, "Human Rights: An Indonesian View," *Far Eastern Economic Review*, December 2, 1977, pp. 22-24.

7 "Indonesia: Devil's Island," *Newsweek*, January 2, 1978, p. 29; David Jenkins, "Indonesia: The Struggle for Survival on Buru," *Far Eastern Economic Review*, December 30, 1977, pp. 12-14.

8 "Indonesia's Island Prison for Families," a Letter to the Editor by Ruth B. Haas, *Washington Post*, November 27, 1976, A14.

9 "Amnesty International Declares Jakarta Holds 100,000 Prisoners," *New York Times*, September 22, 1976, p. 80.

10 Hamish McDonald, "The Ghosts from 'Gestapu.' " *Far Eastern Economic Review*, May 28, 1976, pp. 10-12.

11 For information on these subsequent reports, see, for example, "US Says 6

Nations Curb Rights But Urges That Arms Aid Go On," *New York Times*, January 1, 1977, p. A14.; "Excerpts from State Department's Reports on the Status of Human Rights Abroad," *New York Times*, February 10, 1978, p. A14.

12 "Indonesia Starting to Free Some Political Prisoners," *New York Times*, December 2, 1975, p. 10; Hamish McDonald, "Indonesians to Free Prisoners," *Washington Post*, July 9, 1976, A21, "Indonesia Frees 2,500 Held Since '65 Coup Bid," *Washington Post*, December 2, 1976, A40, and "Jakarta Frees 10,000 Detainees," *Washington Post*, December 21, 1977, A24; "Indonesians Report 10,000 Capitives Freed: Some Suspected Communists Held for 12 Years without Trial," *New York Times*, December 21, 1977, p. 9.

13 David Jenkins, "Indonesia: Opening Doors for Detainees," *Far Eastern Economic Review*, December 17, 1976, p. 26.

14 Pranay Gupte, "Indonesia Accused by Rights Group," *New York Times*, October 19, 1977, p. 2.

15 "Mondale, in Indonesia, Says U.S. Appreciates Freeing of Prisoners," *Washington Post*, May 7, 1978, A30.

The Ford Administration Response to Human Rights Violations in Brazil

Jeffrey D. Merritt

Jeffrey Merritt's research details the issues in human rights with Brazil during the Ford administration and includes the perceptive comments of Ambassador John Crimmins on the diplomacy of that period.

Torture and other human rights violations occurred in Brazil during Gerald Ford's presidency, but less extensively than in the 1969–73 period. A trend toward human rights improvement, bolstered by President Ernesto Geisel's *abertura* (political "opening") and crackdown on army abuses, persuaded the Ford administration that Brazil would manage well without strong American pressure.[1] Not wishing to erode American influence in other areas of U.S.-Brazilian relations, U.S. officials generally avoided public criticism, while favoring quiet intercession and supporting multilateral initiatives. The administration continued military assistance to Brazil and moved to strengthen overall trade and diplomatic relations.

The Morris Incident

Initially complicating the administration's Brazil policy was the arrest, imprisonment, and torture of American Fred Morris by Army authorities in Recife. Morris, a former Methodist missionary and part-time journalist, was accused of subversive activity as a result of his association with known opponents of the Brazilian regime. U.S. officials had known Morris was under surveillance, had satisfied themselves he was involved in no anti-government activities, and had alerted Brazilian authorities in advance of their strong inter-

111

est in Morris' welfare. His arrest and subsequent abuse were therefore taken by the U.S. embassy as a direct challenge to the United States.

The American consulate in Recife, particularly Consul Richard Brown, reacted vigorously to Morris' mistreatment.[2] Following Brown's personal intercession and a strong protest from Ambassador John Crimmins,[3] the abuse of Morris stopped and he was soon released.

The sharp embassy reaction—limited only to Morris' predicament and not to the broader torture issue—perturbed both the Brazilian government and the State Department. Angry that the American embassy gave details of the incident to the U.S. press, Brasilia ostracized Ambassador Crimmins for several weeks.

> The whole government was upset, but the military was furious—the hardline commander of the Fourth Army, the intelligence people in the Army and the Army Minister....They were concerned, first, that we were making such a big thing of this, and second, that, in response to persistent questioning, we had told the press of actions we had taken.[4]

According to several officials other than Crimmins with whom I spoke, Consul Brown was at some point "disciplined" by Secretary of State Kissinger. Ambassador Crimmins described the response of the Department of State to his own action:

> I notified the department by telephone—I think it was Harry Shlaudeman who was deputy assistant secretary at the time—and I told him I was going to...send a strong note. And he said "Well, if you think it's necessary, O.K." Now, what the upper levels in the department felt I don't really know. I received several weeks after the event a rather delphic communication from the assistant secretary which was carefully if not artfully worded. And I wrote back, "Am I supposed to look upon this as some sort of reprimand?" And I never got a reply. It was, as I say, very ambiguously worded. Now, I never talked to Henry Kissinger about this. Kissinger never talked to me about it. And no one in the department ever talked to me about it in any substantive way. I talked to the Brazilian country director about it, but I never received, other than that ambiguous letter, any reaction from the department.[5]

Morris' ordeal and the actions of the American embassy in obtaining his release received a full review by the House International Organizations Subcommittee on December 11, 1974.[6] Chairman Donald Fraser, who had previously expressed concern about Brazilian abuses,[7] said he wished U.S. officials "might be as outspoken concerning the thousands of Brazilians who have been tortured—oftentimes with great severity." He criticized the administration's request for $60 million in FY74 military credit sales to Brazil "notwithstanding the oppression."[8] Morris, who praised the U.S. embassy's action in his case, also recommended U.S. intercession on behalf of mistreated Brazilians and an end to U.S. financial support for repressive regimes such as Brazil's.[9]

Press coverage of the Morris affair kept the Brazilian human rights issue alive in U.S. policy circles when it otherwise might have faded. For in November 1974, Brazilians voted in congressional elections—the freest in ten years. While the results indicated strong dissatisfaction with Brazil's military leadership,[10] the elections themselves underscored the Geisel government's commitment to *abertura*.

An Uneven "Decompression"

The process of *distensão* (controlled relaxation or "decompression") which marked the first phase of the political opening was unsteady, uneven, and subject to occasional reverses in the 1974–76 period. Geisel's turning from Medici's harsher policies emboldened Brazilian intellectuals, church leaders, and lawyers to work for an end to censorship and torture and for a complete restoration of legal processes.[11] Censorship was, in fact, quietly ended in all but a handful of Brazil's newspapers and magazines early in 1975. Geisel refused, however, to fully satisfy the demands of the legal opposition [MDB] for clarifying the fate of "missing persons" and political prisoners.[12]

Part of Geisel's problem was the considerable power of military hard-liners in the government and in the Second Army—security forces which often abused human rights in the name of anti-communism. These repressive forces constituted a virtual "parallel government," strongly opposed to *abertura* and capable of mounting a coup. With Geisel constantly on guard against criticism from these hard-liners, progress on human rights was sometimes slow.

Professor Albert Fishlow contends that "the United States was drawn increasingly into an adversary position" on human rights in 1975, with congressional interest pushing the State Department "into a more active stance than it wished, but still less than the U.S. Embassy in Brasilia counseled."[13]

Fishlow is essentially correct, though department officials themselves differed in their attitudes towards Brazil's situation. From all accounts, Secretary Kissinger did not stress human rights in discussions with Brazil's formidable Foreign Minister Antonio Azeredo da Silveira,[14] with whom he developed a personal correspondence.[15] Nor did Kissinger wish subordinates to press the rights issue. The secretary's well-publicized distaste for "forceful" human rights démarches carried considerable weight within the department's Brazil bureaucracy. Though more inclined to criticize Brazil than Kissinger, Assistant Secretary William D. Rogers generally offered moderate suggestions for diplomatic representations. Human rights officer George Lister of the Inter-American Affairs Bureau (ARA) was more resolute in encouraging the department and/or embassy to speak out.

Ambassador John Hugh Crimmins

Ambassador John Crimmins took human rights seriously, and his philosophy of human rights protection helped to shape U.S. policy toward Brazil for several years, most notably when he served as U.S. ambassador there from 1973 to 1978. For Crimmins, "the overridingly most important aspect of human rights is the integrity of the person....My principal concern in Brazil was always the physical integrity of the person—disappearances, torture, arbitrary arrest, habeas corpus, that kind of thing."[16] Crimmins felt rights relating to political, economic and social progress were conceptually vague, and found them difficult to influence effectively and directly through diplomacy. While not overlooking the political "openness" issue, he referred to it indirectly—"making sure in our USIA output, in my own speeches [that] our experience with a constitutional, open system was put forward with the informed Brazilian public, in effect, noting the differences." He believed this policy was "reasonably successful."[17]

For handling "physical integrity" cases, Crimmins set "ground rules" which were based largely on the "nearness of the U.S. interest." The department "was aware of them and certainly didn't object to them." In cases where a mistreated Brazilian had dual nationality—especially American—the United States would intercede on the basis of that association. Normally the embassy wouldn't "touch at all" cases of "pure Brazilians...where we had no handle." But intercessions would sometimes be made in "pure Brazilian cases which had aroused very considerable interest in the United States." In such instances, where a particular U.S. interest group or member of Congress had inquired, "we would go in on these cases citing the interest in the United States...as a cover for our expressions of concern and requests for information." There were "gradations in this spectrum" as well as "in the level at which we made the pitches," said Crimmins.

> Some cases were handled by the counselor for political affairs with the head of the America section in Itamaraty [the Brazilian Foreign Ministry]; there were some cases that I followed up with the secretary general or even with the foreign minister. It was a combination of the heinousness of the allegation...of the alleged treatment and the strength or tenuousness of the link with the United States that tended to govern the nature and the level at which these cases were brought to the attention of the Brazilian authorities.

This "technique, and it *was* technique," stressed Crimmins, varied from case to case but remained much the same throughout his years in Brazil.[18]

The ambassador conceded that his embassy was in a "much better position to move" on a human rights case when it had the backing of credible institutions such as Congress or major religious organizations.[19] He denied, however, that the embassy never interceded of its own volition. Frequently, U.S. officials would informally raise "questions of a more general, less specific, less specifically supported nature" with their Brazilian counterparts "at a dinner or over drinks....

> Certainly we mentioned that...the Congress is interested or that the church groups of the United States are interested. We almost always coupled this with "this is affecting the image of Brazil in the United States and making it very difficult for us to have the kind of relationship that we want." Now that, to a cynic or to a "red hot," would be interpreted as a cop-out. But it does have meaning....The Brazilian government was very conscious throughout of its image.[20]

Ambassador Crimmins' intelligence and professionalism were widely respected. Human rights activists would have liked greater pressure on the Brazilians. Brazil's military hard-liners and Dr. Kissinger would have preferred a less aggressive style. However, Crimmins provided a sensible, moderate approach to U.S.-Brazilian relations in general and human rights intercession in particular.

The Crimmins embassy interceded perhaps a half-dozen times a year.[21] According to Crimmins, such U.S. representations were normally "received politely and notes were taken. Every once in a while there would be some small challenge to the legitimacy of our interest but nothing like 'This is none of your business. We don't want to talk about it!' " To minimize Brazilian objection, the embassy, as indicated, sought to manifest—whenever possible—a U.S. "angle" to the human rights case it would raise. However, the Brazilians rarely satisfied the embassy "in terms of full reports of what happened" in these cases. "Quite frankly," said Crimmins, "we never expected to get them."[22]

The Herzog Incident and Ednardo Firing

Brazil's most notorious human rights violation of 1975, the torture-death of journalist Vladimir Herzog,[23] had no American angle other than the indignation it aroused in certain U.S. circles. Herzog's death, following a wave of repression and arrests,[24] stimulated tremendous outcry in Brazil and elsewhere for an end to such brutality and for a fixing of blame. Ambassador Crimmins could not remember whether his embassy took up the Herzog case with the Brazilian government "because of interest in the United States," or whether it felt no need to assert the U.S. angle given the loud internal uproar.

Slightly more than a month after the Herzog murder Ambassador Crimmins delivered a major speech in São Paulo on "the history of the sanctity of the person in American constitutional history." The speech, part of the U.S. bicentennial celebration in that city, was favorably reviewed by the audience and "was given pretty heavy press play in São Paulo."[25] Military hard-liners could not have been pleased with this choice of topics. Indeed, when Crimmins resurrected the theme later in the year [in Minas Gerais, following the Carter election]—in a speech in which he quoted from the American Declaration of Independence—he was sharply criticized in some government circles.[26] "The military...reacted as if I were trying to subvert the government," said Crimmins, who cited his two speeches as successful examples of "indirect" commentary on the course of Brazilian events.[27]

Senator Edward Kennedy was among those in Washington who saw in Herzog's murder—and the torture of Morris—a failure of the Geisel government to put an end to human rights violations. Saying he had expressed his concern to the State Department, Kennedy urged the Senate to take these recent events into consideration in considering the foreign aid package for 1976.[28]

President Geisel, seeking to erase any notion that he had given a "green light" to recompression,[29] warned the powerful Second Army commander, Ednardo D'Avila Mello, against a recurrence of such abuses as Herzog had suffered. When a second incident—the "suicide" (killing) of labor leader Manuel Fiel Filho—did occur, Geisel took the courageous step of firing Ednardo. The sacking of such a prominent officer did not go unnoticed by U.S. officials. To Ambassador Crimmins, "this was a major breakthrough from a human rights point of view.... [It] captured and set the tone of the Geisel administration with respect to human rights."[30]

Kissinger's Visit and "Consultation" Accord

Secretary Kissinger's visit to Brazil in February 1976 followed on the heels of this significant human rights development, but had no connection to it. Indeed, the secretary's trip had been several times rescheduled.[31] Its basic objectives were to reassure Brazil's government that the United States remained a purposeful world leader, to clarify American acceptance of Brazil as an emerging world power, to soothe Brazilian resentment over certain American economic policies, and to formally establish a mechanism for future, regularized consultation on bilateral and global issues.[32]

A "secret" February 9 memorandum to Kissinger from Assistant Secretary Rogers reveals keen departmental awareness of continuing human rights controversy within Brazil.

Human rights abuses have been the subject of public outcry by members of the Brazilian Congress, the media, the Church and civic and professional groups but hard-line military elements have resisted Geisel's efforts to control the security apparatus. Tensions aroused last October by the death of prominent TV news analyst Vladimir Herzog to all appearances at the hands of army intelligency [sic] interrogators, and the scandal of a similar death last month, have apparently prompted Geisel to try again....[33]

Noting "the past year's upsurge in political arrests and torture," and President Geisel's efforts to control the security apparatus, Rogers warned Kissinger that it was "too soon...to rule out a military backlash that could once more force Geisel to retrench." Rogers also alerted the secretary to the possibility of Brazil's human rights performance soon becoming "a highly troublesome issue" in U.S.-Brazilian relations as a result of "increasing public and congressional scrutiny."[34]

Geisel's reaffirmation of his *abertura/distensão* program and his dismissal of General Ednardo made the "consultation" accord signed by Kissinger and Silveira slightly more palatable to liberal critics. The agreement naturally fueled talk of a "special relationship" between the United States and Brazil, but its importance—symbolic and substantive—was overstated by the press. The press' attitude was mixed as to the human rights impact of the consultation agreement. Most commentators concluded that Washington's image in the world would only be further sullied by strengthening its association with Brazil's military leaders. Others saw the accord as possibly advancing human rights.

The *Los Angeles Times* said it could be argued that "the new arrangement will give the United States leverage with which to press...for an end to torture and for genuine moves toward democratic rights and freedoms." But it added there was no reason to believe that Kissinger would employ such leverage.[35] Professor Frank D. McCann argued that lending prestige to the Geisel government in this manner would "strengthen the positive drift toward a more open, more civilian government."[36]

Ambassador Crimmins said the agreement was "not a big thing" from the U.S. point of view. Indeed, Washington was "very doubtful about the utility" of such an accord when the Brazilians first pressed for it in 1975.

Through 1975 we didn't pursue this very actively because we believed that this might not be good for Brazil in the sense that it could arouse sensitivities in other Latin American countries. We also made it clear that we were prepared to do this with other Latin American countries...Argentina, Venezuela, Mexico.[37]

Secretary Kissinger himself downplayed the significance of the new arrangement upon his return to the United States, telling congressmen that Washington and Brasilia had been systematically consulting in any event.

The House International Relations Committee did not question Kissinger on Brazilian human rights issues, nor did the secretary offer any observation.[38] In Brazil, Kissinger made several uncritical references to human rights and apparently did not make human rights a prominent issue in his private discussions with Geisel and Silveira.[39] Rogers' memorandum nonetheless suggested several "talking points" on human rights.

—The US policy on human rights is well known and is rooted in the deepest traditions of our society and Western humanistic values.
—US espousal of international initiatives to further human rights is not an attempt to single out or embarrass individual countries; our support for studies of alleged violations is consistent with our belief in the Universal Declaration of Human Rights.
—We admire the Geisel Administration's efforts gradually to bring about a political environment in keeping with the increasing complexity of Brazilian society, and an increasing respect for human rights.
—We are aware how delicate this task is, but we believe in Brazil's bright future and wish the President every success.
—Human rights issues are a matter of widespread concern in the United States, and recent congressional moves to link our economic and military assistance programs to human rights performance could present difficulties in US-Brazilian relations.[40]

Asked at a press conference about human rights in Brazil, Kissinger replied:

It is not my obligation here publicly to discuss internal Brazilian affairs....We have stated our view on the human rights issue repeatedly. The United States supports respect of the individual and democratic governments.[41]

Earlier, he had declared that

there are no two peoples whose concern for human dignities and for the basic values of man is more profound in day-to-day life than Brazil and the United States.[42]

This comment surprised and discomfited some U.S. officials, including Ambassador Crimmins,[43] and angered critics of close U.S.-Brazilian collaboration. The *New York Times*, in an editorial entitled "Hyperbole in Brasilia," declared that Kissinger's "paean of praise for Brazil—and by implication its authoritarian military regime—went beyond the bounds of reason." It argued that the secretary's speech would harm relations with other Latin American nations, give respectability to leftist charges of U.S.-Brazilian collusion and bolster Washington's image as a supporter of right-wing dictatorships.[44] Foreign Minister Silveira attacked the *Times'* editorial as "irresponsible" and as an example of "misunderstanding and injustice."[45]

Brazilian officials, pleased by Kissinger's demeanor, said he had respected Brazil's sovereignty in his talks on "sensitive issues" such as human rights.[46] Kissinger said only that he had learned from his talks with Brazilian officials "their perception of the role of human rights" in Brazil's development.[47]

Human Rights and "Development"

Kissinger and other U.S. officials often viewed Brazil's human rights problems in the context of the nation's overall development picture. American policymakers neither ignored nor minimized the significance of reported human rights violations. But they also appreciated Brazil's enormous task of constructing a sound, high-growth economy, and understood Brazilian arguments that quasi-authoritarian political structures or "guided" democracy best suited such a development phase.

Kissinger recognized Brazil's economic achievements during the seventies. He was also impressed by Brazil's first-rate foreign ministry and the fact that, as Professor Riordan Roett put it, "the Brazilians stood out in international meetings as a voice of reason and moderation."[48] The secretary of state rarely focused on Latin America and, to be sure, Brazil was never at the center of his concerns. Yet by 1976, Roett explained, "Kissinger was very clearly respond-ing to being pushed by people like [Assistant Secretary] William Rogers at the State Department who argued that countries like Brazil required a slightly different way of looking at the world." Certainly, Brazil came to have a higher priority for the secretary than most other Third World countries. In the seven-ties, said Roett, moderate Brazil "loomed as an obvious friend and ally from a Kissinger-Nixon-Ford position," particularly given the United States' "traditional hostility with Argentina, and the rather militant position then being taken by Mexico and Venezuela."[49] That Kissinger and the State Department restrained their human rights criticism followed logically from this perception of Brazil's overall importance and politico-economic posture.

Washington Supports U.N. Investigation

Although Kissinger was reluctant to criticize Brazil's human rights record publicly, the department was not unwilling to see the Brazilian case investigated by the United Nations. Indeed, Kissinger was in Brasilia when it was reported—to his considerable embarrassment—that U.S. representative Leonard Garment had requested the U.N. Commission on Human Rights to take such action.[50] Brazil privately protested Garment's move, but there were no serious diplomatic repercussions.[51]

One State Department official recalled Garment's action clearly, noting that Brazil was the foremost issue that came up in that 1976 Commission and that the U.S. delegation went to Geneva that February with a government-cleared position to support consideration of the Brazilian case by the Commission. This official thought the Morris torture incident a principal factor underlying the U.S. position. As it turned out, the Commission decided to drop the case, although the U.S. voted in favor of discussion.[52]

This was a relatively minor intercessionary episode, but noteworthy inasmuch as it demonstrated the Ford administration's preference for multilateral action in the Brazilian case. At a time of growing congressional attention to human rights, the administration perhaps felt it could build credibility by supporting U.N. discussion and/or investigation of an ally's human rights practices, while avoiding riskier unilateral intercession.[53] It is significant that Kissinger, though chagrined by Garment's unfortunate timing, never disavowed Garment's position. Indeed, later in 1976, Kissinger personally supported strengthening the Inter-American Commission on Human Rights—another multilateral panel with an interest in Brazil. Having supported U.N. investigation of Chilean violations in 1975 and having previously supported U.N. Commission initiatives in principle, the secretary was unlikely to disavow Garment's request for a Brazilian investigation.

Whether Kissinger knew of Garment's specific intention to name Brazil in advance of his Brazilian trip is unclear. He would have known [and perhaps did] had he read the memo prepared for him by Assistant Secretary Rogers. It states that the "U.S. representatives on the Commission are instructed to *support, or if necessary to initiate along with other members, a study of the Brazilian situation*" [emphasis mine]. Rogers' memorandum made clear that this position would be resented.

> While this question will be considered in confidential session a GOB observer will probably be present. The U.S. action is consistent with our global policy and will be welcomed by many concerned Brazilians; it will, however, generate a degree of resentment within the GOB, especially among the military.[54]

The U.N. investigation threat appears to have had a meaningful impact on Brasilia. Brazil's representatives reportedly made strenuous efforts to avoid discussion of the case by the Commission, conferring with practically every Commission member. They even made a formal complaint.[55] It is unlikely that the U.N.'s abortive investigation altered Brazilian government practices. However, Brasilia's sensitivity to human rights intercession was heightened. Brazil sought—and gained—membership in the Commission the following year, and has since been active in advancing a restrictive view of permissible U.N. human rights activity.

Torture Subsides

Human rights violations did not stop abruptly after Geisel's sacking of Ednardo. Indeed, Geisel's struggle to tame Brazil's security apparatus continued. Abuses and 'death squad' activities at state and local levels persisted, but torture and prisoner mistreatment directly involving agents of the federal government subsided.[56] Satisfied that Brazil's government sought to combat abuse through disciplinary action, U.S. officials generally believed intercession to be counterproductive. Some Americans had excused Brasilia's actions all along—even during the worst excesses of the Medici period. Others saw a real difference between Geisel's handling of human rights problems and Medici's and believed it was better to "lay off" than to prod an essentially reformist leadership.

Democrats Remain Critical

Despite improvements at the federal level, reports continued to surface in 1976 regarding mistreatment of Brazilian prisoners—political and nonpolitical.[57] Senator Edward Kennedy remained in the forefront of Americans critical of Brazil, along with fellow Democratic presidential contender, Jimmy Carter.[58] As a result, Brasilia concluded that its best interests required a Republican victory in the U.S. elections.

Kennedy, in a May 10 Senate speech, released documents he claimed had been recently smuggled out of Brazil by political prisoners. Such disclosures of "recent torture," he said, could "only serve to create enormous dissatisfaction with the U.S. Government's recent accord with Brazil and reemphasize[d] the need to act on the basis of our oft-repeated declarations in support of human rights."[59] In April 1976 the senator urged Secretary Kissinger to express concern to Brazilian authorities over the "cassation" [removal of political rights] of two Brazilian congressmen.[60]

The department's noncommittal reply did not satisfy Kennedy. Robert J. McCloskey, assistant secretary for congressional relations, said only that the department appreciated Kennedy's concern for the safety of one of the cassated congressmen and promised "to follow closely any further developments." He did not say whether the U.S. government had interceded in the case.

McCloskey's letter added that

> in terms of general policy, the Brazilian Government is fully aware of the
> position of the Executive Branch, the U.S. Congress, and the American
> public on human rights....U.S. officials have publicly expressed concern
> over reports of torture and mistreatment of prisoners on several occasions
> and have done so privately with officials at different levels of the Brazilian
> Government.[61]

Following his May 10 speech, the senator wrote again, demanding to know
how recently—and in what "form"—the department had publicly expressed
"concern over reports of torture and mistreatment in Brazil." Kennedy also
inquired as to whether the department had evaluated human rights conditions in
Brazil, and whether it considered "the continued reports of torture...a legitimate reason for reevaluating the current request of $60 million for military
support for the Brazilian Government." Kennedy urged "such a reevaluation
and at least a substantial lowering of the amount of military assistance."[62]

Assistant Secretary McCloskey's reply provides insight into State's thinking
on Brazilian developments, specific responses to those developments, and the
overall effectiveness of unilateral versus multilateral intercession.

> The last several years have seen a greater emphasis, both in our internal
> policy formulation processes and in our public policy statements, on the
> importance of human rights considerations....
>
> Human rights considerations are taken into account in our policy plan-
> ning processes and in the programming of U.S. assistance. The issue is
> seldom simple. In many cases it is questionable whether direct bilateral
> pressures for changes in internal structures and practices will produce the
> effects desired. Often this type of pressure generates nationalistic
> reactions which blur the essential question of human rights. The effects of
> such pressures on other important interests in a country must also be
> carefully weighed....
>
> Our private bilateral representations with specific countries, including
> Brazil, have continued. But we also believe that concerted international
> action, through appropriate and adequately supported institutions such as
> the Inter-American Commission on Human Rights...is the most effective
> way to promote wider observance of these norms.[63]

McCloskey said the department's "most recent public statement on human
rights explicitly singling out Brazil was made in testimony before [the House
International Organizations Subcommittee] in 1973." As for military aid,
McCloskey wrote:

After analysis and review, we have concluded that a United States Government move to substantially reduce this [$60 million Foreign Military Sales] credit availability on human rights grounds would be unlikely to further our human rights objectives and would, in addition, adversely affect our basic bilateral relationships and the broad range of our other interests in Brazil.[64]

McCloskey conceded there had been ups and downs in President Geisel's liberalization program,[65] but stressed that since late January 1976

political arrests have decreased, formalized procedures for detention and judicial review have been followed to a somewhat greater extent, and reports of torture of political prisoners seem to have greatly diminished.[66]

McCloskey's letter drew heavily upon reports prepared by the Inter-American Affairs Bureau and Crimmins' embassy. The first formal State Department report on Brazil's human rights situation was prepared in 1975, but Secretary Kissinger refused to allow it to be sent to Capitol Hill. A second report was prepared within the department during 1976, again with considerable embassy input and drafting. It was this report—essentially a Ford administration product—that precipitated a small crisis in U.S.-Brazilian relations when released by the Carter administration in February 1977.

Ambassador Crimmins said that insofar as he knew "there were no changes" made upon the Ford administration's draft by Carter officials.

In fact, I used to point this out to Brazilians, who said that this was all Jimmy Carter's doing. And I said, "Look, the act [requiring the report] was passed in the Ford period. The thing was prepared before the change of government." ...I have the firm recollection that everything was set by early January [1977]....The department introduced some changes, but we thought it was a balanced report.[67]

James Wilson recalled that reports from Crimmins' embassy were generally positive—that "while there were some objectionable elements in the whole picture, it was their feeling that things were getting better instead of worse."[68]

Overview

The Ford administration faced a different situation in Brazil than did the Nixon administration. By the end of 1974, Brazil had essentially crushed its radical insurgency and had demonstrated its capacity for decompression by holding elections and easing censorship. Under President Geisel, further liberalizations were pledged and ultimately occurred, though with reverses. The Brazilian growth "miracle" continued, but sharply higher oil prices threatened not only a slowdown and mounting debt but also additional foreign policy realignment.

Washington responded cautiously to these new realities, stressing consultation to iron out economic differences and better understand Brasilia's new foreign policy positions. The 1974–76 period saw a continuing U.S.-Brazilian military alliance, with the United States providing military assistance each year and allowing Brazil to purchase armaments essentially without restriction. Economic assistance, however, was entirely phased out—more a consequence of Brazil's own economic success than of congressional human rights criticism.

In this period of congressional activism on human rights, certain congressmen—notably, Senator Kennedy and Representative Fraser—continued to monitor the Brazilian situation, speaking out whenever there appeared to be serious abuses or a weakening resolve on the part of the Geisel regime to address them seriously. But overall the human rights trend in Brazil was a positive one, and most congressmen seemed willing to accept the administration's laissez-faire posture towards Brazil as being in the best interests of both nations and the hemisphere. Somewhat forgotten in the furor over Chile, Brazil never became the human rights *cause célèbre* it might have become had the human rights issue blossomed two or three years earlier.

Notes

1 Because of generally forward movement toward political liberalization—including the holding of legislative elections in 1974—and the gradual easing of press censorship, Brazilians themselves were far more able to criticize their government's human rights record than they had been under the previous administration of General Emilio Medici.

2 For an account of Brown's actions—and of Morris' ordeal—see U.S. Congress, House Committee on Foreign Affairs. Subcommittee on International Organizations and Movements, *Torture and Oppression in Brazil: Hearing*, 93rd Cong., 2nd sess., Dec. 11 1974 (Washington: U.S. Govt. Printing Office, 1975), pp. 2-14.

3 Ambassador Crimmins "personally drafted...a very strong note...in effect demanding medical treatment for [Morris], examination of him, and an explanation. And efforts to find the parties responsible and 'punishment.' ...I didn't use that term." John Hugh Crimmins, interview, Kensington, Maryland, July 6, 1982, hereafter cited as Crimmins interview #2. An earlier interview, on July 1, 1982, will be cited as Crimmins interview #1. Crimmins served as U.S. Ambassador to Brazil from August 1973 to February 1978.

4 Crimmins interview #2.

5 Crimmins interview #2. (An official of the State Department Bureau of Inter-American Affairs (ARA) recalled that there were those in Washington who weren't particularly happy with the ambassador's reaction to the Morris incident. The official said he personally believed Crimmins' response had been properly stern. Interview not for attribution.)

6 *Torture and Oppression in Brazil: Hearing.*

7 See Subcommittee on International Organizations and Movements, House Committee on Foreign Affairs, *International Protection of Human Rights...: Hearings*, 93rd Cong., 1st Sess., pp. 187ff.

8 *Torture and Oppression in Brazil: Hearing*, p. 1.

9 Ibid., p. 14. Morris' testimony was partly prepared by a leader of the American NGO contingent seeking to end U.S. support of Brazil's military government. Interview not for attribution.

10 The Movimento Democrático Brasileiro (MDB), the legally sanctioned opposition party, captured 16 of 22 Senate seats and 160 of 364 Chamber of Deputies seats at stake. Stefan Robock, *Brazil: A Study in Development Progress* (Lexington: Lexington Books, 1975), p. 162.

11 Albert Fishlow, "The United States and Brazil: The Case of the Missing Relationship," *Foreign Affairs* 60 (Spring 1982): 914.

12 Thomas G. Sanders, "Decompression," in Handelman and Sanders, eds., *Military Government and the Movement toward Democracy in America* (Bloomington: Indiana University Press, 1981), p. 156.

13 Fishlow, "The United States and Brazil," p. 907.

14 Silveira played a key role in U.S.-Brazilian relations during both the Ford and Carter administrations. Outspoken, strongly opposed to outside "interference" in Brazilian affairs, and prone to "leak," Silveira was described by one official as "one really tough nut." Interview not for attribution.

15 In a toast to Kissinger delivered during the Secretary's February 1976 visit to Brazil, Silveira disclosed that the two ministers had averaged one personal meeting every four months "in the last 22 months [since May 1974]." Silveira declared:
> In the interval between those meetings we have kept our personal contacts, and our foreign ministries are maintaining the practice of trying to keep each other informed on the viewpoint of each government on questions of common interest.

Silveira said a "personal friendship and confidence" had grown "between us" during these two years. U.S. *Foreign Broadcast Information Service* [FBIS], Daily Report for Latin America, 24 Feb. 1976, p. D3. *Jornal do Brasil*, in Portuguese, 20 Feb. 1976, p. 4.

16 Crimmins interview #2.

17 Ibid.

18 Ibid.

19 Crimmins stressed that all embassies received scores, sometimes hundreds, of allegations of mistreatment and that only rarely could these be independently confirmed. "And there is nothing more frustrating than to raise an allegation and to have the allegation blow up in your face." Crimmins said it wasn't "stonewalling the question most of the time" to be cautious about interceding when the allegations lacked a concrete base. This would occur when there was nothing other than "allegations of relatives or political colleagues or coreligionists...." Crimmins interview #1.

20 Ibid.

21 Crimmins interview #2.

22 Crimmins interview #2. Ambassador Crimmins noted two such cases that the embassy had taken up with Brazilian officials—that of Stuart Angel-Jones, a "disappeared" person of mixed [U.S. and Brazilian] parentage, and that of another missing young man, the son of an American Presbyterian minister who had opted for Brazilian citizenship. Ibid.

23 "Herzog died in prison after being picked up by security forces in a roundup of about 200 persons. Though the government insisted that Herzog committed suicide, their refusal to allow an autopsy encouraged belief that he had been killed." Sanders,"Decompression," p. 161.

24 The arrests occurred for a variety of reasons—many having to do with the speed of liberalization and "decompression" thought best by various political and military factions, but some being quite esoteric [e.g., the discovery of Communist printing presses].

Jan Black has concluded that the arrests were "provoked...by the military command's fears of internal subversion on the Portuguese model and by actual or anticipated criticism of economic policies." Jan Knippers Black, *U.S. Penetration of Brazil* (Manchester: Manchester University Press, 1977), p. 252.

25 Crimmins interview #2.

26 "Brazilians Upset by US Envoy," *Washington Post*, Nov. 26, 1976, p. A11.

27 Crimmins interview #2.

28 *Congressional Record*, Nov. 10, 1975, pp. S19527-28.

29 According to Ambassador Crimmins, Geisel had made a speech in August 1975, in which he stressed the need to handle economic and social issues immediately, while delaying for a brief time the political *distensão* process. This, said Crimmins, was interpreted as a backing off, or at least a standing still as a result of military pressure. The military had been alarmed and infuriated by... efforts [of] the newly strengthened opposition to set up a commission of inquiry on torture. And they [the military] made very clear that this was beyond the pale and, in effect, this [was] one of the worst fruits of *distensão*.

Ambassador Crimmins noted that a theory in Brazilian circles held that "pressure from the hard line had induced this slowing down or halting of the process," and that the security apparatus had interpreted Geisel's speech in this light. Crimmins interview #2.

30 Crimmins interview #2.

31 Earlier visits had been rescheduled for reasons having little to do with the immediate state of U.S.-Brazilian relations.

32 Department of State "Briefing Memorandum" to Secretary Henry A. Kissinger from Assistant Secretary William D. Rogers, Feb. 9, 1976, noted these and other "specific objectives."

33 Rogers "Briefing Memorandum," p. 4.

34 Ibid., p. 4.

35 "Brazil: a Special Case," *Los Angeles Times*, Feb. 22, 1976, p. IX2.

36 "The Value of U.S.-Brazilian Consultation," *New York Times*, March 6, 1976, p. 25.

37 Crimmins interview #2. Fishlow wrote that "Brazil pressed for an explicit 'special relationship' in an effort to extract the utmost in its bilateral dealings with the United States, although appreciative that there was precious little to gain." Fishlow, "The United States and Brazil," p. 907.

38 U.S. Congress, House Committee on International Relations, *Report of Secretary of State Kissinger on His Trip to Latin America*, 94th Cong., 2d sess., March 4, 1976 (Washington: U.S. Govt. Printing Office, 1976), pp. 8-13.

39 Robert G. Wesson. *The United States and Brazil: Limits of Influence* (New York: Praeger, 1981), p. 92.

40 Rogers "Briefing Memorandum," p. 14.

41 Jonathan Kandell, "U.S. and Brazil Sign Accord on Ties," *New York Times*, Feb. 22, 1976, p. 12.

42 Ibid., p. 12.

43 Crimmins interview #2.

44 *New York Times*, Feb. 21, 1976, p. 24.

45 *FBIS*, Daily Report for Latin America, 24 Feb. 1976, p. D4. Buenos Aires *Ansa* in Spanish, 1633 GMT, 23 Feb. 1976.

46 Joanne Omang, "Brazil, U.S. Sign Consultative Accord," *Washington Post*, Feb. 22, 1976, p. A23.

47 Ibid., p. A23.

48 Riordan Roett, interview, Washington, June 14, 1982.

49 Ibid.

50 Kathleen Teltsch, "U.S. Rights Aide Assails Third-World Bloc of U.N.," *New York Times*, April 2, 1976, p. 4.

51 Ambassador Crimmins said he could not "recall any impact of [Garment's] statement on the visit." Crimmins interview #2.

52 Interview not for attribution.

53 The Ford administration's policy of supporting international organization investigations of human rights violations was initiated in 1975. It purportedly applied to all countries—allies and adversaries alike.

54 Rogers "Briefing Memorandum," pp. 13-14.

55 Interview not for attribution.

56 According to a senior American official, there was no incident known to the U.S. embassy in Brasilia "after 1976" in which the federal government of Brazil was involved or appeared to be involved. The official conceded that there continued to be abuses at the state level, however. Interview not for attribution.

57 See Jack Anderson, "Torture of Political Prisoners Continues," *Washington Post*, March 27, 1976, p. E14; and Bruce Haendler, "Torture Eased But Brazil Still Crushes Dissent," *Washington Post*, April 4, 1976, p. A12.

58 Carter was an early opponent of the Kissinger-Silveira consultation agreement and openly denounced Brazil's nuclear agreement with West Germany. Carter's aides and backers also made a number of remarks critical of Brazil prior to the election and during the transition.

59 *Congressional Record*. [Remarks of Senator Kennedy], May 10, 1976, pp. S6754-58.

60 Senator Edward Kennedy to Secretary of State Henry Kissinger, Washington, April 19, 1976. Personal files of the author.

61 Robert J. McCloskey to Senator Edward Kennedy, Washington, May 5, 1976, personal files of the author.

62 Senator Kennedy to Assistant Secretary McCloskey, Washington, May 11, 1976.

63 Robert McCloskey to Senator Kennedy, Washington, July 30, 1976, personal files of author.

64 Ibid.

65 McCloskey wrote: "Developments in Brazil with respect to human rights and political liberalization have been mixed since 1974. The first year of President Geisel's administration saw significant relaxation of media censorship, congressional elections which were essentially free of interference or manipulation and which produced gains for the recognized opposition, and a reduction in the incidence of arbitrary arrest and reports of gross mistreatment of political prisoners. This positive movement declined in 1975 with the discovery of Communist Party printing presses and a resulting 'anti-subversion' campaign." Ibid.

66 Ibid.

67 Crimmins interview #2.

68 James Morrison Wilson, Jr. (former coordinator for human rights and humanitarian affairs), interview, Washington, Oct. 14, 1982.

Chapter 11 ARGENTINA

U.S. Human Rights Initiatives Concerning Argentina

Patrick J. Flood

No human rights situation created greater concern in Washington than that of Argentina in the 1970s. The author was part of the sustained bureaucratic and diplomatic effort to bring outside influence to bear in that country.

The Department of State made a serious, sustained effort during the Carter administration to bring U.S. influence to bear on behalf of improved observance of human rights in Argentina. Notwithstanding the difficulty of identifying direct cause-and-effect relationships in international affairs, I am convinced that these initiatives contributed to a substantial decline in human rights abuses.

The absence of international public authority means that foreign government authorities cannot be ordered to respect universal human rights standards. They must be persuaded to do this, and the means of persuasion are diverse and often indirect. Moreover, it is not simply a matter of the interaction of two governments; in the case of Argentina, domestic and international human rights organizations, the press, and other governments played an important part in moving the Argentine military regime away from repression. This essay concentrates on the role of the U.S. government, which in practice meant the Department of State and the American embassy in Buenos Aires. Within the department, the policy effort was led by the Bureau of Human Rights and Humanitarian Affairs, in which I served from September 1978 until June 1980.

On the whole, the department made good use of the available policy instruments and opportunities. There were times, however, when the push and pull of bureaucratic forces representing other U.S. national interests produced a mixed message about our priorities and detracted somewhat from the overall

The views expressed in this article do not necessarily reflect those of the U.S. Department of State.

129

impact of our human rights effort. I will touch on these internal debates only to the extent that it is necessary to explain something about the context of a given decision; this article is not about inter-bureaucratic dynamics. Finally, I will discuss a few potentially useful policy initiatives that we did not pursue because of the constant press of urgent day-to-day business, and I will offer some general recommendations on how to conduct an effective human rights policy.

Philosophy

The underlying rationale for U.S. human rights policy is that objective universal human rights standards have been recognized by the international community, especially in the Universal Declaration of Human Rights, and are valid for all countries. Moreover, the international community as a whole and its member states have an obligation to take measures to see that these standards are observed in practice. We wanted the Argentine government to understand and respond constructively to the fact that human rights were now a main strand of our foreign policy and that, for us, good relations would henceforth depend importantly on practical respect for human rights; "business as usual" would not be carried on while serious abuses continued.

In Argentina as elsewhere, it took some time, and reinforcing action, before it could be understood that this was not just a passing rhetorical fad but a primary component of the long-term U.S. approach to the rest of the world. For this reason, we in the Human Rights Bureau argued within the department that a steady, sustained effort was a prerequisite for the credibility essential to success. Although we should be prepared to respond positively to genuine, lasting improvements in human rights practices, any premature or excessive reaction would be taken as a sign of halfheartedness and thereby undercut the achievement of our policy goals. We needed to emphasize firmness over flexibility until we could be sure that a strong, sustained improving trend was clearly underway.

Principal Policy Initiatives

Although I will deal in roughly chronological order with each of the various channels through which we sought to discourage human rights abuses, it should be borne in mind that several of these means were in use simultaneously at most points during the period covered by this article. The bilateral diplomatic channel, for example, was employed in this effort more or less constantly. A week did not pass without discussion of broad human rights issues or of specific cases, either in Buenos Aires or Washington or both. My point is that an effective policy requires the integration and coordination of several mutually reinforcing efforts over an extended period.

Military Credits, Sales, and Training

Congress, exasperated by the continuing epidemic of human rights abuses and the failure of the Argentine regime to respond constructively to several high-level diplomatic approaches in 1977, legislated an end to the military supply-and-training relationship, to take effect in the autumn of 1978. In my view, this congressional action was fully warranted by the human rights situation and, more important, helpful to our efforts to convince Argentina's rulers that we were serious and that administration policy had the full backing of Congress.

Until the legislative ban finally went into effect that autumn, the Argentines probably doubted that we would go through with it. A high-level mission to Argentina in early 1978, led by Under Secretary David Newsom, warned the Argentines what would happen, and consultations continued during the succeeding months in a search for a way to satisfy the requirements of the law and achieve human rights progress while avoiding the necessity to break this traditional relationship. However, the terror continued in Argentina, and we had no basis on which to ask Congress for a postponement of the ban. It went into effect as scheduled.

As the Argentine military traditionally preferred U.S. equipment and training, and needed spare parts for equipment they already owned, we believed they would have an incentive to begin taking important measures in the human rights field when the practical impact of the cutoff began to be felt. Because restoration of the military-supply relationship would be a strong symbol of political approval, benefitting the regime's position at home and its image abroad, we made it clear throughout the Carter administration that any possibility of reestablishing this link could come only after fundamental, lasting human rights improvements. (We had already stopped selling police equipment in order to reduce our ties with that element of the repressive apparatus. Breaking the military-supply link was an even more important step both materially and symbolically.) In 1981, the relevant legislation was modified to permit the president to resume the military-supply relationship upon certification to the Congress "that the Government of Argentina has made significant progress in meeting internationally recognized principles of human rights."

Multilateral Bank Loans

During 1978, we had been abstaining on Argentine loan applications in the World Bank and the Inter-American Development Bank on projects not directed toward the fulfillment of basic human needs. At the beginning of 1979, disappearances were still occurring at a high rate, headless bodies were once again washing up on Argentine beaches, as they had on several occasions in 1976–78, and the number of political detainees remained in the thousands. The Human Rights Bureau became convinced the U.S. should start voting "no" on

Argentina's applications for loans other than for basic human needs, as a signal of our deep concern at the persistence of these violations. Although some other bureaus argued against toughening our stand, Deputy Secretary Warren Christopher agreed that we should vote no.

A few days before the voting on the next set of loans, we informed the Argentines of our decision and of the reasons for it. As a result of subsequent discussions, understandings, and assurances, we decided to maintain our abstention. For the next few months, every time we reported a new disappearance to the Argentine government, there was prompt and effective action, and the missing were found (usually in jail, but alive and accessible by family and lawyers). Unfortunately, this good behavior began to lapse as new unresolved cases started to occur later in the spring, although at nowhere near the rate that had prevailed in 1978 and earlier.

At least for a few months, U.S. firmness—in the form of a prospective "no" vote—had a tangible positive effect. This is somewhat remarkable, in view of the fact that a U.S. "no" would not have been sufficient to defeat the loans; in fact, it would have counted the same as an abstention, because a majority affirmative (weighted) vote is needed for approval. The importance of the prospective shift lay in its political symbolism and in the fact that a U.S. "no" could perhaps have stimulated enough other switches—even from "yes" to "abstain"—to defeat the applications. Such an outcome would have been a staggering political defeat for the Argentine regime.

Although we could have shifted to a "no" as soon as any new unexplained disappearance occurred, the Argentines continued to assure us that they were actively investigating these few unresolved cases; as we hoped that these efforts would turn out as successfully as those earlier in the year, we decided to wait and see. Also, sometimes weeks passed before we heard of a new case, thereby suggesting that perhaps we had seen the end of this phase of the problem (but not, of course, of the problem of locating the thousands who had previously vanished). By August, attention on all sides had shifted to the impending visit of the Inter-American Commission on Human Rights, which was already seized with these recent cases and with the thousands of earlier disappearances. It was time to see what the commission could do about these and other problems.

Inter-American Commission on Human Rights of the Organization of American States (IACHR)

The IACHR had asked as early as 1977 for permission to conduct an on-site visit to Argentina. The authorization finally came in September 1978 in connection with the "EXIM Affair" (described below). Approval of the visit meant that for the first time the Argentine regime accepted that it was answerable to the international community for its human rights practices, and that the international community had a legitimate interest in the matter. Before the visit, the authorities took a number of steps to improve the physical conditions of confinement of political detainees. Reports of mistreatment began to decline.

For these reasons, the visit was clearly a success, although it was unable to make headway in resolving disappearances. Moreover, the commission produced an objective, well-documented public report. An impartial, official hemispheric body had now laid the facts on the public record and had recommended specific improvements. The hemisphere would be watching Argentina's compliance with these recommendations. Argentine policymakers were beginning to accord more weight to the country's international reputation, and the visit was a factor in stimulating a trend toward better observance of human rights.

Export-Import Bank (EXIM)

In mid-1978, the State Department decided to invoke the human rights provisions of the EXIM legislation to deny financing for the large Yacyreta hydroelectric power project in Argentina. Technically, the denial applied only to an early phase of the financing process and was therefore more of a delay than an outright refusal.

As it was the first use of the human rights provision of the EXIM law, the political impact was considerable. In the U.S., the temporary denial touched off a massive lobbying campaign in the executive branch and Congress by the American firms who stood to lose contracts worth several hundred million dollars. There was consternation in Buenos Aires, as the message began to be understood that "business as usual" could no longer be taken for granted while serious human rights abuses persisted. (As the arms embargo would not come into effect until several months later, and we had not yet begun to reexamine our voting position in the multilateral banks, the EXIM "hold" was the first visible sign that we were prepared to back our words with material actions.)

After a great deal of back-and-forth, the Argentine government announced its acceptance of an on-site visit by IACHR, and the U.S. announced that EXIM financing would now go forward. For obvious reasons, neither side publicly linked the two decisions. As the State Department had been pressing for acceptance of the IACHR visit, we were pleased with this aspect of the outcome.

However, this turned out to be the only time the Human Rights Bureau was able to obtain a policy decision to use the EXIM mechanism. The department leadership was reluctant to invest the necessary political capital and energy in future battles with domestic interests and their supporters in Washington. The Human Rights Bureau continued to review EXIM cases and to set forth our objections for the record, but as a policy instrument the EXIM lever had effectively fallen from our hands. Several months later, Congress even changed the law to make it practically impossible to fight a human rights case over EXIM financing.

United Nations Commission on Human Rights

We decided that the first priority for action in the UN human rights field was to establish a mechanism that could help end disappearances in Argentina and elsewhere and to provide a neutral means for governments to transmit information to families about the fate of their missing relatives.

An international mechanism made sense for three reasons: 1) governments would presumably prefer to cooperate with a multilateral organization of which they were members rather than appear to be submitting to bilateral pressures; 2) the problem had clearly reached international dimensions: credible reports of disappearances were coming in from countries in nearly all regions of the world; and 3) it was risky to expect that successive U.S. administrations would be prepared to invest the same amount of political capital on this particular problem.

The effort bore fruit at the UN Commission on Human Rights in early 1980, when the commission adopted a resolution establishing a five-member working group with the authority to intercede quickly in cases of reported disappearances and to clarify the facts surrounding both new and old cases. Establishment of the group was the major U.S. goal at the session. The five members were to serve in their individual capacities and not as representatives of their governments, thereby depoliticizing the group's operations to the maximum possible extent.

The group's ability to initiate action immediately upon receipt of information, to determine how much of its work should be treated in confidence and how much made public, and to function on a continuous year-round basis constituted significant innovations in UN human rights practice and have been indispensable ingredients of the group's remarkable record of achievements. Its public reports provide a glimpse of the way in which its rapid intercession has helped to locate at least some individuals and thereby to save their lives. These successes occurred principally in situations where the disappearance had just occurred. In the case of Argentina, the working group has had no better results than anyone else in clearing up cases of persons who disappeared in the early years of the military regime. The existence and activity of the group, however, has probably contributed to the decline in the practice of disappearance in Argentina and elsewhere.

Diplomatic Channels

In our day-in, day-out diplomatic contacts in Washington and in Buenos Aires, we emphasized the high priority we attached to human rights issues. In addition to démarches on broad fundamental issues—halting disappearances and torture, accounting to families for their disappeared relatives, and release of political detainees—we raised a large number of individual cases. If they involved disappeared persons, we were typically told only that the authorities had no information about them. With political detainees, however, we had better results. As the vast majority were uncharged with any crimes, we strongly urged their release, often under a "right-of-option" provision of the Argentine Constitution which permits uncharged executive detainees to choose exile as an alternative to continued imprisonment. We even established a special U.S. entry quota for such individuals. Although the Argentine authorities turned down our requests in many "option" cases, and dragged their feet in many others, we were able to facilitate the release of at least some people in this way. Right-of-option cases were a major part of our high-level diplomatic dialogue in Buenos Aires.

The "squeaky wheel" approach to human rights diplomacy—badgering the authorities about a limited number of prisoners in whom we have a particular interest—is an important component of an overall effort, because it usually gets results that benefit at least some human beings and because it allows our interlocutor government to demonstrate some degree of responsiveness to our concerns even before it comes to grips with the more basic issues involved. The release of Jacobo Timerman is probably the best-known example of this approach; there were few conversations with Argentine officials in which we did not mention his case, and his release in the autumn of 1979 was an important event.

I made an official visit to Argentina in April 1979 to discuss U.S. human rights policy with Argentine officials, human rights organizations, and other nongovernmental organizations and individuals and to obtain firsthand experience of the human rights situation. Occasional (and I stress *occasional*) visits from a Washington policy office reinforce, and thus assist, the work carried out by our embassies on a day-to-day basis.

My visit provided an occasion for senior Argentine military and civilian officials to hear our message from someone "fresh from Washington," that is, someone directly involved in the policymaking process. I received a careful hearing from the Secretaries-General of each of the three armed services,* and I listened to them in turn. I believe that our exchange enriched their understanding of the scope and depth of our commitment to a serious human rights policy and our understanding of their attitudes.

The human rights groups with whom I met appreciated the fact that the Department's Human Rights Bureau had sent someone to Buenos Aires at that time. (It had been a year since Assistant Secretary Derian's last visit.) This was most vividly illustrated during my impromptu meeting in a park with about 300

---

* Roughly speaking, the third-ranking officers in each service. Two of them eventually became members of the ruling junta. General Bignone became president of Argentina.

members of the Mothers of the Plaza de Mayo (the mothers of the disappeared). As I approached the group at its weekly gathering, I recognized and greeted one or two women whom I had met on their visits to Washington. Others quickly gathered around me, wondering aloud who I was. After my initial explanation that I was from the Department of State in Washington seemed to leave them in some doubt about what that meant, I said simply "I work for Patricia Derian." That was all the identification they needed. They all cheered and made it clear that they didn't want me to leave. I said I brought them greetings from Ms. Derian and reassurance that we were still working hard to help find their loved ones and would not give up. As we were under police surveillance, and the police had in the past attacked gatherings of the Mothers, I thought it best not to prolong our meeting. I told them I would be happy to meet with them individually and took my leave. (I did see several of them later.) I think that even these small symbolic acts are important in letting human rights victims know that the United States really cares what happens to them.

The Afghanistan Connection

The hope of inducing Argentina to participate in the grain embargo against the USSR, following the Soviet invasion of Afghanistan, created new pressures within the administration to relax our human rights policy. The Soviets were trying to capitalize on Argentina's estrangement from the U.S. by supporting Argentine positions in UN fora and by making overtures in other areas. This alarmed the White House, which sent two high-level missions to Argentina in early 1980 to explore what could be done to rebuild our relationship.

The two missions, headed by General Andrew Goodpaster (in January) and Ambassador Gerard Smith (in March) unfortunately resulted in confusing the Argentines about our priorities. Although General Goodpaster raised our human rights concerns strongly, he mixed up some key details about what we were seeking at the UN Human Rights Commission (whose session was about to begin), thereby complicating our already difficult task at the commission's Geneva meeting. Although we were able to sort that out, the fact that Ambassador Smith barely mentioned human rights during his mission in late March left the Argentines with the impression that human rights were no longer near the top of our policy agenda. The Argentines now felt that they could use the Afghanistan crisis to keep us off-balance on human rights issues. Although they joined the Olympic boycott and voted in the UN General Assembly to condemn the Soviet invasion, they did not participate in the grain embargo.

White House Policy Review

The Afghanistan crisis prompted the White House to order a thorough interagency review of U.S. policy toward Argentina in the spring of 1980. At this time, a policy paper I had drafted a few months earlier was working its way through the State Department and had already acquired considerable support. This spadework facilitated the preparation of policy recommendations to the president, who reaffirmed the essential elements of our human rights approach, including continued administration support for the U.S. arms embargo and for at least abstention on multilateral bank loans, as well as for our efforts in the OAS and the UN. At the same time, he also approved a recommendation calling for more frequent consultations with our European allies and friends on Argentine human rights issues and on possible joint or parallel approaches. Approval of this document brought together in one place a set of guidelines that greatly assisted day-to-day decision making.

Assessment

I am convinced that U.S. efforts contributed significantly to a reduction in the level of human rights abuses in Argentina. It is equally clear to me that nongovernmental groups and organizations in Argentina and abroad, as well as other governments, international organizations, parliamentarians, and the press also played important complementary roles. I think we could have done better in some areas.

a) *Military sales*: The U.S. was alone in taking a strong, clear-cut stand on this issue, although one or two of our Western allies may have reduced their sales slightly on human rights grounds. However, the "business as usual" approach of most of our Western friends and Israel tended to dilute the impact of our own restrictions. The amounts were not small—over a billion dollars a year. In Washington, the Human Rights Bureau sometimes heard the question, "Since our friends are selling, why shouldn't we get our share of the business?" The question should have been, "Why don't we try seriously to convince our friends that this is an issue where money isn't the most important value, and where a joint effort can help significantly to attain the objective we all profess to seek?" Because of the effect of the Afghanistan situation in the overall geopolitical atmosphere, little was done to pursue this idea.

b) *Multilateral bank votes*: We did not lobby our allies for support for our position in the banks. Instead, we simply informed them of our position, and usually on the eve of the vote—after they had already reached their own decisions. In cases where we told them earlier, even this low-key informational effort probably influenced some votes some of the time. A more active lobbying effort could have been much more effective.

c) *Joint démarches*: We seldom organized joint démarches with our European friends on human rights issues, although in Buenos Aires our embassy conducted a working-level exchange of information with them on these matters. We might usefully have tried to organize occasional high-level joint démarches. The Argentines, sensitive to their international image, were attuned to Western European signals as much as they were to our own approaches. Most Argentines feel close cultural ties with Western Europe, from which their grandparents or great-grandparents originated.

General Policy Conclusions

1) When we have a worthwhile policy objective, we should be prepared to make our commitment felt in as many areas of our bilateral and multilateral relationships as possible. Otherwise, it is difficult to expect other governments to take our concerns seriously into account in reaching their own policy decisions.

2) We should be prepared to stick it out for a sufficiently long period; we can't expect results overnight. If we overreact to cosmetic or transitory improvements, we convey the impression that our policy commitment is not all that deep or lasting. Communication is the essence of any effective foreign policy. This is why we should not break or suspend diplomatic relations except in the most extreme circumstances, but it is also why we must ensure that our diplomatic message consists of deeds as well as words. Diplomatic exchanges are neither an end in themselves, nor are they a sufficient means to attain our ends in a serious situation. They are an essential element of an overall approach.

3) We should not overlook the fact that most governments want good, friendly, mutually beneficial relations with the United States. It is not too much to expect that this relationship be based on a mutual observance of shared values, particularly when these values have been consecrated in internationally valid documents. "Good relations" are not an end in themselves—if they are, then the relationship is based on inherently shaky ground. It is not a coincidence that our best relations are with countries which respect human dignity and human rights.

4) We should also bear in mind that most countries want very much to be regarded as civilized, decent members of the family of nations. Even the worst violators of human rights go to great lengths to defend their conduct in international forums. Some care more than others about their international reputation, but they all care to some extent. It is not too much to expect that governments earn their good name through practical observance of the norms they have pledged to uphold. We should not be afraid to say this to our interlocutors.

5) It is important that all U.S. government officials, regardless of their particular technical or specialized professional interests, include human rights matters in their discourse with officials of a country that we are trying to persuade to accord greater respect for human rights. If specialists talk only about their specialities, the impression is left that human rights are the concern of only a part of the U.S. government.

6) As in any human undertaking, we are not going to succeed every time.

The turnaround on EXIM demonstrated the domestic limits of the human rights policy. Argentina was the right place to test these limits, but experience showed that the costs—in terms of being able to sustain an effective human rights policy —outweighed the benefits. Any foreign policy requires domestic support. As EXIM is essentially a subsidy to American business rather than foreign assistance, it was never a particularly promising policy instrument. We tried it and achieved something, but in the process we had to decide that it was not worth trying again.

7) We should look early, carefully, and long at multilateral institutions that might play a role in improving the situation. Multilateral and bilateral initiatives strengthen each other. Only a fully integrated approach has a reasonable chance of success. Moreover, we can share *some* of the burden of promoting human rights with multilateral institutions. In the long run, they should take over more and more of the action responsibility for promoting and protecting human rights. Strengthening these institutions should be a major U.S. policy goal.

8) We should bear in mind that a strong U.S. human rights position, because it identifies us with universal and enduring values, will engender lasting pro-American attitudes among significant sectors in foreign countries. Our struggles against Nazi and Communist totalitarianism were, and continue to be, rooted in human rights concerns. Our identification with the cause of human rights will be remembered positively when the "dark night of oppression passes in any country; then we will see that the "bad relations" with the oppressor regime were a small price to pay for living up to our professed commitment to human dignity and human rights. The benefits to the United States thus extend far beyond merely "feeling good about ourselves"—although I frankly see nothing wrong in practicing what we preach, wherever we can.

It is right to ask whether a foreign policy is effective, but it is a mistake to assume from the outset that a policy that enables us to honor our values is somehow unrealistic and ineffective, and therefore wrong as statecraft. Our human rights policy initiatives toward Argentina demonstrated that a value-oriented policy can produce positive results.

Postscript: As this article was being completed, Raul Alfonsin, a founding member of the principal Argentine human rights organization—the Permanent Assembly for Human Rights—was elected president of Argentina by an absolute majority. Mr. Alfonsin was an outspoken advocate of human rights during the period of military rule (hardly a risk-free position during that era) and gave considerable attention to human rights issues during his campaign. It is not unreasonable to think that Mr. Alfonsin's courageous commitment to human rights played a role in his remarkable election victory. I suggest that this development could be instructive to U.S. policymakers who are called upon to weigh the relative importance of human rights issues in framing our approach to despotic regimes.

The View From Embassy/Pretoria

An Interview with Ambassador William B. Edmondson

*The existence of apartheid in South Africa and the strong domestic con-
cern in the United States have made human rights in that country an
issue through several decades. William Edmondson, who served as U.S.
ambassador in Pretoria from June 1978 to July 1981, tells in an interview with Frank Meehan and David Newsom how the Carter administration sought to exert influence there.*

MEEHAN. The purpose of this interview is to examine the process of pursuing a
policy on human rights in a country where, from the American perspective,
there are very serious problems in the relationship between the government and
many citizens and non-citizens within the country. You have been in South
Africa twice, as deputy chief of mission and as chief of mission. As you look
back on it, were there any important differences in American embassy approaches to questions of human rights in South Africa between your service as
DCM and later as ambassador?

EDMONDSON. No. I can see where, in some circumstances, there would be, but
this would depend largely on the relationship between the ambassador and the
DCM. I was very fortunate, as a DCM, in serving two ambassadors who were
very open with me; they had very different styles (and personal views) in the
matter of human rights, but the perspective I had as a DCM and as an ambassador was essentially the same. The policies of the administrations I served
were different.

I suspect that if you asked the same question of others who served at the
embassy, you might find differences in the experience and perspective of the
junior officers according to the ambassador under whom they were serving.

The views expressed in this interview do not necessarily reflect those of the U.S.
Department of State.

NEWSOM. We might begin by looking at the basic mission of an embassy, assuming, as I think we must, that human rights are a part of our diplomatic agenda both by reason of legislation and by reason of the interest in this country. How would you describe the mission of the embassy in Pretoria as you perceived it in this field?

EDMONDSON. Let me begin with a more general comment on what I see as the mission of any embassy or consular post with respect to human rights. I think there are probably three different aspects. First, a particularly important part of an embassy's mission is to report as accurately as possible, as completely as resources permit and as requirements demand, on the human rights situation in the host country. This reporting must cover how human rights abuses or restrictions affect that country's internal and external affairs, including its political, economic and social development, as well as its relations with the United States. Since our concern is humanitarian as well as diplomatic or political, reporting should also cover departures from generally accepted human rights standards, particularly departures that are frequent or flagrant.

The second aspect of the mission is to convey U.S. public attitudes and policy on human rights questions to the government and people of the country of accreditation, as accurately and as effectively as possible and as forcefully or as gingerly as is required to be effective.

A third aspect, flowing from the second one, is that the embassy must call upon those in it to seek to influence human rights attitudes and practices in the receiving country, in accordance with U.S. policy, by whatever programs and representations seem most likely to be effective without harming other essential U.S. interests.

NEWSOM. Let me follow on your comment and Frank's question. Did you find in South Africa that there were certain aspects of this issue that could only be left to the ambassador, some which were more appropriate to junior officers in the embassy, and some that were more effectively handled by the consulates rather than by the embassy? I remember in my own experience in South Africa realizing that there were things, for example, that the officers of the consulate general in Johannesburg seemed able to do that were more difficult for officers from Pretoria to do.

EDMONDSON. I think the distinction is probably greater among the officers of different ranks and different functions than between the embassy and the consulates. There is a distinction in the latter case, but I think that is due primarily to location. There are three consular posts in South Africa; one is partly a diplomatic post because the embassy is sometimes located there. The three consular posts are Durban, Johannesburg, and Cape Town. There are differences in the makeup of the population in each of those areas. There is strong interest in

Durban, for instance, because of the Indian population and because it is near the homeland of the Zulus, led by Chief Gatsha Buthelezi. In Cape Town, the concentration is on the colored population. The views of the white parliamentarians from that area are of interest since they tend to be, perhaps, more liberal than some of those from other areas. In Johannesburg, South Africa's major industrial center, there is greater concern with the large urban black population, that of Soweto, Alexandra, and other urban townships, as well as with the mining industry, the black mineworkers, and so on.

Pretoria had a smaller black population in its suburbs, but the embassy considered Johannesburg as also within its constituency of occasional reporting contacts, even though it was primarily in the consulate general's reporting area. So, in many respects, the differences between the consulates and the embassy were simply a matter of location and of access to the different elements of the population.

The other aspect of the question relates to whether there are things that the ambassador might do more appropriately than a junior officer, or vice versa. I would say yes. Contacts at a high level in government or at sensitive levels of leadership either within government or the general population are best left, I think, to the ambassador and senior officers who are more closely attuned to policy sensitivities, both those of the host government and of the U.S. government. On the other hand, junior officers can much more easily make contact and carry on friendly relationships with certain elements of the population, particularly black elements, with less notice than the ambassador or DCM would receive.

Junior officers, for instance, do a good deal of reporting based on contacts with black students, or Afrikaner students, or young workers; an ambassador simply cannot deal effectively here, partly because of distinctions in position, and partly because of age. There are different levels of the society with which each element of the embassy can work better, and I suspect that is true in other areas of the world.

MEEHAN. So reporting human rights situations in South Africa was clearly an important part of the embassy operation and of the operation of the consulates. What sort of resources did you devote to it, in terms of overall mission effort?

EDMONDSON. I would say probably a very considerable proportion—noting that we are talking about human rights in South Africa in the very broadest sense—because human rights problems can either be at a political level or at a very personal level and both exist in South Africa. At the political level you have what is known as "grand apartheid," including such things as the homelands policy, citizenship rights, and influx control. At the personal level you have "petty apartheid," consisting of separate, often very unequal, social facilities and other instances of racial discrimination. Between those two ends of the continuum, there are many forms of racial discrimination and human rights abuses that may stem from but are not necessarily a legal part of the system—abuses such as prisoners beaten in jail and similar human rights violations. But it is important to know why this occurs. Is it because of political corruption in a country? Is it because of racial tension? I think in South Africa you had both. So human rights reporting ranged everywhere from the reporting on what, in any other country, would simply be a political trend (but still has to do with human rights in South Africa), right down to what would be an individual aspect of the social policy of a society. I would say that, in one way or another, almost all of our reporting had some element of human rights.

MEEHAN. And your sources were good? I mean you felt that you were getting to the real information on this?

EDMONDSON. Essentially, I think so. One is never really satisified anywhere with sources. It is like scholarly researchers; they never have enough information. Basically, the quality of one's information is dependent upon the number and quality of one's sources, which in turn depend upon the degree of access one has to various elements of the population. For the mission as a whole, I believe our access was reasonably good.

NEWSOM. In some embassies, there is the practice of assigning one officer whose primary task it is to report on human rights problems. Did you do that in South Africa?

EDMONDSON. Yes, but it was for that aspect of human rights problems which I referred to earlier as the personal aspect, i.e., "petty apartheid." I asked the consular officer, who was free in Pretoria to do other work, such as political and sociological reporting, to undertake the responsibility of following "petty apartheid" in particular. That officer also followed such matters as arrests and detentions, police brutality, forced relocations, "pass law" violations, and the activities and findings of various associations and groups in South Africa that were interested in human rights. He also reported on legal and social changes away from apartheid restrictions. In that sense, yes, we had a human rights officer. But at the other end of the spectrum, the political counselor and other officers spent a lot of time on international problems, such as Namibia, and also on what the philosophy of the government was concerning the future of South Africa, particularly its constitutional future. They also reported political parties' attitudes and positions regarding civil and political rights for the various racial groups.

Let me go a little bit further into that. There were officers who spent much of their time on black contacts and interests while others concentrated on white contacts and politics. Thus, we had some degree of specialization. One officer, for instance, was concerned primarily with the politics of parliamentarians, who were white. The same officer also had black contacts, but his responsibility was to follow the national political parties and learn their views on political matters, including their views on racial questions, human rights questions, and so on. Another officer was concerned primarily with Namibia, but also followed some aspects of black politics, and occasionally some concerns of the white parliamentarians.

MEEHAN. On a human level, did you deal with people who were free to talk, who were not afraid, on such things as petty apartheid? Was there evidence of pressure being brought against them to avoid you?

EDMONDSON. No, quite the contrary. Though many aspects of South Africa are those of a closed society, it is not a closed society in terms of people speaking with foreigners, as I would imagine Eastern Europe to be. There is a great deal of freedom of speech, although there is a degree of press censorship. If you raised questions in the area of police or military actions, some people clammed up. The papers did have censorship restrictions. But in terms of what was happening in the country on apartheid, or the constitutional future, or racial feeling, people spoke very freely, very openly. In fact, the Afrikaans-speaking community liked to talk politics; they liked to argue; they liked, for instance, to take issue with the American position. They liked to try to explain the situation and the history in South Africa—that blacks in South Africa are different from blacks in the United States (usually phrased as "your blacks are different from our blacks"), but they argued this freely. In fact, you could have a mixed function in the diplomatic sphere where you got quite vigorous arguments going, and as long as you kept it under reasonable control they all went away and said how much they enjoyed talking with people from other races.

MEEHAN. I was thinking more of blacks or people of mixed race being free to say things?

EDMONDSON. Generally speaking, I believe the blacks felt quite free to speak to us, although there was more reserve on the part of those who were more radical. In other words, those who felt that the United States was "in bed" with South Africa (and that, of course, was how some saw the policy of the United States), were more reluctant to talk, partly because of hostility, partly, perhaps, because they felt the officer discussing things with them was interested simply in intelligence. To the extent that young, more radical blacks were associated with what the South Africans consider questionable associations, they might be much more guarded about what was said. But I generally found that younger, more junior officers in the embassy could, simply by being friendly and sympathetic listeners, encourage an open discussion of political issues.

Generally, as I said earlier, I think we had pretty good access. That was changing, partly as a result of the change in the U.S. administration and in policy statements before I left South Africa. Access to the black community was becoming more difficult in 1981.

NEWSOM. To what degree in your work in the human rights field in the embassy did you feel you were in good communication with the Department of State and others in Washington? Obviously, this is a matter of great American domestic interest. Did you feel that you were kept reasonably aware of the different attitudes and currents in this country that had a relationship to how you dealt with South Africa and how South Africa reacted to American policy and to events in the United States?

EDMONDSON. On the whole, I think the communications were quite good, perhaps exceptional. I think at that time, and it still continues today, there was good reporting of major articles and editorial opinion carried in the American press. It was particularly important to us to have, as rapidly as possible, any kinds of press statements that might be made by the State Department's spokesperson, for instance. So an arrangement was worked out—and continues today as far as I am aware—for posts to get an advance copy of the guidance prepared for the noon press briefing. The department might caution that the guidance had not been used and was subject to correction if and when it was used, but the practice was still helpful. Occasionally, we would get material that had not been raised in the noon briefing, but that was still available for us to use in conversation with officials or with individual journalists in South Africa.

Sometimes, it would have been more effective had it been used in the noon briefing, because then we could use it more naturally and in a far more public fashion. This was a frequent source of embassy frustration. It is often harder for the embassy to raise such issues in the country where accredited, since embassies don't usually have regular, let alone daily, press briefings, and are usually not being pestered by local newspersons to comment on local human rights matters. When an embassy uses such material without either the impetus of local questions it must answer *or* a U.S. statement it can quote (e.g., something said in the daily briefing), the impression is created that it is the embassy *only* that is giving an extra special plug to its viewpoint.

Because South Africans often tend to interpret diplomats' statements as more personal than official, a statement from clearly official levels in the United States was probably given greater credibility than one issued only by an embassy in South Africa. This doesn't mean to say that they did not regard statements by the ambassador or other embassy officers as official, but simply that they felt it might be tinged with the personal views of those officers.

NEWSOM. In many of the most difficult human rights situations that we have faced in our diplomacy, there is always the question of the basic objective, whether it is to reduce the association of the United States in the minds of a substantial part of the population with a regime that is identified with human rights excesses, or whether it is to influence the course of events. These two things are not necessarily mutually exclusive; but, in some cases, if you are excessively vocal in an attempt to reduce your identification with the regime, you can also reduce your capacity to influence the regime. What would you say, in your mind, was the principal objective of our human rights efforts in South Africa?

EDMONDSON. That is a difficult question because you are outlining a traditional diplomatic dilemma: whether to speak out and be truthful with the government and people to which one is accredited, and thus risk their ceasing to listen, or whether to hold back one's views and thus, perhaps, gain greater confidence? The answer changes, perhaps, from one administration to another. I think there is a basic difference today, between the policy of the Carter administration and that of the Reagan administration. The idea of "constructive engagement" has become kind of a slogan that is taken to mean more perhaps than it does in its simple words. We know that in earlier administrations there have been phrases such as "communication" and "dialogue."

The main answer to your question is that this is a matter of the policy of the administration. It is quite possible, I think, for an administration to be too much on a soapbox, too much in the focus. In the other extreme, though, it is perhaps equally bad in modern-day diplomacy to sit and say nothing about excesses. I think American policy demands that we voice the attitudes of the American public.

It is important that the ambassador on the spot have the backing for what he says in the public statements made by officials of the government, by congressmen, newspapers, and so on. The most effective tool in a society like South Africa is to show that it is not just the ambassador speaking personally, but it is the American people. I think most countries around the world, like it or not, do realize that the United States is a democracy, that the government of the United States has to represent what the majority of the people want. That is not always easy to distinguish, because there are other things that enter into our policy.

When there is a clear expression from Congress, clear views throughout the nation in editorials and in public statements, and a clear expression on the part of the administration, either at the cabinet or subcabinet level, then the ambassador has merely to point to these, explain what they mean, and interpret them for the foreign government and society. Then, I think, the diplomat's views are much more readily taken as being valid.

If the embassy presents a different picture than the one projected by the government in Washington, then it is unlikely that the diplomacy will be effective.

NEWSOM. Here in this country there are those who say the United States is supporting the South African regime, that the United States is identified with the regime as it has been identified with regimes like that of the Shah and Somoza, etc. Did you have the feeling that there is a problem as far as the United States is concerned diplomatically in South Africa in that a large number of important figures, particularly in the black community, feel that the United States is closely identified with and in a sense supporting the South African government?

EDMONDSON. This changes with the changes in the policy of the administration in Washington, sometimes even when they are minor changes. No matter what administration is in office, there will be a certain element of the population in South Africa, both black and white, that will suggest that the United States leans one way or the other. I think it is inevitable that, as a great power, we are seen (or assumed) to favor someone, and so people read our statements to be evidence of closeness or hostility, one way or the other. There are many American statements against the current political system in South Africa that will be regarded as increasingly hostile by certain white groups and possibly even some black elements. But there are so many differences and variations of opinion and viewpoint about South Africa itself among the various racial groups in South Africa that you can always count on someone feeling that the United States is on the wrong side. That is not a direct answer to your question. In South Africa, the more radical blacks who have already decided that only violence will bring about change and who feel that all foreign entities should help with some kind of pressure will regard any diplomatic relationship with the Government of South Africa as not helping their cause. To the extent that the United States seems to withhold its criticism, then there is a larger group that suggests that we are too close to that government.

MEEHAN. How important, as you look at it now, is the U.S. factor in the whole human rights situation? Are we seen by any part of the South African population as having a major role, or are we seen as an important factor but not one that is really going to move things?

EDMONDSON. No single factor is really going to move things in a decisive way. The U.S. role is significant but not the major one, and it is impossible to pinpoint the exact degree of U.S. influence. In my opinion, the United States is not without influence in any South African racial group. There is a desire for approval within every group, and that seems particularly true among the Afrikaans-speaking community. There are elements at the two extremes, that is, among the most conservative white elements and the most radical black elements, who would say the United States is not relevant and really believe it. There are others toward those two extremes who would say the United States is not relevant, but they don't really mean it. There is still a desire on the part of a very large part of the knowing public, black or white, to have some kind of relationship with the United States or to have the United States see their side of the problems in South Africa. They want the approbation of the United States as a world power just as they want it from other outside powers, including those in Europe and the Third World. The outside world does have an influence upon the thinking of South Africans.

One of the advantages of maintaining a relationship—or engagement, communication, access, whatever you want to call it—is to wield whatever degree of influence we can through this means by letting the South Africans know what it is the outside world thinks of them. That does not mean we will change their actions very quickly, but I believe it has some influence. At the very least, it gives South Africans—black, white, and colored—a window onto the outside world, prevents their isolation, and gives other countries' representatives a window to look into South Africa to see what is going on. I think that is important for understanding in both directions. If you look at it only in terms of access, the ability to convey the viewpoint of the outside world makes the South Africans think more self-consciously about their actions than they ever would in isolation.

NEWSOM. Let me ask one question on the tools of the trade. Obviously, we have all carried out diplomatic tasks relating to human rights in different parts of the world—Frank in Eastern Europe, myself in Southeast Asia, and you in South Africa—and in each case we encounter a somewhat different set of obstacles because we are dealing with sensitive internal problems. What would you say, Bill, were the special problems or inhibitions that exist for U.S. diplomats in South Africa in carrying out the human rights objectives of any administration?

EDMONDSON. If I can work from the philosophical to the practical, I would start out by saying that I think the special problems in South Africa stem largely from the circumstance that human rights abuses originate from an all-pervasive clash of different races and cultures and tend to be like the human rights abuses of war or of military occupation, for instance. Abuses occur, as I suggested earlier, both at the political level, where one finds "grand apartheid," and the personal level, where one finds discrimination and "petty apartheid." Throughout, both types of apartheid have been institutionalized in the form of legally based, caste-like social taboos, that, like the historical forms of racial segregation and discrimination in the United States, are accepted to a large degree by most of the population. Historically, that has changed. What this meant for diplomats in South Africa some years ago was that it would have been impossible to think of going into a black area without a pass, without observing the laws and rules of apartheid.

During the times that I was there, we had reached the point of ourselves using diplomatic immunity to violate many of these taboos. In fact, we forbade our officers to observe them in certain circumstances. Even though the action might be frowned upon, we preferred to go without a pass into, say, Soweto, to see a person under banning orders, provided that we weren't going to get that person in difficulty. Even with diplomatic immunity, the very existence of apartheid rules and regulations and taboos that closely regulate the black part of South African society made it difficult for diplomats to move around and have the kind of access needed to meet these people and learn who they were.

We started many years ago—and there is a progression in American policy since World War II—with Fourth of July parties to which, for the first time, American ambassadors started inviting blacks. The South African reaction was originally very negative, and one American ambassador was told officially that, in effect, in Rome you must do what the Romans do.

MEEHAN. When did we start with this?

EDMONDSON. I would say in the period of the sixties, the Kennedy period, but some contacts were even earlier. The South African reaction on the official level was one of hostility at first. Private whites came. After a while, civil servants started to come. But I think it was only in the seventies that cabinet ministers started to come to our Fourth of July parties. While I was there, the foreign minister attended, and it became quite acceptable for ministers to be seen at parties where there were blacks and coloreds as well as whites. At some point, in addition to the Fourth of July parties and increasing steadily with almost every ambassador, the embassy encouraged more and more mixed representational affairs, whether dinners or receptions.

Receptions were easier. While I was ambassador and earlier as DCM, I encouraged and the ambassador supported my having officers avoid anything other than a mixed affair. That was not always practical. Blacks sometimes found it difficult to come all the way from Soweto, for instance, but increasingly we had a reputation for having mixed parties. And then we found that other foreign embassies started to have mixed parties as well. Beginning with their national days, the Canadians, the Australians, the British, the Germans, and eventually the French were all having multiracial parties.

In the early seventies we first assigned black officers to South Africa, and that is now more or less standard practice.

NEWSOM. To what extent did you feel that the embassy had an obligation to private American citizens and groups who wanted to make contact with human rights organizations and individuals in South Africa? Did you feel that it was part of the embassy's general task in this field to help private citizens meet with human rights activists, with black leaders, with colored leaders, and so forth?

EDMONDSON. I would say very definitely yes. The only caveat I would add is that we considered it important to offer any Americans the opportunity to meet different elements of South African society. In fact, it was sometimes interesting to expose a conservative American to one of the more reactionary, racist white South Africans. Even if they were quite conservative, Americans found that they looked and felt pretty liberal next to the South African. And then they might meet representatives of various groups of liberal white South Africans as well as representatives of various black groups. What we found is that Americans who have not followed the situation closely tend to oversimplify a situation that is extremely complex in South Africa.

That is true also of some American officials. One of the first things that we as an embassy tried to do was to broaden their horizons and their understanding of the different groups so that they could come away feeling that they had talked to the different sides. We left it to them to decide, but I think it was interesting that Americans tended to react very similarly. The conservative Americans tended to move to a more liberal position; the very liberal Americans often tended to move to a somewhat more conservative position. What they found out was that there were Afrikaners who were very serious and well meaning in their attitudes, who were very concerned about having a better scciety for all, and who, though they may have been misguided in their discriminatory views, were sincere in wanting a fairer system.

By the same token one found that Americans who thought that everything was going well in South Africa and that the government was dealing well with the blacks often discovered some of the more horrible aspects of apartheid. They also, I think, came away with a better appreciation of the degree of change—that is, the changes that are taking place and those that are not. This, too, is a very complex subject.

Using the Tools of Human Rights Diplomacy

NEWSOM. Let's turn to some of the specific diplomatic tools that an ambassador and an embassy have at their disposal in pursuing human rights objectives. Perhaps you could comment on the effectiveness of some of these as you saw them—for instance, direct démarches to senior officials of the government expressing an official American view on some aspects of their human rights circumstances. Is that an effective diplomatic tool?

EDMONDSON. It can be a very effective tool. It is not so much whether you make démarches but how and how frequently you make them. It is a matter of doing so selectively and with an appreciation of what the likely reaction is going to be. I don't mean that simply because you estimate the reaction would be hostile you would not make the démarche. But rather, more importantly, you do not repeat the same kind of démarche so that they start turning you off. This is a particularly important thing. So, you pick and choose, in a sense, which ones are more likely to be taken seriously by them.

Thus, you take the more flagrant cases, say a racial abuse or some other abuse that may not have started as a racial abuse but was based on the treatment of prisoners by police, an abuse that you could bring to their attention and seek to convince them how wrong this was. You began to hit them where it hurt. While they might react quite defensively and with all kinds of excuses and reasons, you would come away with some reason to believe that they probably were determining to themselves: let's not have that happen again.

In those circumstances, démarches played a very important role.

NEWSOM. It is always difficult to generalize, but let us take a hypothetical circumstance in which there has been a serious riot and you have been asked by Washington to express the hope that such activities can be curtailed and the idea that the excessive use of force is going to cause problems. Would the South African authorities have felt compelled to give publicity to these démarches? Would you have felt compelled?

EDMONDSON. I can't remember any case where the South Africans gave such publicity. There were cases where the U.S. side gave publicity, but this was largely done in the United States and then repeated by the embassy. This seemed to us the most effective way to have the matter made public. The major ire of the government, if it was there, was then directed at the government of the United States as a whole rather than simply the American embassy or the officers delivering the démarche.

In general, we did not make the démarche public unless it was a particularly flagrant thing and we wanted to get it on the record even before it got to Washington. That was fairly rare. Sometimes we might have answered a press question which made it clear that we had made representations on a certain subject. It is difficult to generalize.

MEEHAN. That raises the question of the old chestnut of public diplomacy and quiet diplomacy. I think most practitioners would feel that you have to do both, depending on the circumstances; but as you look back at your own experience there, what do you feel about the merits of quiet diplomacy as opposed to public diplomacy?

EDMONDSON. As your question suggests, it is not an either-or proposition. I think you have to use both, and selectively. There are good reasons at times for private diplomacy. If the government is already sensitive to the fact that they have done something wrong, it doesn't necessarily help to chastise them publicly, but it does help to let them know that there is deep concern about a subject in the United States and to express interest, even put pressure on in any way you can, to get them to take steps so that this kind of thing will be prevented. It is often much easier to present it as being in their interest if you do so privately.

At the same time, there are two outside elements that you have to keep in mind. First and foremost, perhaps, for any administration is the attitude of the public in the United States. I think that the American public wants to see that our representatives are indeed representing their views to foreign governments. That is necessary and must be taken into account. The other thing is that when there are deep divisions within the other country, and you want to keep access to both sides, you have to make your representation public so that those who feel that the representations would be in their favor are allowed to know it, other than privately. Letting it be known privately is not nearly so effective as letting it be known publicly.

In South Africa the great majority of people are black. Therefore, it behooves us—at least on certain occasions—to make it clear publicly what the policy of the United States is.

So, while I say to use both public and quiet diplomacy selectively, it is very difficult to define the criteria more exactly. These are the parameters.

MEEHAN. As I was listening to you, it seems to me what you were saying, in a way, was that in practice in the South African situation you shade off on the side of public diplomacy, but without excluding private diplomacy. You act in terms of perceived U.S. needs there. The point you make about the importance of reaching a majority of the population, that sort of shades you off, does it not, to public diplomacy?

EDMONDSON. I am not sure that it does. I think you have probably already, in your previous studies, found diplomacy described as an art and not a science. In that sense there is a certain touch to this, a feel. When diplomats say this, political scientists and others trying to be much more scientific and professional will sit back and say that this is not professional. But in fact a great deal goes into that feeling. It can be done with specific analysis. What is the effect of a specific statement on a specific incident going to be? What is the effect of not making a statement? Which is going to be more effective with the public, and which is going to be more effective with the government?

The reason you make your representation public, apart from U.S. domestic politics and the interest of the U.S. public in knowing, is to allow the various publics of the foreign country to know and thus continue to have your access. One of the criticisms directed against constructive engagement, as some people currently interpret it, is that it appears too one-sided. The engagement is more intense and visible with the South African government and its supporters, this argument runs, than it is with the opponents of the government.

In diplomacy, whatever the situation is, the ideal thing is to have contacts and continuing access among all elements of the population. You need to know what the opposition is thinking, as well as the supporters of the government. In a situation where you actually have conflicts, you have to be in touch with insurgents or, in this case, with an oppressed racial group. You are not going to achieve that unless they feel that there is some way they can influence the attitude of the United States—that you are at least in some degree sympathetic. So you have to try to convey sympathy to the good points on all sides.

That is not always easy, because we tend to see things and become emotionally or idealistically involved in a right side as opposed to a wrong side. Even in a situation as tragic as the South African one, and I am sure this would be true of many other countries, the right isn't always on one side and the wrong isn't always on one side. The best form of diplomacy is to indicate an independent objectivity. The groups inside the country may not agree with it, but at least they can see that you are not totally committed to one side or the other. That is the element that you have to measure carefully when deciding whether and when you are going to make your representations public so all these groups will know, or whether you are going to keep them private. In the case of a private representation, it may be that your calculation is that it will be far more effective if kept private. Under previous administrations, as well as this one, the U.S. did not make public all its representations.

NEWSOM. In that line, can you generalize at all on whether the public statements made in Washington were helpful or not helpful in your direct dealings with the South African government? For example, you are going to see the South African government on an issue and the noon briefer in Washington has already made a pronouncement saying that we oppose apartheid and we view with deep regret such and such an incident that has just taken place. Is that helpful to your mission and in influencing the situation, or does it arouse feelings on the other side? I realize it is difficult to generalize, but there is a basic point here.

EDMONDSON. Generally speaking, I would say it is more helpful than not, but it can sometimes be harmful. An official U.S. government statement, at either the cabinet level or elsewhere in the Department of State, that is known to be official and carefully calculated, can be extremely helpful. A statement can be very unhelpful that is made by some more peripheral official, often someone in another capital, perhaps, trying to impress a different audience.

At the same time, even a more extreme statement made by a member of the public or a member of Congress can possibly be helpful. You can convey that to the government as being a result of their own failure to make their policies clear or to do the right thing.

Too often, either because there are other matters of greater concern in Washington or because the Washington officials don't want to give unnecessary offense or make an issue bigger than it should be in the world press, the task of conveying disapproval is left to the embassy on the spot. If one approaches this question from the "good-guy/bad-guy" strategy that is sometimes used, generally speaking, it is better to let the ambassador and the embassy seem to be the good guys and Washington the bad guys. That is an overgeneralization, but, occasionally, as I have said, an embassy isn't given the kind of official statement that would be helpful in demonstrating that its representations are based on strong instructions from home.

NEWSOM. Another technique in pursuing human rights objectives in the foreign country is for the embassy to work indirectly through private individuals and organizations to reinforce its views and those of the United States. To what extent did you find this kind of indirect communication, if indeed it was used, helpful in getting across the seriousness with which the United States regarded some of these issues?

EDMONDSON. I think it is indeed very helpful. There are various ways of doing it. You have the assistance of the United States Information Service, which deals not only with the press but with many other elements of the population, the university faculties, students, businessmen, cultural leaders. All elements of a mission, whether it is the agricultural attaché, the ambassador, the political officer, the consular officer, or USIS, can play a role in this.

It is important to be in touch with parliamentarians in terms of the influence on direct policy. What you may find is that there is a certain imperviousness on the part of the government to influences within their society but outside of government. This can happen anywhere, and this is also true in South Africa. It is not a total imperviousness at all times, but it is a very strong one. That means that you have to work on these things as a long-term project. In that connection, work with the supporters of government, who may still be critical at times, or with the press is important. Increasingly in South Africa, one found that what was at one point a very uncritical Afrikaans press became more and more critical, or more willing to look at different sides of the issue. They still remain supporters of government, but to the extent that you had some very astute journalists and analysts of public affairs, it was as important to get in touch with them as it was with the opposition press. At the same time, you could find that the opposition press would be influenced by your sharing with them, on a non-attributable basis, analysis and viewpoints that they could use in order to influence public opinion.

The human rights groups could be of great value, primarily in obtaining information and understanding the situation, but also from time to time in influencing their members as to what kinds of statements or actions would be most effective.

MEEHAN. Were the embassy or the consulates the subject of hostile media comments on account of the human rights activities that were conducted? And if so, was this a major factor in your handling of the situation?

EDMONDSON. Very definitely yes. It was an important factor, an important part of the environment. It did not necessarily influence our actions. One tended to be extremely careful.

I would say the point to be most careful about is the point of accuracy, to know your own facts. I have mentioned earlier the harm that could be done by peripheral official statements, whether in Washington, Europe or elsewhere, and those were most harmful when they were inaccurate. They may not have been based on embassy reports, but they were based on idealistic and somewhat emotional conceptions of what these complicated problems were. In such instances, the people in the country pin it on the embassy and pin it on the United States government.

MEEHAN. On the question of the media and the embassy, it seems to me that there are two points. One is what you might call generalized hostility directed against U.S. human rights policy. But what I had in mind were attacks specifically directed at the embassy for activities that it had undertaken in the human rights field; that is, apart from policy, say, approaches to blacks, contacts with people that conservatives might consider radical elements.

EDMONDSON. It will take some time to be specific, but I could say that I do have a fairly sizable file of clippings of personal attacks in the Afrikaans-speaking press on me as ambassador. I took great pride, however, in having been defended by one of the Afrikaans papers where I had some very good contacts. Some of these papers seemed to take great pleasure in attacking me during the last several months of my presence in South Africa, largely because I was a holdover from the Carter administration six months into the Reagan administration. Even though I was trying faithfully to convey the policy changes and policy attitudes of the new administration, I am sure that there were elements both within the National party and the National party press that wanted to convince the administration that it should remove me and send someone that would be more visibly friendly. I was too closely associated with the previous administration and its much stronger criticism of the situation in South Africa.

This had odd twists because sometimes the attacks were unthinking. On one occasion I went into Soweto to make a brief presentation of books at a cultural center there and made a statement that I thought was really quite moderate and as apolitical as I felt it politic to be in the middle of Soweto. There were very few white reporters; there were several black reporters, including a stringer for a paper in Zimbabwe. He presented the remarks that I made in a way that would appeal to Zimbabweans as being critical of apartheid, and they got played back and picked up by Afrikaans-speaking newspapermen and portrayed as being very hostile, which they were not. In fact, I saw my remarks distorted from what was pretty much an apolitical statement into another attack on the South African government, which was not the case. But there were so many people prepared to believe that I personally was hostile to white South Africa that it was indeed getting to be obvious that I could no longer be effective with that element of the population of South Africa.

NEWSOM. Would you say a word about the degree of difference in the reaction and effectiveness of an approach made specifically on behalf of an individual or a specific situation, whether it is Nelson Mandela or Crossroads, and a démarche made in general terms about the position of the United States with respect to apartheid. Does one get a sharper reaction than the other? Is one more resented than the other?

EDMONDSON. I'm not certain. I think that you can have both situations. It's usually easiest to have an incident of some sort on which to peg a representation. Whether the démarche is generalized to apply to a particular practice in South Africa and represents American pressure to eliminate problems like this or whether it is particularized to what is happening to an individual depends on circumstances. If it is a particularly egregious case of injustice to an individual, I think you can make that démarche and have it understood. Here again, the démarche is much more likely to be received in a clinical diplomatic fashion if it is made at an official as opposed to a cabinet level in the South African government. Those at the cabinet level, depending on the personality, tended to invoke more argument about the practices of apartheid.

NEWSOM. Were you ever told that this is none of the business of the United States government?

EDMONDSON. Interestingly, I was not. The implication was there occasionally. But by explaining the deep concern of the American people with the situation, one usually found that the South Africans listened. They didn't like it always, but they listened.

NEWSOM. In broad terms, if you were speaking to a successor going to South Africa, what would you say would be the limits of diplomatic techniques in dealing with human rights situations? Are there any generalizations that you can make about: "You can do this, but don't do that?" Are there definable limits in what you can effectively do in a situation like South Africa? If, for example, I were talking to someone about going to some of the Southeast Asian countries where I have served, I would say: "You can raise any case of an individual provided you have some basis, some credible basis for raising the case—a member of Congress has asked about it, questions have been raised with the State Department by outside groups that have an interest—but if you go in as an ambassador and say: 'I'm interested in the case of such and such,' then, you are likely to get: 'Well, this is an internal matter.' "

EDMONDSON. Generally speaking there is a certain similarity in South Africa. I would say at least that your hand is strengthened, as I suggested earlier, by a statement of concern in Washington or by evidence of congressional concern. Immediately, you have the ability to point to that as the reason you are conveying your views to them. You usually put these in terms of the views of the American public generally, as represented by the government and yourself, rather than as your own personal views. There are times when, I think, you can express to certain individuals within the government some personal views as to how abhorrent something is. They have become so used to hearing this from Americans that they are not particularly surprised. Even so, you can get a cool reception.

Coming back to your original question of whether there are limits, I think there are, but I think they are movable, and, to some extent, expandable. I think it is up to the good diplomat to explore those limits, to keep pushing them out by arguing that the matters at issue involve basic human rights.

One can also take a legal viewpoint. If you have, in addition to congressional interests, a clearcut violation of individual rights as recognized in a UN declaration on human rights around the world, I think you have every reason to point to that as another major element of your concern. If an arrested person has been beaten, you may concentrate on the beating rather than the arrest because you do not always know the circumstances. If there has been action taken by the police in a demonstration and persons are killed, I think you always have a basis to express concern if there have, for instance, been reports of undue resort to violence. Probably, the [1985] case involving press reports about police officers giving conflicting testimony as to what instructions they had and what the circumstances were under which they fired at a crowd near Uitenhage is a good example of where there is a lot of leverage for the outside world to use.

For the first time, the South Africans are beginning to examine their own methods. The fact is that, until recently, they have not given a great deal of concentration to the use of, say, water guns or other nonlethal means of riot control (as far as they've gone has been rubber bullets), but I think they are now becoming very concerned about the integrity of their police and whether they're honest in saying they had stones thrown at them. Also, there is concern whether the police had the equipment to deal with the low level of mob violence, as opposed to firearms. In almost all the circumstances of shootings in South

Africa, there has not been a great deal of evidence of any shots from the mobs. Rock throwing can be dangerous, but it can be protected against. You can make those kinds of arguments with serious officials. I might add that, in the case of all these démarches, you have a much better reception from persons in the Department of Foreign Affairs—in effect, the foreign ministry —and with the foreign minister himself than you would with other elements of government, because they understand the foreign attitudes around the world. But you are not always certain how accurately and how effectively any representation has been conveyed to other members of the government, to the cabinet and elsewhere. You have to try to make similar representations in a less formal sense to parliamentarians and others.

NEWSOM. What is the South African reaction when an official raises a question brought to the surface by a nonofficial organization, such as Amnesty International or the International Commission of Jurists?

EDMONDSON. It tends to be somewhat hostile. However, if it is on an event that is well known, it is not rejected, but tends to be accepted. For instance, if Amnesty International raises the issue of an individual who has been missing, I have never had any difficulty in presenting that to them and asking for information. I would often be assured that they would check into it and give me what information they had. I should add too, however, that while they might have assured me they would check into it, it might take a number of further inquiries to get the information. The answer might always be that they still don't have it. This kind of approach wasn't always effective.

NEWSOM. In the past, and, I presume, still, it has been the practice of some American organizations like the Lawyers Committee for Civil Rights under Law to funnel funds into South Africa for the defense of people that are tried either under the Pass Act or under some harsher restrictive laws. First, if you can comment, does the embassy get involved in that type of transaction? And secondly, what is the South African attitude toward it?

EDMONDSON. The embassy did not become involved in these essentially private transactions. There are enough open channels and sources within South Africa for cooperation with lawyers and so on. We often were aware of such private ties or were in touch with the civil rights lawyers and others involved, from whom we got a lot of our information. But we did not act as a channel. We felt, in fact, that it could conceivably endanger those channels if we were to try to help. That doesn't say that we didn't have projects of our own in the human rights area, self-help types of projects; but we were very careful that these were projects that increased the awareness of the South African public of the importance of human rights, the importance, particularly, of due process, and of education in the field of human rights, and not those subjects that could be seen as elements of political opposition.

NEWSOM. Did you have some funds for self-help projects?

EDMONDSON. Yes, from AID, for human rights projects. Not USIA funds, though we had an extensive program of educational and cultural exchange under USIA.

NEWSOM. What kind of human rights projects would you undertake?

EDMONDSON. One project we supported was that of a women's group to disseminate information on women's rights. These were primarily black women, but women who were concerned with their rights. Most projects were carried out in cooperation with organizations in South Africa. In some cases, it was merely a matter of assisting them with the elements of communication, for instance, or training, or bringing lecturers.

NEWSOM. Did you have any role in the relations between the AFL–CIO and trade unions in South Africa?

EDMONDSON. Aside from assisting in exchange programs, none in a direct sense. There was a labor attaché and there was cooperation, but no channeling of funds.

NEWSOM. Did AAFLI [the African-American Free Labor Institute], the AFL–CIO organization through which funds are channeled for technical assistance, operate in South Africa?

EDMONDSON. No, they operated more in some of the adjacent countries like Botswana. They were not acceptable at the time I was in South Africa.

MEEHAN. I know you feel congressional interest growing and increasingly important, leading as you know to congressional visits. What about those congressional visits in terms of the embassy's activities in the human rights field? Were they apt to give a push to what the embassy was doing? Were they a major help, a major hindrance? How would you see them?

EDMONDSON. They ran the full range of what you suggested—helpful and harmful. Sometimes you had an individual congressman who wanted to make a point, either favorable to the South African government, on the one hand, or totally supportive of the opponents of apartheid; these interventions weren't always too helpful. The congressman also made life difficult who arrived and insisted on issuing statements or seeing people in a way that the South Africans saw as, in effect, fomenting a demonstration or opposition.

There were occasions when congressmen were denied visas. We worked very hard on such cases. Sometimes we were successful at overcoming these restrictions, and at other times we were not. One congressman, who was held temporarily in the transit area of the international airport, wanted the embassy to post a press statement. This was very difficult for us because he wasn't allowed entry into the country to have his own press conference. That's one extreme. The other is a case when some of the members of a congressional subcommittee came and we arranged a whole series of appointments and interviews. One of them was with a minister of the government. He proceeded to give them a very biased line on the good aspects of apartheid and what they were doing. The chairman of the congressional committee, afterwards, wanting to appear to be very receptive, said how pleased they were to have "the straight dope" after receiving so much "misinformation" from the Department of State and the American embassy. That wasn't very helpful either; it certainly undercut the effectiveness of the American ambassador.

NEWSOM. Were there some occasions where congressional visits opened doors for you that you were not normally able to open as the embassy?

EDMONDSON. Not really, though they sometimes helped us use doors we had already opened. In answering your previous question, I was explaining what the extremes of the congressional visits were and I didn't explain what the mean was. Most congressional visits were, in fact, very helpful in that they consisted of congressmen who were truly interested in learning as much as they could about different aspects of South Africa, be they parts of the economy or the social-political conflicts in South Africa. There were many congressmen who came with good sharp questions. They assisted in improving entrée that we often had, but I don't know of any openings they gave us that we didn't have to some degree. What they did was to help us groove those channels a little better. They gave us something to invite people to see, or people to meet. They gave us an excuse to use contacts we already had. They also gave us the ability to go with a congressman into Soweto, for instance, under circumstances that the government might otherwise have questioned.

Whatever the actions of the visitors, one unhelpful extreme was the person who wanted to try to make a public statement, wanted to go in and solve the South African situation. That tended to be resented, not only by the government of South Africa, but by South Africans black and white. There are conflicts among all the elements of the population. Any American or any outsider who comes in and says, "I have the solution; all you have to do is get together," is going to find resentment. There was a down side to some of those visits, but I would say the great majority who simply wanted to meet liberal Afrikaners, reactionary or conservative Afrikaners, radical blacks, moderate blacks, who wanted to get into all aspects of society, were simply helping us do what we already very much wanted to do.

MEEHAN. Do those comments apply in a way to American media interests and coverage of the South African situation? I don't mean those that originate in the U.S., but the kinds that come from special missions, special correspondents being sent out to do the South African story, that kind of thing. Did that have much of an impact on what you were doing?

EDMONDSON. Not while I was there. I think there have been a few instances since where there has been some advantage to it. There is good press representation in South Africa and the embassy maintains a good relationship. The press often had extremely good contacts that we could use and vice versa. I think there was some reinforcement between diplomats and journalists.

NEWSOM. One of the legislatively mandated parts of our human rights policy consists of the annual human rights reports. How did you handle those in the embassy? Did you use those as a basis for any kind of approach to the government? Did you give copies to the government? Was it a problem to explain why they were being issued?

EDMONDSON. When the first ones were done it was a problem. But as we explained that this was a statuatory requirement levied upon us by Congress, I think we gained understanding. We weren't volunteering all this nasty information about the country publicly, but we were being made to issue a report by Congress. Our interest was to make that report as accurate as possible from our point of view. They didn't always agree that it was accurate, but it was not a major problem. It was somewhat difficult in the earlier stages, which I suspect is not a problem now, to try to get an advance copy to the government so that they would not be taken by surprise by publicity given to the report when it was issued by Congress here. At the same time, the State Department had a legitimate interest in not making this public or circulating it before it had in fact been given to Congress. So there was a dilemma there. I think that probably is less of a problem now than it was then.

NEWSOM. Did you ever seek to use those as a basis for a démarche to the government on any specific aspects of their policy?

EDMONDSON. Not really, largely because they were an historical presentation of a previous year's events. It was something in the past. It was our own report and not some press report, not something new. Often, if representations were due, they had already been made. We could make reference to it, but I can recall no situation where we used that as a tool, ourselves, with South Africa. It was true, from a different stance, that the distribution of the report discreetly to different elements of the population other than government in South Africa was useful in showing that we did report on and take notice of the human rights situation in South Africa. It was very useful in that regard.

NEWSOM. Did the government ever take issue in an official way with any of the major facts or findings in those reports?

EDMONDSON. I cannot recall that it did in an official way. I think that unofficially, when there was press publicity, there were responses, but not in a way that they would take us to task officially.

MEEHAN. Bill, at an earlier stage in our conversation, you were saying, I think, that other embassies, other Western European embassies, plus Canada and Australia, in the matter of social contact in South Africa began to follow an American lead in broadening the range of contacts. This leads me to ask: Did you as the American ambassador have a feeling that other Western friends and allies were what I would call 'closely supportive' of our human rights policies and the tools we used to advance them? Or did you have the feeling of a rather clear, deliberate distance taken between us and them?

NEWSOM. Or were any of them active in their own right in pursuing human rights issues?

EDMONDSON. I think I can say all of the above. There were some that were closely supportive and active in their own right. And there were others who, though not attempting to distance themselves per se, followed policies that were not akin to the kind of policies we followed. There were countries, in fact, whose policies at the United Nations and whose public statements occasionally elsewhere in the world were quite a bit stronger even than those of the United States; but when it came to being on the front line, they accepted at least the practices of apartheid—they held black tie dinners only for whites—and didn't make the efforts that I think we and certain other countries did. I mentioned earlier the Canadians and Australians, both of whom had programs of their own. Often they were simple programs to indicate support to people in the townships, to provide art exhibits or other evidences of trying to have a relationship and understanding with black South Africans. There were occasions on which they had junior officers who got into difficulty because of visiting the areas that were normally restricted, just as sometimes our people skirted the regulations.

NEWSOM. Did you ever work in cooperation with any of these embassies?

EDMONDSON. There was some cooperation, but not to the degree of being a project coordination or collusion if looked at from the South African point of view. But one of the popular things we had done, through USIS, was to sponsor a jazz group and occasionally sponsor black art groups. Again, I mentioned the Canadians and Australians, and they participated in these and invited us, indeed, to participate with theirs. So they would come when we were having a group of people who were interested in jazz—and that included not just black South Africans but white South Africans as well. Incidentally, when there was entertaining in the diplomatic circle among the junior officers, you found some of those same people involved—right across the board, including the British, French, Germans, and others. Yes, there was cooperation.

There was a different kind of cooperation in a couple of situations. That was where there were active boycotts on the part of South Africans in which the diplomatic corps joined. Two of those I might mention were the Nico Malan Theatre in Cape Town, a Kennedy Center-like facility, which was originally closed to blacks and subsequently segregated. At one point they decided they would open it to coloreds on Tuesdays and Thursdays and whites on Mondays, Wednesdays, and Fridays, or something like that. This was quite ridiculous, so eventually it was opened to everyone. But during the period that blacks could not go at all and during most of the period when it was still segregated, the diplomatic corps for the most part—not all members perhaps—joined in a boycott that was sponsored by many white South Africans. And that was not just the liberal whites, but included some other whites as well. This helped, I would imagine, the beginning breakdown of some of these elements of apartheid.

The same thing occurred with the Breytenbach Theatre in Pretoria. A boycott was begun, particularly when the play *Golda* was being shown and the Israeli ambassador was incensed that it would have been shown to a segregated audience or only to blacks at one time and whites at another. He refused to go and was joined in an effective boycott by the diplomatic community.

NEWSOM. One final question. Were there instructions from Washington on the human rights situation that you ever felt were unrealistic in light of the local situation?

EDMONDSON. For the most part, I can't think of any. No. There were occasionally statements that we wished had been coordinated with us before they were made, or at least that we had been given advance warning or notice of. But as far as démarches and so on, while we sometimes felt that Washington wasn't always as appreciative as they might have been of the difficulties in making approaches (the fact that we were the ones who had to take the cold shoulders, so to speak), I don't think that we ever really had any unrealistic instructions.

NEWSOM. This has been, from our standpoint, a very good review of the various techniques. Are there any other parts of the process of human rights diplomacy in South Africa that you feel we have not mentioned that should be mentioned?

EDMONDSON. I mentioned earlier the importance of reporting as one of the aspects of a mission's policy on human rights questions. Reporting is an important part of diplomacy everywhere; to explain the human rights situation in a country is very much a part of that. In South Africa, the human rights problems, or the racial problems, pervade the whole society, and, therefore, pervade all your reporting. Because South Africa is a matter of such importance to the American people, and because there are so many emotional attitudes toward it, I thought it was extremely important that reporting be complete, that no officer be stymied in reporting what he or she saw or in calling the shots. At the same time, I regarded it as equally important that that reporting be in language that was as objective and clinical as possible.

Therein, I think lies an important aspect of diplomatic technique that could also be applied to representations and statements. That is, one often reads or hears others speak about a "racist" South Africa; and it is easy to use such epithets or emotive adjectives. I am not denying for a moment that South Africa is racist, but it does not help continued communication to use those kinds of adjectives. Thus, one of the elements of reporting is to stick to nouns and leave adjectives out, because if you do it correctly, the nouns will speak for themselves and people can draw their own conclusions as to how bad the situation is. The best advice really is to try to be as clinical as possible and be unemotionally involved.

The recent television film on Wallenberg, the Swedish civil rights activist in Eastern Europe during the Nazi persecution of the Jews, showed that it was important to maintain a relationship and in that relationship, while being frank about those things that we abhor, avoiding intemperate language. This sounds like a contradiction in terms but I think it is quite possible, and it is a traditional aspect of diplomacy. You say what you mean but you choose those words carefully. It is not to say that you don't call a spade a spade, but you don't have to call it a bloody spade.

MEEHAN. It is an aspect that most people don't like very much, apart from the practitioners themselves.

NEWSOM. And those in Washington that have to read the messages. Were you ever embarrassed by any revelations in Washington of sources or information in those reports that came back to haunt you in South Africa?

EDMONDSON. Not directly, although I think there were some instances; and these were not a matter of official revelations of Washington officers, but more of unofficial contacts people had at political levels in Washington—where we had reason to believe that some of the critical views and analysis expressed by the embassy were in fact conveyed back to South Africa. But on the whole, I would say no.

NEWSOM. Bill, thank you very much.

Multilateral Diplomacy: The Madrid Review Meeting

Lynne A. Davidson

In the Madrid Conference on European Security and Cooperation in 1980–83, nations of East and West sought to reach agreement on approaches to human rights issues. Ms. Davidson illustrates, in this account, the application of multilateral diplomacy to such issues.

To the success of our hopeless task!

> — *Yuri Orlov, toasting the formation of the first Helsinki Monitoring Group, Moscow, 1976*

Largely due to an East-West impasse over contentious human rights issues raised by brutal Soviet and Czech efforts to suppress citizens groups monitoring their governments' violations of the Helsinki accords,* the first CSCE review meeting in Belgrade ended with a terse communiqué containing no new measures. The second review meeting in Madrid began on November 11, 1980 in the wake of the Soviet invasion of Afghanistan, under the threat of an invasion of Solidarity Poland, and amidst growing public concern in the West about intensified repression of human rights activists in the East.

Goals and Strategies

The United States was chiefly interested in advancing human rights issues at the conference by holding the East accountable for violations of the Final Act and forcing it to pay a political price for such misconduct. The neutral and nonaligned (NNa) European states and our NATO allies, fearing that a repeat of Belgrade at Madrid would significantly diminish the stature of the CSCE

---

* The 1975 agreement adopted by the 35-nation East-West Conference on Security and Cooperation in Europe, held in Helsinki, Finland, as discussed in chapter 3 above.

process and exacerbate East-West tensions, were extremely desirous to end the Madrid Meeting with a balanced and substantive concluding document. Adding to the complexity of the negotiation for the United States was the fact that many West European and NNa governments, under growing domestic pro-disarmament pressure, were anxious that the Madrid Meeting provide an impetus for improvements in East-West relations as well as for the invigoration of arms control negotiations. This led to a push to include in the final document of the meeting a mandate for a Conference on Military Confidence- and Security-Building Measures and Disarmament in Europe (CDE). The West reasoned that the USSR and its allies, then involved in a European "peace offensive" aimed at deflecting the INF* deployments scheduled to begin in late 1983, had a stake in bringing the Madrid Meeting to a successful conclusion in order to show the world that détente was still viable.

Procedure and Principle

To accomplish their interdependent goals at this multilateral negotiation, it would be crucial for the United States and our allies to develop and maintain a strong and united NATO position and to engage in concerted consensus-building efforts with the NNa countries. Under CSCE rules, adoption of a concluding document requires unanimous assent of the thirty-five participating states. Ultimately, therefore, it would be necessary to reconcile polarized NATO and Warsaw Pact positions.

During the preparatory phase of the Madrid Meeting, the NATO countries were determined from the outset to negotiate an agenda and procedures for the main meeting that would provide for a thorough and candid review of Final Act implementation by the signatories, as well as for discussion of new proposals on how best to strengthen the Helsinki process. For its part, the East sought to deflect criticism of its extensive human rights transgressions by diluting the procedures which had permitted a comprehensive implementation review at Belgrade. Manipulation of procedural rules was seen as an important means by which East and West respectively could attempt to retard or advance the negotiation of matters of human rights principle.

Soviet stonewalling at the preparatory stage on procedural questions quickly cemented allied unity and encouraged allied, neutral and nonaligned nations to take steadfast positions against Soviet and East European violations. The pattern of frequent NATO caucusing and informal consultation with the NNa set during the preparatory meeting was to serve Western interests throughout the course of the three-year meeting. Also, a Soviet-induced procedural deadlock, which suspensefully continued for four days into the main meeting proper, raised false fears that Moscow had decided to scuttle the CSCE process. The procedural drama provided grist for the mills of the international press,

---

* Intermediate-range nuclear forces.

which saw the Madrid Meeting as a test of Moscow's political commitment to maintain workable East-West relations in the post-Afghanistan era. The Western delegations skillfully played back this interpretation to the East in order to exact procedural concessions and break the deadlock.

The Implementation Review

The agenda finally produced by the preparatory meeting allowed sufficient time for a thorough implementation review. From November 11 through December 19, 1980, the West, joined by most of the NNa, and despite East bloc protestations that human rights criticism constitutes interference in internal affairs, meticulously documented the East's worsening violations. Often, Western and NNa delegations illustratively cited the names of individual victims of such repression. Since all but the opening and concluding ceremonies at CSCE meetings are closed sessions, Western delegations made a habit of releasing the texts of their critical speeches to the waiting press (including Western radios broadcasting to East bloc audiences) gathered at the conference center. Separately and together, NATO delegations held frequent press conferences at which the Western approach to the talks was explained and publicized.

Once the time specifically designated for the implementation review was over, the West exercised its prerogative, safeguarded by procedures painstakingly established at the preparatory stage, to expose and condemn in plenary and in subsidiary negotiating bodies Soviet and other Eastern violations as they occurred throughout the rest of the three-year meeting. The thus extenuated implementation review became the chief mechanism by which the West and sympathetic NNa countries could defend the integrity of the Helsinki process by holding the East publicly liable for abrogation of Helsinki commitments.

New Proposals

The new major agenda item of the meeting was the consideration of new proposals to complement or reinforce already existing commitments in all the areas or "baskets" of the Final Act. In all, over eighty proposals were put forward. Both East and West strongly advocated their respective proposals for a post-Madrid security forum, while the West also emphasized its jointly drafted human rights-related proposals.

Despite twenty-two weeks of negotiations, from January through July 1981, the thirty-five states could not reach consensus on how to synthesize these proposals into a substantive and balanced concluding document. Two key issues were at the heart of the impasse, human rights and military security. The West insisted that improvement in the military security area had to be balanced by adequate progress in human rights; the East was reluctant to make any human rights concession and rejected outright many of the West's proposals. Important differences also arose over the nature of a post-Madrid security forum, originally presented in separate proposals by France on behalf of NATO and by Poland for the Warsaw Pact. On December 16, 1981, the NNa countries offered the first of two formal-compromise draft concluding documents in an attempt to find a common denominator for the Eastern and Western positions.

Martial Law in Poland

The declaration of martial law in Poland on the night of December 12–13, 1981 had already doomed the NNa draft to failure. The crackdown in Poland brutally violated eight out of the ten fundamental principles set forth in the Final Act to guide relations among states. Western and NNa delegations delivered speeches condemning the massive human rights abuses taking place in Poland. The devastating scope and nature of these violations were only beginning to become apparent to the outside world as the Madrid Meeting recessed on December 18, 1981 for a winter break, and the delegations returned to their capitals for consultations on the crisis. The credibility of the entire Helsinki process was at stake.

Having joined a consensus prior to the imposition of martial law to continue the talks on February 9, 1982, the United States and our NATO allies faced a situation in which further negotiation of a concluding document was politically insupportable. While all NATO countries recognized that a return to business as usual at Madrid in February was out of the question, there were nuances of difference in approach to the new session. The United States, Canada and some West European countries believed that this session of the Madrid meeting should be used solely to criticize violations in Poland and then be recessed as soon as possible to avoid the appearance of conducting normal negotiations. Other West European countries at least initially preferred to keep the meeting going in order to help keep the spotlight on Poland and to avoid giving the impression that the West was responsible for cutting off the East-West dialogue.

Meanwhile, in the weeks prior to the resumption of the session, the East, desiring to split the Western alliance and draw a curtain over the Polish crisis, let it be known that they proposed to conduct negotiations as usual at Madrid and that they would view the NNa draft concluding document as an acceptable basis for ongoing negotiations toward eventual agreement. At the same time, the East warned that it would not tolerate any discussion of the Polish situation, as this was completely beyond the purview of the meeting and constituted unwarranted interference in Poland's internal affairs. The Eastern strategy was unsuccessful, the important differences of approach among the NATO countries having been largely eliminated through consultation.

On February 9, 1982, in a dramatic departure from standard practice, NATO foreign ministers, together with their counterparts from NNa states, led their delegations back to Madrid, returning not to negotiate but to deplore. The session was characterized by stubbornly repeated condemnations, in plenary, of martial law and of other East bloc violations and by icy silence in the real negotiating fora, the drafting groups. The East's efforts to split NATO unity and to avert sustained Western criticism about Poland by means of procedural maneuvering backfired. It having become evident that negotiation was neither possible nor appropriate, consensus was finally reached for early adjournment on March 8, 1982, with a new round of negotiations not scheduled until November 9, 1982. It was hoped that during the long recess conditions would measurably improve in Poland and elsewhere in the East so as to create an atmosphere more conducive to negotiation in the fall.

The NATO Package

The interim witnessed: no improvement in Poland, where Solidarity was outlawed by *diktat*; a marked deterioration in the human rights situation in the Soviet Union, where the Moscow Helsinki monitoring group had been forced to disband and emigration continued to plummet; and a serious setback in Romania, where a highly restrictive "education tax" on prospective emigrants had been imposed. The United States therefore regarded the chances for agreement in Madrid during the fall 1982 phase of the meetings to be virtually nil. For domestic and international reasons, however, our NATO allies saw merit in a return to negotiation; they wished to achieve a mandate at Madrid for a security meeting in advance of INF deployments in order to assuage concern at home over the further deterioration of East-West relations. With improved relations, our allies further reasoned, the West might have some leverage to ease human rights conditions in the East. Yet, the United States was adamant that no attempt be made to justify the resumption of negotiation by glossing over the darkening picture of East bloc human rights violations.

The West's solution was a package of jointly tabled new proposals and amendments for inclusion in the NNa compromise text. The new Western formulations, targeted at the worst Eastern rights abuses, included language relating to: trade union rights and the right to strike; Helsinki monitors; religious liberty; an experts' meeting on human rights; an experts' meeting on human contacts; radio jamming; working conditions for journalists; and freer access by citizens to foreign diplomatic missions. The Western package soon became the focus of discussion in the drafting groups, where the merits of each of the Western proposals and amendments were argued on the basis of the continuing violations from which they sprang. Thus, the implementation review was perpetuated in another guise. In response, the East now embraced weaker NNa proposals on human rights which had antedated martial law. However, several of the NNa, sympathetic to the West's humanitarian aims, supported the Western language in substitution for their own.

Quiet Diplomacy and Public Protest

As he had from the beginning, but now more intensively as the push for final agreement gathered momentum, the U.S. head of delegation, Max Kampelman, engaged his East European and Soviet counterparts in private human rights exchanges. For example, he held discussions with the Romanian head of delegation about the "education tax."* Also, in a succession of exchanges with the Soviet delegation chief on the periphery of the meeting, Ambassador Kampelman made a determined effort to persuade the USSR that it should make concrete humanitarian gestures, i.e., release prisoners, permit increased emigration, etc., in order to ease ultimate agreement on a concluding document at Madrid. Underscoring this U.S. aim, on December 16, 1982, just two days before the session ended, Secretary of State Shultz took the occasion of a bilateral visit to Spain to emphasize publicly that the United States was actively seeking a successful outcome at Madrid which would involve humanitarian deeds by the East in addition to Eastern agreement to more human rights promises on paper.

The next phase of the meeting commenced on February 8, 1983. Increasingly, the NNa and the East appeared able to accept the NNa compromise draft 'as is' or with only minimal changes. NATO was prepared to focus efforts on negotiating a concluding document containing the essence if not the letter of its package. To further agreement, smaller negotiating bodies were tried, which did not produce dramatic results, but did make limited progress. So as not to give rise to false optimism, the United States and other NATO countries spoke out in plenary about intensified repression in Poland, Romania and the USSR.

End Game

On March 15, 1983, the NNa presented their second effort at a compromise draft, which omitted important Western proposals and which the Western countries found especially lacking in the human rights dimension. The Western alliance was now faced with the task of working out a common position on the revised NNa document. While all Western delegates were in basic agreement that the text was deficient, there were some differences over the scope and number of desired changes; the United States wanted more revisions than its allies. After intensive consultation, the NATO allies again arrived at a package of changes which they presented informally to the NNa and the East.

In a damage control maneuver, on May 6, 1983, the Soviets abruptly declared their readiness to swallow the NNa revised draft whole, without any changes whatsoever. Showing caution and admirably maintaining unity, the NNa and those of our NATO allies that were most hungry for agreement still did not take the bait, willing to hold off accepting the tempting offer and to let the

* See the author's account in chapter 15 of the 1982 most-favored-nation review of Romania's emigration practices.—Ed.

human rights language ripen a bit longer. On the day it was announced, the impact of the Soviet initiative also was blunted by the entirely coincidental arrival at the conference center of Avital Shcharansky, wife of imprisoned Soviet Helsinki monitor Anatoly Shcharansky, together with a large group of press. A Soviet press conference, scheduled to give added impetus to the effect of the Soviet offer, was cancelled, having been eclipsed by the media attention given to Mrs. Shcharansky.

Finally, on June 17, the Spanish prime minister, acting in his capacity as leader of the host country, announced a further compromise initiative, which cut the remaining issues down the middle but which met the key U.S. demand for an experts' meeting on human contacts. On this basis, agreement on a 38-page concluding document was reached by all the participating states except Malta (which was to withhold consent until September 8). The agreement came as a result of a surprise decision from Moscow reversing the previous Soviet position of stubborn opposition to the human contacts meeting. For all intents and purposes, the substantive dimension of the Madrid negotiation was now over and closing ceremonies were scheduled for September 7–9, 1983.

Curtain

It had been hoped that formal adoption of the Madrid Concluding Document would have an ameliorating effect on the climate of East-West relations. But the summer's papal visit to Poland and the formal lifting of martial law had been followed by a spate of legislation passed by Poland's rubber stamp parliament tightening internal controls. Also in the interim, arrests in the USSR increased, and the only positive gesture made by the Soviet Union—permission to emigrate was given to the Pentecostal families who had taken refuge five years earlier in the U.S. Embassy in Moscow—fell woefully short of the kind of deeds the United States had worked for in Madrid.

Then, only days before the final ceremonies, the Soviet shootdown of a Korean passenger plane sent East-West relations into another tailspin. The closing speeches by Secretary Shultz and other Western foreign ministers, both NATO and NNa, were replete with condemnation of this brutal action. The response of Soviet Foreign Minister Gromyko, who not only defended the action but threatened future "intruders" with the same fate, only served to increase the tension. The long-heralded bilateral meeting at Madrid between Shultz and Gromyko, which had been widely viewed as an occasion to reduce hostility and move forward in the area of arms control, concentrated instead, at U.S. insistence, on the airliner incident and other Soviet human rights violations.

Results and Conclusion

Thus, the Madrid Meeting ended on September 9, 1983 much as it had begun, in a darkening East-West atmosphere. The lengthy concluding document, full of promises for improved East-West relations and containing the mandate for a post-Madrid Conference on Confidence- and Security-Building Measures and Disarmament in Europe, was largely over-shadowed by the renewed confrontation.

The history of the Madrid Meeting was in a sense a chronicle of tragic developments. There had been virtually no change for the better in East bloc behavior. Yet, for three long years at the meeting, Western countries succeeded in focussing world attention on the human tragedies taking place. The East had been forced to pay a political price for violations of the Helsinki Final Act.

The concluding document that finally emerged from the Madrid Meeting is a balanced and substantive document which reflects the West's purposeful pre-occupation with humanitarian questions. New or strengthened provisions fall largely in those areas—human rights and human contacts—where experience has shown that the greatest problems exist. The modest textual advances over the original accords that were won include oblique references to Helsinki monitors and direct reference to the right freely to establish and join trade unions (a legacy of Solidarity), to enhanced religious liberty, to measures against terrorism, to better working conditions for journalists, and to improved procedures for family reunification.

Provision was also made for six specialized or "experts" meetings on a variety of subjects, including one on human rights in Ottawa in 1985, another on human contacts in Berne in 1986, and a "Cultural Forum" in Budapest in 1985. A successor to the Belgrade and Madrid review conferences is to be held in Vienna beginning November 1986. In addition, a commemorative meeting was set for Helsinki in 1985 marking the tenth anniversary of the signing of the Final Act. These meetings create, in effect, a continuing framework for the consideration of a broad range of East-West issues between and among the thirty-five participating states. Most importantly, they keep the door open to the possibility of making some concrete human rights progress when the international climate is propitious.

Chapter 14 THE SOVIET UNION

Human Rights Diplomacy in the Communist Heartland

Roberta Cohen

As the author says, "There are formidable obstacles to overcome" in conducting human rights diplomacy in the Soviet Union. As she demonstrates, however, the walls can be breached.

There are formidable obstacles to overcome in applying human rights diplomacy to the Soviet Union, a totalitarian state largely closed off to foreigners which relies on rigid internal controls and a secret police to suppress any efforts at reform. The nature of the system, on the one hand, makes it largely impervious to human rights initiatives from abroad. On the other hand, because domestic recourse is nonexistent, outside assistance is essential. Soviet scientist Andrei Sakharov and other beleaguered dissidents consistently turn to the outside world for support in pressuring the Soviet government to fulfill its human rights obligations under the Helsinki Final Act and United Nations Human Rights Covenants.

If human rights initiatives are to be successful, they must be limited in objective. While the USSR has changed considerably since the utter lawlessness and mass executions of Stalin's day, it is doubtful that human rights efforts will affect in any meaningful way the fundamental nature of the Soviet system or make it more open or democratic. Moreover, Western leverage is extremely limited. There are, however, areas susceptible to influence. International pressure, carefully applied by governments, intergovernmental organizations and nongovernmental groups can achieve important results for individuals and groups. Human rights actions over the past fifteen years have resulted in the release of political prisoners, increased emigration of minority groups, exit visas for dissidents, and improved access to information both for Soviet citizens and the West.

It is by and large during periods of détente or relatively low tension between East and West that the Soviets have exhibited willingness to make human rights concessions. During such periods, the Soviets are more likely to gain political and economic concessions from the West. Détente additionally creates opportunities for the West to exert pressure. Governments as well as private groups and citizens are brought more regularly into contact with Soviet society, enabling them to make their concerns known.

Conversely, when relations chill and East-West tensions mount, crackdowns on internal liberalization, reform and contacts with the West invariably follow. It is therefore not surprising that during what George Kennan has described as the "dreadful and dangerous" state of U.S.-Soviet relations today, there have been next to no human rights concessions, and dissent and contacts with the West have been harshly suppressed.

Although it has been argued, especially by former Secretary of State Henry Kissinger, that raising human rights concerns could well risk good U.S.-Soviet relations and even arms control, subsequent administrations have rejected and disproved this view. President Carter pursued human rights concerns with President Brezhnev while successfully negotiating the SALT II agreement in 1979. President Reagan in 1982 publicly affirmed with regard to the Soviet Union that "the persecution of people for whatever reason" must be "on the negotiating table or the United States does not belong at that table." His secretary of state raised both arms control and human rights issues in his first meeting with Soviet Foreign Minister Shevardnadze in 1985 on improving bilateral relations. Both administrations have encouraged human rights initiatives on behalf of Soviet dissidents. The varied tools of human rights diplomacy employed by governments, international organizations and NGOs are discussed below.

Quiet Diplomacy

Quiet diplomacy can be decisive in family reunification and emigration cases and in alleviating the plight of dissidents. One of its most dramatic and productive results has been the exchange of prisoners. In 1976, the Nixon administration gained the release from prison and emigration to the West of Soviet dissident Vladimir Bukovsky in exchange for Luis Corvalan, the imprisoned head of the Chilean Communist Party. Three years later, in 1979, the Carter administration negotiated the release of five leading dissidents for two Soviet spies. The dissidents included Jewish, Baptist, and Ukrainian prisoners and the high-interest Helsinki monitor, Alexander Ginzburg.

Because the Soviets do not have a uniform approach to dissidents —imprisoning some, harassing others, allowing still others to leave—Western governments have some chance of success when raising individual cases. Thus, discussions between a U.S. delegate to the UN and the Soviet minister of justice in 1979 resulted in the commutation of the death penalty for two Jewish prisoners. Intercessions by U.S. officials with Soviet ILO representatives in

1980 secured an exit visa for rearrested trade union activist Vladimir Borisov. The Soviet decision to make adequate supplies of flour available to urban Jewish communities for Passover in 1978 followed Secretary Cyrus Vance's raising the issue in 1977. The Reagan administration's sustained diplomacy on behalf of the Vashchenkos and the Chmykhalovs, Pentecostal families living in the U.S. embassy for five years, resulted in both families' receiving permission to emigrate in 1983. Initiatives by members of Congress have also helped. Senator Kennedy announced, following his 1978 visit to the Soviet Union, that the USSR had agreed to reconsider eighteen family reunification and emigration cases.*

But most diplomatic initiatives do not succeed. During the latter half of 1979 alone, the Carter administration made over one hundred representations to Soviet officials, twenty-seven in human rights cases, forty in family reunification cases and over sixty in matters such as travel, marriage and media representation. Only a small percentage of these cases were resolved.

Some U.S. officials have argued that an "American angle" should underlie official U.S. discussions with the USSR. The U.S. should raise only family reunification cases involving Americans; Jewish emigration should also be included because of its domestic political importance. Such cases might not be dismissed out of hand by the Soviets as interference in internal affairs and would more likely produce results. Fortunately the Carter and Reagan administrations have rejected this approach on the grounds that all human rights issues in the Soviet Union are legitimate subjects of concern, especially in view of the signing by the USSR of the Helsinki Final Act setting forth a wide range of human rights for Soviet citizens. Moreover, intercessions on behalf of dissidents seeking their rights under these agreements can at times yield positive results.

Quiet diplomacy has often been effective when linked to Soviet economic and political objectives. Thus, in the early 1970s, when the Soviet Union sought increased trade and technology from the West, and also wanted to contain an explosive internal situation, they increased Jewish emigration. They raised it from 1000 in 1970 to 33,500 in 1973. In 1974, the exiling of Solzhenitsyn, the halting of a campaign against Sakharov, and the granting of permission to Pavel Litvinov and the Panovs to leave all reflected the Soviet desire for better political and economic relations with the West. Certainly it was no accident that the signing of the SALT II agreement in 1979 coincided with the highest rate of Jewish emigration ever allowed (51,320) and the resolution of many family reunification cases. In 1983, the Reagan administration lost an

---

* After this book had gone to press, the Reagan administration negotiated the release and emigration to Israel of Anatoly Shcharansky on February 11, 1986 as part of a prisoner exchange. —Ed.

important opportunity when it failed to raise human rights cases during its negotiations with the USSR for a long-term grain agreement.

Public Statements

Public statements have proved effective when quiet diplomacy has failed. In 1981, following the failure of several diplomatic initiatives, the Reagan administration issued a public statement about Sakharov's hunger strike. It expressed concern about Sakharov's health and urged the USSR to allow Lisa Alexeyeva, for whom he was fasting, to join her husband in the United States. Because the statement identified a specific problem, dealt with specific persons and suggested a remedy, it proved effective. It no doubt played a role in the Soviet Union's decision to allow Lisa to emigrate and save Sakharov's life.

Other statements by the Reagan administration have not been so effective. Its bellicose condemnations of communism have been too easily dismissed as political propaganda. Branding the Soviet Union "the focus of evil in the modern world," or describing a cutback in Jewish emigration as "an unmitigated case of evil" lends credence to the view that the administration is interested in using human rights only as a weapon in its anticommunist crusade. The administration's failure to make many statements about countries other than the USSR reinforces this view and cuts into its credibility.

Public statements are important because they focus international attention on human rights violations and embarrass the government concerned. In the case of the Soviet Union, they also serve the important function of telling the truth. Soviet authorities frequently discredit dissidents. Public statements enable the truth to be heard both abroad and in the USSR through foreign broadcasts and by "samizdat" circulation.

There is ample evidence that at given times the Soviet Union is sensitive to world public opinion. In 1972, the Soviet government revoked an education tax on visa applicants after public protests. In 1981, the Jewish scientist Viktor Brailovsky received a less severe sentence than expected (five years internal exile) following an international outcry. The Soviets have proven especially vulnerable when foreign Communist party leaders, eminent international figures or peace spokesmen have publicly criticized its practices. Leonid Plyushch, a mathematician incarcerated in mental hospitals for 2½ years, was permitted to emigrate in 1978 after the French Communist party voiced objections.

Soviet human rights activists insist that without public protest Soviet dissidents would be subjected to much harsher treatment. They point out that Helsinki monitors Tikhy, Marinovic, Matusevich, and Petkus, about whom few or no public protests were lodged, received particularly harsh sentences. They further note that after the loudly protested Orlov and Shcharansky trials, a definite hiatus in arrests occurred and milder sentences were meted out to other Helsinki monitors.

At the same time, the Soviet Union does not want to be seen as caving in to foreign pressure, especially from the United States. Thus public confrontations about particular prisoners can at times result in more severe sentences for those prisoners. Yuri Orlov might be a case in point. But there is sufficient evidence to support the view that public protests do serve as a restraining influence on Soviet actions.

Sanctions

The absence of military or economic leverage with the Soviet Union means that there are few effective sanctions. The Jackson-Vanik amendment of 1974 represented the first attempt to place human rights conditions on the Soviet Union. The amendment sought by legislation to regulate the right of emigration from the USSR by linking most-favored-nation (MFN) treatment to eased emigration. It was an appropriate response to the systematic Soviet denial of visas to Jews seeking to emigrate and to the harassment, intimidation and pressure to which they were being subjected. Although some blamed the "confrontational" amendment for the USSR's subsequent reduction of Jewish emigration, the Soviet government accepted its terms, according to Secretary Kissinger. The reasons for the USSR's scrapping of the U.S.-USSR trade agreement in 1975 was the Stevenson amendment, a more severe sanction. It put a ceiling on credits to the Soviet Union, causing the Soviets to calculate that they would not gain enough in trade to make emigration worthwhile.

The Jackson-Vanik amendment in fact turned out to be quite useful in the case of Romania. When the Romanian government imposed an educational tax on would-be emigrants in 1983, the Reagan administration threatened to end Romania's MFN status. This readiness to apply sanctions resulted in Romania's rescinding the tax.*

Were Jackson-Vanik ever to be repealed, it should be done only in the context of an agreement with the Soviet Union and other communist countries that assured freer emigration in exchange for MFN.

Cutbacks in technology sales and in scientific exchanges are other sanctions that have been used against the Soviet Union, at times effectively. The National Academy of Sciences' threat in 1973 to cut back its exchanges with the USSR reportedly resulted in the Soviets' decision not to arrest Sakharov. The U.S. government, in response to the stiff sentencing of Soviet scientists Orlov, Shcharansky and Ginzburg, cancelled four official visits to the USSR in science and health, postponed several scientific exchange activities and held up the sale

---

* See chapter 15 for Lynne Davidson's account of the Romanian case.—Ed.

of high technology equipment. Although these actions did not modify the sentences, they may have contributed to the milder punishment meted out to other monitors subsequently tried.

Some human rights activists have urged the complete halting of exchanges rather than their interruption to protest human rights violations. However, limited sanctions make eminently more sense. Most importantly, they assure that lines of communication remain open to Soviet scientists, Soviet dissidents and Soviet leaders. Most Soviet dissidents fear the complete closing off of contacts with the West as possibly leading the USSR to return to the closed society of the past. The more limited sanctions also have the benefit of making it possible to respond to improvements. A postponed visit can more easily be rescheduled than a halted exchange.

The partial grain embargo imposed against the Soviet Union after Afghanistan was also explained by the U.S. as a protest against Sakharov's exile to Gorky. It is noteworthy that Sakharov himself has opposed such embargoes on the grounds that food should not be used for political purposes. Because the embargo was unilateral and undercut by the allies of the U.S., it did not succeed in modifying Soviet behavior and hurt American farmers to boot. However, its lifting without reference to Sakharov or human rights conveyed the damaging message that human rights was of less concern to the Reagan administration than making money. The U.S. representative to the Helsinki Review Conference in fact publicly complained that this action undercut his efforts to gain human rights concessions from the USSR.

The failure of the administration to use economic leverage for human rights has not been confined to this instance. It resumed phosphate and ammonia sales to the Soviet Union, approved the sale of tractors and oil-drilling equipment, and even considered the repeal of the Jackson-Vanik amendment, without any linkage to human rights objectives. These actions have been a net loss for the Soviet human rights movement.

International Organizations

Soviet refusal to abide by most human rights provisions of the Helsinki Final Act has created much disillusionment, even cynicism, over the Act. Nonetheless, the review conferences to monitor compliance do provide the most significant international fora for publicly airing human rights abuses in the USSR. For the first time, Western delegations have been able to meet with their East European counterparts to publicly discuss the full range of Soviet human rights violations. In doing so, they have drawn the attention of the press, world figures, and public opinion to the Soviet record. Moreover, they have publicized not just general violations of the principles, but the plight of the individual victims of Soviet repression. In the month of December 1980 alone, the U.S. delegation at Madrid raised by name the cases of sixty persons subject to persecution in the Soviet Union and Eastern Europe.* In May 1985 in Ottawa, the U.S. publicized the cases of one hundred seventy Soviet, Czech and Polish dissidents. The review conferences thus have established human rights as a legitimate and lasting element of East-West diplomacy. The concluding document of the 1983 Madrid meeting in fact contained stronger language than the Helsinki Final Act about trade union rights, family reunification and access to consulates.

At the same time, most Western energy at review conferences has expended itself in public debate. Serious diplomatic initiatives on behalf of individuals and groups appear to have been neglected or at least to have yielded few or no results. From December 1982 to June 1983, only three divided family cases on the U.S. representation list were resolved. Within the Soviet Union, the campaign of repression against all forms of dissent intensified in severity and essentially destroyed what was left of the human rights movement. If the Helsinki Final Act is to have any meaning in real terms, greater reliance will have to be placed in future on hard diplomatic bargaining. The U.S. and other Western governments will have to link progress in human rights cases more consistently and vigorously to progress in other areas of interest to the Soviets that are covered by the Final Act. A higher priority in Western strategy will have to be given to diplomatic negotiation to achieve more concrete results for human rights.

Strenuous efforts on the part of governments and nongovernmental organizations will be needed to galvanize support for debate and action in other international fora on Soviet practices. The efforts of Western trade unions have paid off in the International Labor Organization (ILO). Soviet forced labor has been publicly debated and denounced and Soviet practices condemned in written reports. More recently, ILO pressure resulted in a 1982 invitation to send an on-site mission to the USSR to examine charges of forced prison labor being used to construct the Siberian gas pipeline. Soviet restrictions on trade union rights have been another source of friction between the USSR and the ILO.

In other international organizations, Soviet human rights offenses have not come to the fore. The United Nations Commission on Human Rights did place the Sakharov case on its agenda in 1980 but failed to take action on it, and in 1981, allowed the case to lapse. Nor has the commission acted on any other Soviet human rights issue. A UNESCO committee after much deliberation took the very weak step of requesting information from the Soviet Union on Sakharov's status.

The main reasons for the reluctance of UN bodies to confront the USSR have been Third World need of East bloc votes for issues of importance to them, Third World fear of having their own records scrutinized, and Third World hesitance to confront the Soviets. The USSR, unlike the West, brooks no criti-

---

* See the case study on the Madrid review conference in chapter 13 above.—Ed.

cism. In addition, some Third World states have bought the Soviet line that Soviet violations are mere Cold War inventions. However, largely as a result of NGO and Western prodding and the difficulty of consistently avoiding one part of the world, the UN Human Rights Commission did begin in the 1980s to act on human rights violations in East European states other than the USSR, such as Poland, and to deal with issues that could be applied to the Soviet Union. These have included the political abuse of psychiatry and the right of private groups to monitor compliance with human rights treaties. These are significant steps that should be strengthened and expanded.

Soviet ratification of international agreements, such as the Human Rights Covenants and Racial Discrimination Convention, provides important opportunities to other states parties to press the USSR for compliance. U.S. failure to ratify these agreements has denied it a role in this process. Unfortunately, the Reagan administration has set back chances for U.S. ratification by expressing opposition to these treaties. It has ignored the lesson of Helsinki that participation can be a plus for human rights. The U.S. Postal Service has been able to press Soviet officials on non-delivery of mail because the U.S. is a party to the Universal Postal Union. Joint action with other postal services would be even more effective, especially if financial penalties and public exposure were threatened.

Nongovernmental Organizations

NGOs, like Amnesty International, the International League for Human Rights and Helsinki Watch,* have documented and published Soviet violations, brought complaints to governments and intergovernmental bodies, and mobilized public opinion on behalf of individual prisoners and refuseniks through media campaigns. They also have undertaken bold actions to assist individual dissidents. In 1971, the League announced the affiliation of the Moscow Human Rights Committee and became the first international NGO to recognize that association with a private group of Soviet citizens could assist them. When Committee member Valery Chalidze was threatened with arrest, the League was able to help him secure an exit visa. NGOs also have provided material support to Soviet prisoners and their families. They have maintained telephone and mail communication. The International Human Rights Law Group has produced legal opinions on the trials of prisoners for publication and distribution to the Soviet Procurator General.

NGOs have published information on Soviet human rights received from dissidents for redistribution in the Soviet Union and abroad. The most im-

---

* See also appendix E.—Ed.

portant of these publications has been the "Chronicle of Current Events," published in English by Amnesty International. They have spurred professional groups such as scientific organizations, psychiatric associations and book publishers to take action on behalf of their persecuted colleagues. Thus, in the 1970s, scientific groups began to threaten scientific cutbacks on human rights grounds and to refuse to participate in exchanges; these actions at times restrained Soviet authorities. For example, they probably prevented Sakharov's arrest in 1973 and won exit visas for physicist Veniamin Levich and mathematician Valentin Turchin.

In 1980, most American publishers boycotted the Moscow International Book Fair because of the arrest or exile of many writers, but attended a Moscow Book Fair in Exile reception in New York, organized by the Association of American Publishers. This action may not have freed anyone from prison, but it may have prevented others from being arrested.

The World Psychiatric Association's stinging condemnation of Soviet political abuse of psychiatry in 1971 helped lead to the abatement of this practice in 1974 and 1975. Its subsequent resumption thereafter resulted in member associations' investigating and documenting violations, interceding with Soviet authorities, and finally threatening to expel Soviet psychiatrists from the WPA. The Soviets, to avoid further public scrutiny and possible expulsion, walked out in 1983. Their withdrawal from the 65-nation body was generally viewed as a firm admission of guilt, a discrediting of their practices and a blow to their prestige. The jolt may some day bring a reappraisal of the practice of forced incarceration of dissidents in psychiatric hospitals.

Jewish organizations in many countries have also played a prominent role in publicizing specifically the plight of their co-religionists, holding demonstrations and vigils, and making the issue of Soviet Jewry an important one on the East-West agenda. Many successes in Jewish emigration can be credited to their efforts. The World Council of Churches on the other hand has limited its activities to "quiet diplomacy" on behalf of its co-religionists in the USSR, presumably to maintain the official Russian Orthodox Church's participation in its councils. When asked by Soviet Christians to take vocal stands, WCC officials have argued that to do so would not be effective. Various other human rights NGOs, while active elsewhere, also carefully avoid publicized actions on human rights in Eastern Europe. Their reasons generally seem to have been to enhance their standing, even credibility, with communist and Third World countries and to protect their consultative status at the United Nations from Soviet attack.

Failing to promote human rights in the Soviet Union not only misses opportunities, but lends credibility to Soviet propaganda that there are no major violations in the USSR and that NGOs who expose them are politically motivated and proponents of the Cold War. The most striking case occurred in the mid-1970s when the former Secretary-General of the International Commission of Jurists, Sean MacBride, visited the USSR while serving as Amnesty International's chairman. He publicly expressed doubt that there were any political dissidents in mental hospitals, despite abundant evidence to the contrary. Amnesty International disassociated itself from its chairman's remarks. Mr. MacBride went on to become United Nations Commissioner for Namibia, presumably with Soviet support.

Mobilizing Local Support

The relationship that developed between the Soviet human rights movement of the 1970s and the outside world of NGOs, media and foreign governments made the world aware of Soviet human rights conditions, led Western governments and even Communist parties to undertake initiatives to assist victims, and proved decisive in many human rights cases. For example, the transfer of imprisoned biologist Sergei Kovalev to a prison hospital where his life was saved was the result of appeals by Sakharov, published in the West. The emigration of the Chudnovsky family, refused exit permits and assaulted on the street, was also the result of Sakhrov's calling upon the wire services, newspapers, radio stations, mathematicians, governments, and public organizations to support their right to leave.

The severe KGB crackdown of the 1980s on human rights groups and their connections with the West is testimony to the effectiveness of these groups. It makes the maintenance of ties with them even more important. Keeping up contacts with dissidents enables governments and NGOs to assist them and makes needed information available. It was thus important that the U.S. ambassador to Moscow, during the intensified campaign of 1981–82, visited the children of several dissidents threatened with reprisals. Embassy officials also warmly and visibly received Mrs. Sakharov. The U.S. sent observers to the trials of Kovalev and Brailovsky. High administration officials, including the president, met with Soviet dissidents at the White House. In contrast, Ambassador Malcolm Toon's efforts in 1978 to restrict embassy contacts with dissidents, reportedly to protect U.S. personnel, worked against human rights initiatives at a time when there was little appreciable risk to U.S. interests.

Conclusion

The resumption of a serious and civil discourse between the U.S. and the Soviet Union would contribute to a more conducive atmosphere for the promotion of human rights. The U.S. government would of course have to make specific human rights cases an important part of the dialogue, and the Soviet government would have to deem human rights concessions in its interests. New strategies should also be developed to deal with changed human rights conditions in the USSR. Most human rights groups have been disbanded and most of their spokesmen exiled or imprisoned. It is the end of an era that achieved a substantial amount for human rights. Reappraisals are again due, just as new appraisals in the 1960s produced a new policy of establishing contacts with dissidents. Defeatism, although exhibited by some Western officials and foreign policy observers, is just what Soviet authorities want. Governments, international organizations and NGOs must sustain the struggle, create new openings and stand ready to take advantage of each new opportunity.

Romania, CSCE and the Most-Favored-Nation Process, 1982–84

Lynne A. Davidson

One of the tools of influence employed by the United States is the offer of most-favored-nation status. In this piece, the author shows how this has been used effectively in combination with the Helsinki process in the case of Romania.

What Archimedes said of the mechanical powers may be applied to reason and to liberty. 'Had we,' said he, 'a place to stand upon, we might raise the world.'

—*Thomas Paine*, Rights of Man, 1791

Romania is one of the few East Bloc countries with which the United States has significant economic leverage to affect human rights conditions. The principal instrument of that leverage has been the annual review by the president and Congress to determine Romania's eligibility to receive most-favored-nation trading status in conformity with Section 402 (Jackson-Vanik amendment) of the 1974 Trade Act.

In the annual MFN reviews, the multilateral goals of CSCE dovetail with bilateral interests. The Helsinki accords intrinsically link the development of international trade to the exercise of fundamental human rights and freedoms. That same idea is inherent in the Jackson-Vanik amendment, which prohibits the awarding of MFN trading status to Communist countries that deny citizens the right or opportunity to emigrate or impose more than a nominal fee connected with emigration. The law also gives the president authority to waive the prohibitions, subject to congressional approval. At present, the terms of Section 402 are applicable only to the Peoples' Republic of China, Hungary and Romania. (China, Hungary and Romania were the only Communist nations to enter into bilateral trade agreements with the United States following enactment of Jackson-Vanik and, therefore, are the only East bloc countries subject to its terms.)

Under Jackson-Vanik, the president must submit his recommendation on whether or not to extend and use his authority to waive Section 402 for each applicable country by June 3. Following receipt of the president's recommendation, Congress has the power to terminate a country's MFN status by taking action within sixty days after July 3. The Subcommittee on Trade of the House Ways and Means Committee and the Subcommittee on International Trade of the Senate Finance Committee traditionally schedule public hearings to afford the executive branch and interested NGOs a chance to air their views and concerns before the issue is decided by Congress.

Each year since Romania's trading status first came up for annual review in 1975, the president and Congress have concluded that, despite Bucharest's flawed record, humanitarian aims would be better served by the renewal of MFN status than by its denial. As long as Romania continues to violate human rights, however, the possibility of disapproval is real, although the probability that the president or Congress will disapprove varies from year to year, depending on the degree of Romania's responsiveness to U.S. concerns. Technically, the letter of Section 402 subjects only Romania's emigration performance to scrutiny. However, the spirit of the legislation embraces wider human rights considerations. Thus, the MFN process also has been used as a means to address Romania's persisting human rights violations involving the freedoms of conscience and expression, religious liberty and minority rights.

The Role of the Helsinki Commission and Other Interested Parties

The MFN review mechanism pulls into play the whole panoply of executive bilateral relations. The U.S. Helsinki Commission, a focus of executive, legislative and private human rights activity vis-a-vis Romania on a year-round basis, has played a decisive role in coordinating the humanitarian aspects of the MFN review. The commission serves as a clearinghouse on human rights information for Congress and NGOs. It works in concert with other government agencies, particularly the State Department, to promote humanitarian aims. Under Chairman Fascell's direction, the commission maintained constructive and steady dialogue in the form of exchanges of letters and the presentation of case lists to Romanian officials, liaison with the Romanian embassy, and close contact with Romania in multilateral CSCE meetings (Belgrade and Madrid), bilateral CSCE consultations (Bucharest, 1979) and CSCE spin-off fora (U.S.-Romania Human Rights Roundtables in Bucharest, 1980 and in Washington, D.C., 1984). And each year, during the House and Senate MFN hearings, the chairman and other Helsinki commissioners present detailed testimony on the state of human rights in Romania.

A review of the MFN process in the years 1982–84, from the commission's standpoint as a key participant, offers an illustration of just how this delicate operation is played out.

The Darkening Climate in 1982

In 1981, the MFN review was fairly routine, but by 1982 the climate for MFN renewal for Romania had darkened. After Poland's debt crisis, enthusiasm had lessened in the West for trade with Eastern Europe's shaky economies—and Romania's was considered to be one of the shakiest next to Poland's. Also, in late 1981 and early 1982, Romania cast further shadows by taking repressive measures against activist Christians, by showing inadequate responsiveness to congressional intercessions on behalf of intending emigrants, and by letting Jewish emigration fall to unacceptably low monthly levels. Through the work of the Helsinki Commission and other organizations, this poor human rights record came to the attention of Congress in the early months of the year, provoking several members of Congress in April and May to collect signatures on letters to Presidents Reagan and Ceausescu expressing concern about human rights conditions in Romania. At the same time, several private organizations geared up their lobbying efforts.

The President's Cautionary Message

Then, on June 2, President Reagan issued a tough message to Congress concerning extension of MFN to Romania. While he recommended that the MFN status be renewed in 1982, the president stated his concern about Romania's emigration record and the need for its reexamination. The president acknowledged that emigration from Romania to the United States had increased sixfold since the waiver had been put into effect and that the maximum number of emigrants admissible under U.S. immigration procedures had been permitted to leave Romania for permanent settlement in the United States over the previous twelve-month period. At the same time, however, the president cited certain problems, including the fact that the Romanian government had not improved its emigration procedures, which he called "cumbersome and plagued with obstacles for those who merely wish to obtain emigration application forms." The president said that he had weighed these humanitarian concerns within the context of the satisfactory state of overall U.S.-Romanian relations and concluded that, on balance, the aim of Section 402 would best be served by a renewal of MFN in 1982. He then added that he intended to inform the Romanian government that unless a noticeable improvement in its emigration procedures were to take place and the rate of Jewish emigration to Israel were to increase significantly, Romania's MFN renewal in 1983 would be in serious jeopardy.

Although the president's message to Congress on MFN renewal focused on

emigration matters, the administration's concern for the full range of human
rights issues involving Romania was underscored on June 3 by State Department Deputy Press Spokesman Alan Romberg, who noted that the United States
"has continually made our human rights concerns known to the Romanian Government." These concerns include "the persecution of some religious groups in
Romania, the arrests of believers for attempting to bring in Bibles, reports of
discrimination against minorities and the lack of access by private Americans to
see for themselves whether the reports of political and religious persecution are
indeed true."

Romania Lobbies on the Hill

Even prior to these cautionary comments from the executive branch, the new
Romanian ambassador evidently got the message from some quarters (not least
Helsinki Commission Chairman Fascell) that Romania was in for a hard time in
Congress on MFN renewal. Romanian responsiveness to expressions of U.S.
concern about specific emigration cases began to improve. The Romanian
ambassador took an intensive lobbying effort of his own to the Hill. A number of
long-standing emigration cases raised by Chairman Fascell and other members
of Congress were quickly resolved. Significantly higher numbers of Jews were
given emigration approval for Israel. The actual number of Jews arriving in
Israel also jumped. The emigration processing of large numbers of Christian
families, including activists, was stepped up appreciably. However, progress
was made on a case-by-case basis, rather than in terms of systemic reform. The
great majority of intending emigrants, whether they wished to settle in the
United States, the Federal Republic of Germany (the destination of the vast
majority) or other Western countries, still had to endure seemingly endless
procedural obstacles and harassment in contravention of the Helsinki accords
and other international agreements.

Helsinki Commission Efforts

Congressional offices in contact with the Romanian embassy frequently
turned to the commission for briefing material on Romania and pointers on the
most effective use of the MFN tool. Following meetings with the Romanian
ambassador and other embassy officials, these offices would keep the commission informed about developments. This feedback enabled the commission and
the interested executive agencies (State, the NSC and Commerce) to keep up
with the Romanian embassy's lobbying campaign and to correct any misleading
impressions about conditions in Romania that may have been created. All in all,
the commission's efforts significantly affected the review process, helping to
ensure that the human rights information received by most Hill offices was
accurate, that these offices acted in an informed way, and that there was a degree
of coordination between the efforts of the executive and legislative branches.

Congressional Action

Despite the last-minute efforts by Romania to bolster its record, disapproval motions on Romanian MFN were lodged in both chambers of Congress, and Romania's human rights record was roundly criticized during the House and Senate hearings, scheduled respectively for July 12–13 and August 10, 1982. Themes sounded repeatedly in testimony during the House hearings, including that submitted by Helsinki Commission Chairman Fascell, were that while cyclical jumps in emigration statistics coinciding with the MFN season were welcome, they also implied a cynical manipulation of emigration flow by the Romanian authorities; and that many members of Congress would not be content with improvements in emigration levels alone, but expected to see progress in other humanitarian areas if Romania were to earn MFN renewal in 1982. Although disapproval motions in both houses were pending, most members of Congress wisely concluded that the threat of disapproval might be more effective than its execution. Therefore, congressional decision makers tended to delay making their final decision, waiting to see if Romania would make further strides to improve its performance before the Senate-side hearings and the deadline for final congressional action were reached.

Disapproval Averted

In the interval between the House and Senate hearings, higher monthly levels of Romanian emigration were registered through July and into August and a number of cases of interest to particular members of Congress were resolved. Then, in an unprecedented response to heightened congressional and public concern, eleven prisoners of conscience arrested for the unauthorized acquisition and distribution of Bibles were included in an amnesty of twenty-seven individuals. Romania also agreed to begin a series of discussions in August with the Conference of Presidents of Major American Jewish Organizations and later in the fall with the U.S. government on improving the emigration process.

At the Senate hearing on August 10, Helsinki Commission testimony acknowledged that Romania had made some forward steps in recent months, but noted continuing concerns. The commission called for sustained progress in emigration and other human rights areas throughout the course of the next twelve months instead of the familiar cyclical fluctuation. On August 12, the Committee on Ways and Means reported the House disapproval motion adversely. On August 13, Helsinki Commission Co-Chairman and Finance Committee Chairman Robert Dole introduced a "Sense of the Senate" resolution, drafted by a team of Helsinki Commission and Finance Committee experts. It was cosponsored by the senators on the subcommittee as well as those who had lodged the disapproval motion against Romania, thereby negating the disapproval action. The resolution called upon the U.S. government to seek credible assurances that Romania would improve its emigration procedures and charged that Romania had continued to violate the human rights and fundamental freedoms of citizens, particularly those belonging to religious groups and national minorities. Lastly, the resolution directed the U.S. government to "pursue these concerns with the Romanian Government and in appropriate international fora, including the Conference on Security and Cooperation in Europe." The resolution was presented as "an expression of congressional concern directed to a fundamental plank in our bilateral relationship."

The House voted down its disapproval resolution on August 18, shortly before Congress recessed. Romania's MFN status thus was permitted to continue for another twelve-month period, but with stated congressional reservations and obvious erosion of support for its extension. After Congress reconvened in the fall, the "Sense of the Senate" resolution passed on September 24.

A Few Steps Forward, a Major Step Back

Meanwhile, building on the groundwork laid during the MFN review, the Conference of Presidents of Major American Jewish Organizations began talks with Romanian officials in Washington in August and continued the discussions in Bucharest in September. Assistant Secretary for Human Rights and Humanitarian Affairs Elliott Abrams engaged in an initial round of talks in Bucharest on October 6–7. These discussions resulted in Romania's agreement to respond definitively to emigration requests within six-to-nine months. Romania also promised to cease harassment of would-be emigrants.

However, Romania's good faith participation in these talks was thrown into serious question when on November 1, 1982, the government issued a new "education decree," which required *inter alia* that emigrants reimburse the state in hard currency for the cost of education beyond the compulsory ten-year level. On November 9, State Department spokesman John Hughes said: "By imposing this draconian measure, beyond the average citizen's ability to pay, the Romanian Government appears to be closing the emigration door to most citizens. If that is the case, the Romanian Government has gravely jeopardized its ability to retain its Most-Favored-Nation status." The Jackson-Vanik amendment excludes the imposition of more than a nominal tax in connection with emigration.

Protest at the Madrid Meeting

In fact, the education tax was by no means the only, albeit the steepest, barrier to emigration that the Romanian government had erected since it first received MFN status from the United States in 1974 and signed the Helsinki accords in 1975. The decree affected *all* prospective emigrants from Romania, not just those destined for the United States. Ethnic German emigration to the FRG and Jewish emigration to Israel were seriously restricted by the tax, and strong protests were lodged by both governments with Bucharest. At the same time, the FRG, the United Kingdom and The Netherlands as well as the United States pointedly criticized Romania's action at the Madrid Meeting of the CSCE as being contrary to both the letter and the spirit of the Helsinki accords.

The Stakes and the Strategy

Having issued the education decree at the beginning of November, Romania delayed implementation until February, when emigrants who had received exit papers after the announcement of the tax were to begin departing the country. During this period, the United States government proceeded to drive home the message to the Romanian government on the occasion of numerous high-level exchanges, including a January 1983 trip to Bucharest by Under Secretary of State Lawrence Eagleburger, acting as special presidential envoy, that actual implementation of the decree would result in loss of MFN. According to a Commerce Department study, termination of MFN would have meant that seventy-five of Romania's top eighty exports would become significantly less competitive because of the higher tariffs to which they would be subject without favored status. Twenty-nine of Romania's eighty most important exports to the United States would have been forced out of the market by tariff increases in the 30–50 percent range. During the first year following termination, it was estimated that Romanian exports to the United States would have been about $200 million less than otherwise (1982 Romanian exports totaled $340 million). Expiration of the waiver also would have rendered Romania ineligible to receive U.S. government credits and credit guarantees. As a result of Romania's lost hard currency–earning exports and its propensity to balance bilateral trade with Western countries, the Commerce Department also estimated that U.S. exports to Romania could have been reduced by as much as $200 million per year. In all, some three hundred American companies doing business with Romania would have been affected.

Trying to leave the door open for a change in the Romanian position, President Reagan on March 4, 1983 signaled his intention to terminate Romania's MFN status and other benefits effective June 30, 1983, if the education repayment decree were to remain in force on that date. Making the announcement several months ahead of the termination date gave U.S. importers time to protect their interests. It also gave Romania some more time to reconsider its action. Both Romania and the United States knew that once lost, MFN could not easily be rebuilt, since the initial conditions Jackson-Vanik requires a country to meet in order to acquire (or in this case, reacquire) MFN status are much tougher than those governing its extension once gained. In all likelihood, Romania, which had been given its status in 1975 when the rosy glow of détente still suffused the East-West atmosphere, would not be able, nor would it be willing, to meet Jackson-Vanik requirements in the bitter wake of termination.

Nonetheless, U.S. law was explicit. The credibility of the oft-stated U.S. commitment to defend the principle of freedom of emigration was being put to the test. By imposition of the "education tax," Romania had to understand that it had gone beyond the point the U.S. *could not* permit it to go and still carry on bilateral business as usual. The administration and Congress were prepared to act upon this principle despite the undesirable consequences termination of MFN would have for the bilateral relationship. Just as importantly, Israel and the FRG displayed this same resolve in their reaction to the education tax. The education tax then became the focus of a series of bilateral discussions.

A Way Out

In mid-May, Romanian Foreign Minister Andrei came to the United States and met with Vice-President Bush, Secretary of State Shultz and other officials. At the end of the month, FRG Foreign Minister Genscher paid a two-day visit to Bucharest for talks with President Ceausescu. Afterwards, although he publicly denied there was any link between the two matters, Genscher announced that "a satisfactory solution" to the emigration issue had been found and that the FRG had agreed to go ahead with rescheduling Romania's bilateral debt (the FRG is Romania's largest Western trading partner). The two matters were *not*, as East Europeans are fond of saying, coincidental.

Then, in his annual message to Congress on MFN extension, on June 3, 1983, President Reagan similarly announced that he had "received assurances from the President of Romania that Romania will not require reimbursement to the state of educational costs as a precondition to emigration, and that Romania will not create economic or procedural barriers to emigration," and recommended that MFN be extended for another twelve months. According to Jackson-Vanik procedure, the ball was now in Congress' court. Hearings in the House and Senate were scheduled for July 14 and 29, respectively. Disapproval motions had been lodged in both chambers.

The Congressional Review in 1983

In its unofficial advisory capacity, the Helsinki Commission took the position that nonapplication by Romania of the education tax was a necessary, but *not* a sufficient, condition for congressional agreement to extend MFN again in 1983. On the Hill, the memory of the stormy 1982 MFN review was fresh, as was its aftermath: the imposition of the education repayment decree. Once burned by Romania, Congress was twice shy about taking the new assurances on faith. The commission's advice to interested members of Congress was to wait for the promises to be translated into practice before supporting a continuation of MFN for another year.

The commission further recommended that quality of emigration should be stressed over quantity of emigrants. In terms of sheer numbers, Romania had compiled an acceptable record. Emigration levels for the first six months of

1983 looked fairly good. Romania had broken the cyclical pattern of lower emigration levels in the off-months and significantly higher levels in the months just prior to and during the annual MFN review. However, the pattern of harassment and procedural and economic obstacles for intending emigrants persisted. These practices, Chairman Fascell insisted, should be stopped. Furthermore, longstanding cases supported by the Helsinki Commission, members of Congress and the State Department should be given priority. The resolution of such cases would be a real indication that the new presidential understanding was being translated into practice.

A final remaining problem was Romania's woeful human rights record in other areas. In its exhaustive November 1982 *Report on Implementation of the Final Act*, the Helsinki Commission had observed: "The fact that nothing has been done to ameliorate the bleak human rights situation in Romania during the last two years of the Madrid Meeting provides graphic evidence that the Romanian authorities view the CSCE process strictly in terms of foreign policy and trade objectives and in no way as a commitment to respect and protect the human rights and fundamental freedoms of their people." Furthermore, the Fourteenth Semiannual Report on CSCE Implementation by the President to the Helsinki Commission, covering the period December 1, 1982 to May 31, 1983, described "repressive policies on human rights matters," citing "extensive harassment in Romania of religious, political and cultural dissidents," particularly "active persecution of individual Protestants and dissident Orthodox priests" and "the beating and harassment of ethnic Hungarian dissidents."

Chadha

Right in the middle of all these evaluations and preparations for the 1983 MFN review for Romania, the Supreme Court unexpectedly issued a decision that cut much of the ground away from under the Congress. In the case of *Immigration and Naturalization Service v. Chadha*, the high court held that the one-house veto by Congress of executive action is unconstitutional. Among the hundreds of disparate pieces of legislation, domestic and foreign, called into question by the June 23 decision, was the one-house disapproval mechanism prescribed under Jackson-Vanik. Given *Chadha*, the president's MFN recommendation could now be disapproved by Congress only through passage of a bill or a joint resolution—a far more laborious procedure than the one-house veto. For all practical purposes, the congressional MFN lever had been rendered less efficient. Action on the pending disapproval motions sputtered out and it was soon obvious to all—including the Romanians—that Romania's MFN status would be permitted to carry for another year.

After *Chadha*, it was important for both the executive branch and Congress to send a clear message to the Romanians that human rights considerations would continue to figure heavily in the bilateral decision-making process. Consequently, Helsinki Commission Chairman Fascell and Commissioner Heinz, also a member of the Senate Subcommittee on Trade, met separately with the Romanian ambassador and stressed the connection between the fulfillment of human rights and emigration obligations under the Helsinki Final Act and congressional support for MFN and other bilateral issues. It was pointed out to the ambassador that these obligations referred not only to the impropriety of the Romanian emigration tax but the whole gamut of questions covered by the new presidential understanding between Reagan and Ceausescu. On the occasion of his brief trip to Bucharest on September 18–19, 1983, Vice-President Bush emphasized the importance the administration attaches to human rights in the development of U.S.-Romania relations.

The CSCE Human Rights Roundtable

Another major occasion to send a message to the Romanians that U.S. interest in human rights is shared by the executive and legislative branches was the second U.S.-Romania Human Rights Roundtable held in Washington, D.C. on February 27–28, 1984 in conformity with a recommendation in the Madrid Concluding Document. The first roundtable, a voluntary CSCE spinoff forum, had taken place in February 1980 in Bucharest. In addition to State Department and Helsinki Commission participants, members of the U.S. delegation included representatives from other executive agencies and, in the case of the 1980 meeting, private Helsinki Watch representatives. In 1984, Deputy Foreign Minister Maria Groza headed the Romanian delegation and State Department Human Rights Assistant Secretary Elliott Abrams, the American contingent. Romanian Ambassador to the United States Mircea Malitza and U.S. Ambassador to Romania David Funderburk also served on their respective delegations.

In order to maximize the chances for discussion of concrete problems and minimize possibilities for Romanian philosophizing about human rights, on the advice of the Helsinki Commission the United States delegation took care to tie the agenda for the roundtable to specific provisions of the Helsinki and Madrid CSCE documents. Accordingly, each side addressed the agenda items by relating its own domestic experience in fulfilling Helsinki and Madrid pledges on human rights. By using this approach, the U.S. participants were able to draw their Romanian counterparts into extensive discussion of the full range of human rights problems in Romania. Throughout the frank exchanges the United States emphasized that the true value of the roundtable lies less in the words that are exchanged than in the deeds that follow. In particular, Helsinki Commission Staff Director Spencer Oliver stressed that violations of the human rights provisions of the Helsinki and Madrid agreements seriously weaken the credibility of the Helsinki process in the eyes of the public.

The 1984 MFN Review

To exert effective leverage in 1984 because of *Chadha*, Congress had to make known its concerns in the months *before* the presidential decision was to be reached, rather than after. The roundtable set the stage for the 1984 presidential MFN decision by signaling congressional concerns to the Romanians early, and giving them time to make improvements before the June deadline for the presidential recommendation. Members of Congress often referred to the roundtable as a convenient reference point when directly raising their humanitarian concerns with the Romanians and the White House.

On May 31, President Reagan issued his 1984 MFN recommendation to extend Romania's waiver for one more year. In his accompanying message to Congress, the president reported that emigration from Romania to all countries had more than doubled and emigration to the United States had increased ninefold since 1974. Progress was noted in the numbers of people receiving exit documentation and in the shortening of the processing time for passport applications. However, President Reagan acknowledged that "there are still many problems in the emigration area."

Next, on June 4, the State Department released the President's Sixteenth Semiannual Report on CSCE Implementation to the Helsinki Commission, covering the period December 1, 1983 to March 31, 1984. In the section on Romania, the report stated that Romanian observance of basic human rights (as distinct from emigration) provisions of the Final Act had been poor. It indicated that "the number of incidents of government harassment of Protestants, particularly Baptist pastors, substantially increased" during the reporting period and noted "the publication by government-supervised publishing houses of a number of anti-Semitic articles, poems and a book." Romania's fulfillment of Madrid pledges was deemed mixed at best.

At the urging of the Helsinki Commission and other concerned governmental and private human rights organizations, despite *Chadha*, on August 8, the Senate Subcommittee on International Trade held MFN hearings to demonstrate Congress' year-round interest in human rights and its continued control over MFN decision making. Breaking a ten-year tradition, however, the House Trade Subcommittee did not call MFN hearings in 1984. The Senate hearings took place in a bilateral climate heavily influenced by Romania's much-acclaimed participation in the Los Angeles Olympics, which were boycotted by all the other East bloc countries.

In his opening hearing statement, Chairman Danforth made it clear that "(t)he Committee takes its responsibility for overseeing this provision (the Jackson-Vanik amendment) of U.S. trade law with the utmost seriousness, and I think it is fair to say that this year, our perseverance appears to be paying off." Danforth noted "significant improvements" in Romanian emigration performance. He went on to say, however, that despite increases in the numbers permitted to emigrate, "procedural obstacles to emigration remain, where prospective emigrants continue to face delays and harassment. Certain longstanding emigration cases which have enjoyed support in the United States remain unresolved." Danforth called for improvements on the broader human rights front, citing problem areas such as prisoners of conscience, restrictions on freedom of expression, anti-Semitism, religious liberty and minority rights. The testimony of the vast majority of the nongovernmental witnesses focussed in detail on various persisting problems.

Members of Congress other than Chairman Danforth present at the hearing were Finance Committee Chairman and Helsinki Commission Co-Chairman Robert Dole and subcommittee member and Helsinki Commissioner Heinz. Helsinki Commission Chairman Fascell submitted detailed written testimony for the record. Senator Dole emphasized that "the Supreme Court's decision in the *Chadha* case may have invalidated the legislative veto provided for in the Jackson-Vanik amendment, but it has not diminished the Committee's interest in the freedom of people to emigrate from Eastern Europe."

Speaking in his dual trade subcommittee and Helsinki Commission capacities, Senator Heinz asserted that "the Jackson-Vanik amendment has had a positive impact on the lives of the peoples of...Romania." Heinz further stated: "I realize that our deliberations today cannot be divorced from our policies toward Eastern Europe as a whole. While it is important to recognize Romania's occasional independence on certain foreign policy issues, our values compel us and the Jackson-Vanik amendment commands us to call Romania to account for its continuing violations of human rights and fundamental freedoms. At the Olympic opening ceremonies, those gathered in the stadium deservedly gave a warm reception to the athletes from Romania, the only Warsaw Pact nation not to join the Soviet boycott. But the stirring Olympic drama does not, and should not, draw our attention away from the desperate human dramas taking place back in Romania. The anguish of divided families, the persecution of rights activists and the plight of political prisoners remain deep and abiding concerns."

For the written record, Helsinki Commission Chairman Fascell chronicled Romania's human rights performance for the preceding twelve months, pegging improvements and shortcomings to specific provisions of the Helsinki accords and Madrid Concluding Document. He pledged that the Helsinki Commissioners "will continue to pursue these abiding human rights concerns both in Congress and within the Helsinki framework." Chairman Fascell further called upon the Romanian Government to:

— release Father Calciu, a Romanian Orthodox priest imprisoned since 1979, and other prisoners of conscience;
— authorize the construction of more churches, the matriculation of more seminarians, the importation and dissemination of more Bibles, the legalization of the Uniate Church;

— permit dissenting Baptist pastors to preach and to carry out their other pastoral duties without further harassment;

— take steps to ensure that government-supervised printing houses will not again publish anti-Semitic literature;

— show sensitivity to the cultural and educational needs of national minorities and cease the harassment of minority rights activists;

— resolve family reunification and other human contacts cases in which the United States has expressed a longstanding interest;

— and otherwise permit Romanian citizens freely 'to know and act upon' their rights as set forth in the Helsinki and other international agreements.

On August 10, Congress recessed until early September without having passed a bill or joint resolution of disapproval, thereby permitting the presidential decision to stand and Romania to retain its MFN status for another year. Word subsequently reached the West that the Romanian government had quietly released Father Calciu, Romania's most famous prisoner of conscience, on August 20, three days before Romania's National Day, an occasion around which amnesties tend to be timed. While the immediate steps leading up to Father Calciu's release have not yet become known, it is certain that the combined intercessions by a succession of U.S. administrations, members of Congress, Helsinki Commissioners, Western and NNa governments and private human rights organizations in this country and abroad finally succeeded in bringing the Romanian government to the conclusion that its interests would be better served by ending Father Calciu's imprisonment than by continuing it.

That Father Calciu has been under house arrest since his release from prison and is prevented from communicating with Western embassies directly concerned with his welfare and efforts to emigrate attests to the frustrating "two steps forward, one step back" nature of human rights gains in the East bloc context.*

The MFN Review and Beyond

Before the 1985 MFN season, the legislative branch was considering a move to rebuild Jackson-Vanik procedures so as to ensure the amendment's constitutionality and continued effectiveness. In the meantime, the administration, Congress and the Helsinki Commission continued to seek to promote human rights objectives for Romania by utilizing a variety of other tools. Not the least among these is the six-week CSCE Human Rights Experts' Meeting in Ottawa in May–June 1985. Useful opportunities in addition to the yearly MFN reviews are presented by such CSCE gatherings as the Cultural Forum in Budapest

---

* Father Calciu was released from house arrest and permitted to emigrate to the United States in August 1985.—Ed.

(October 1985), the Human Rights Contacts Experts' Meeting in Berne (April 1986) and the Vienna Review Meeting of the CSCE (November 1986).

Assessment of the MFN Mechanism

Although it is a useful instrument, Jackson-Vanik is no magic wand. It is unrealistic to expect the annual MFN review to produce instant institutional change in Romania. The MFN tool should not be regarded merely as a stick to brandish disapprovingly once a year. Nor should the carrot of MFN extension be regarded as an unqualified seal of U.S. approval. Rather, Jackson-Vanik is a specialized tool of leverage—an instrument to be applied with a steady hand from one MFN review to the next and in conjunction with other human rights policy instruments such as CSCE in order to accomplish concrete, if limited, objectives: the reunification of families, the release of prisoners of conscience, easements in the plight of human rights activists and some improvements in the way the Romanian government treats segments of the population.

The foregoing account should not leave the reader with the erroneous impression that those attempting to operate the Jackson-Vanik mechanism always employ it prudently and effectively. Actually, during the annual MFN reviews, many hands, not all of them working in synchrony, attempt to operate the same lever. Thanks to the cooperative efforts of policymakers and staff of the executive branch, Congress and the Helsinki Commission, more often than not MFN has been used as a constructive, rather than destructive, tool.

Appendixes

Appendix A

The Contributors

ROBERTA COHEN was U.S. deputy assistant secretary of state for human rights in 1980–81, following service as a State Department human rights officer in 1978–80 and before that, in the nongovernmental sector, as executive director of the International League for Human Rights, 1972–78. She is a member of the Council on Foreign Relations, the U.S. Helsinki Watch Committee, and the advisory committees of the International League for Human Rights and the International Human Rights Law Group. Among her published writings on U.S. human rights policy are articles in *Human Rights Quarterly*, *Virginia Journal of International Law*, and in the 1979 book *Human Rights and American Foreign Policy*. In 1985 she was honored by the U.S. Information Agency for her work in reestablishing a U.S.I.A. program in Addis Ababa, where she served as public affairs advisor at the U.S. embassy.

LYNNE A. DAVIDSON has been staff assistant for human rights of the U.S. Commission on Security and Cooperation in Europe since 1977. Her responsibilities at the Commission include: Poland and Romania country desks, Soviet Jewry, public affairs and liaison with nongovernmental organizations, and planning for follow-up meetings of the 35 Helsinki (CSCE) signatory states. She has served on several U.S. delegations to CSCE meetings: Madrid (1980–83), Ottawa (1985), Helsinki Tenth Anniversary (1985), and the Cultural Forum (1985) in Budapest; and has participated in related bilateral consultations with Hungary (1979) and Romania (1979, 1980). She received a B.S. in Foreign Service from the School of Foreign Service at Georgetown University (1975) and was twice an exchange student at Leningrad University under the auspices of the Council on International Educational Exchange.

WILLIAM B. EDMONDSON, a career officer of the Senior Foreign Service, was U.S. Ambassador to the Republic of South Africa from May 1978 to August 1981, deputy assistant secretary of state for African affairs, 1976–78, and minister-counselor/deputy chief of mission in Pretoria, 1974–76. His other assignments have included Tanzania (then Tanganyika), Switzerland, Ghana, Zambia, and, in the Department of State, work in international organization affairs, intelligence and research, educational and cultural exchange, and

203

African affairs. Ambassador Edmondson is currently deputy program inspector general of the Department of State. He served in the U.S. Army, 1944–48, then received an A.B. with High Distinction from the University of Nebraska in 1950 and an M.A. from the Fletcher School of Law and Diplomacy in 1951.

PATRICK J. FLOOD is a career Foreign Service officer who has worked extensively in human rights and international organization affairs and in Eastern Europe and Latin America. His overseas assignments have included Mexico City, Budapest, Lima, Poznan, Geneva, and his current post, Warsaw, where he is serving as counselor for political affairs. During Washington assignments, he has dealt with UNESCO, Cuban affairs, Soviet and Eastern European affairs, and human rights. In the period covered by his contribution to this book, he was in charge of South American, Caribbean and OAS affairs in the Bureau of Human Rights and Humanitarian Affairs. Mr. Flood holds an A.B. in philosophy from Providence College and an M.A. in European history from Georgetown.

WILLIAM H. GLEYSTEEN, JR. was U.S. Ambassador to the Republic of Korea from 1979 to 1981. A Foreign Service officer from 1951 to 1981, specializing in Northeast Asia, he served as deputy assistant secretary of state for East Asian and Pacific affairs in 1974–76 and again in 1977–78, and was detailed as a senior staff officer to the National Security Council in 1976–77. Other Foreign Service assignments included Tokyo, Hong Kong and Taipei, where he was deputy chief of mission, 1971–74. Other Washington posts included deputy director of the Office of United Nations Political Affairs, 1966–69, and director of the Office of Intelligence and Research for East Asian and Pacific Affairs, 1969–71. Ambassador Gleysteen was director of the Asia Society's Washington Center in 1981–83 and currently works as a consultant. He is a member of the Council on Foreign Relations and the boards of a number of organizations and companies focused on Asia. He served in the U.S. Navy in 1944–46 and is a graduate of Yale University, B.A., 1949, M.A., 1951.

DAVID C. McGAFFEY, a member of the U.S. Foreign Service since 1967, has served in the Philippines, Pakistan, Afghanistan and Iran. In 1976–79 in Iran, he served during the revolution as principal officer in charge of the U.S. consulates in Tabriz and Isfahan, then as political affairs officer at the embassy in Tehran. In Washington he has served in the Office of the Secretary, the Bureau of Intelligence and Research, and as coordinator for political studies at the Foreign Service Institute, where he helped create the Mid-Level Professional Development Program. He is currently on detail to the Voice of America as deputy chief of the division broadcasting to North Africa, Near East and South Asia. Mr. McGaffey has a B.A. from the University of Detroit (1964) and an M.P.A. from Harvard (1980), and is currently a doctoral candidate at Johns

Hopkins. His specialty is cultural analysis and negotiations. Among several departmental citations he has received is an Award for Heroism in Iran.

FRANCIS J. MEEHAN was appointed U.S. ambassador to the German Democratic Republic in August 1985. A career diplomat since 1951, he was U.S. ambassador to Czechoslovakia in 1979–80 and ambassador to Poland from 1980 to 1983. In 1983–85 he was research professor of diplomacy at the Institute for the Study of Diplomacy, Georgetown University. Among his Foreign Service posts have been Frankfurt, Hamburg, NATO/Paris, intelligence research, Moscow, and Berlin. In the State Department he served as director of the Operations Center in 1967, and as deputy executive secretary, 1967–68. He has served as deputy chief of mission in Budapest (1968–72), Vienna (1975–77) and Bonn (1977–79), where he had earlier served as counselor (1972–75). Ambassador Meehan served in the U.S. Army in 1945–47. He received an M.A. from Glasgow University in 1945 and an M.P.A. from Harvard in 1957.

JEFFREY D. MERRITT, a former Congressional Research Service analyst, writes from Washington on human rights and refugee affairs. He is an annual contributor on these subjects to UNA-USA's *Issues before the General Assembly of the United Nations* and is the author of the book *Day by Day: The Fifties* (Facts on File, 1979). Mr. Merritt holds M.A. and M. Phil. degrees from Columbia University, where he is to receive his Ph.D. in political science in 1986.

CHARLES W. NAAS was director of Iranian affairs in the Department of State from 1974 to 1978, minister-counselor at the embassy in Tehran, May 1978–April 1979, and chargé d'affaires, April–June 1979. A career Foreign Service officer from 1951 to 1981, he also served in Pakistan, India, Turkey and Afghanistan. Other Washington assignments included the Bureau of Intelligence and Research, Bureau of Personnel, Pakistan and Afghanistan desk, political and security affairs at the United Nations, and the policy planning staff. Mr.Naas served in the U.S. Army Air Corps, 1943–46, has an A.B. from Clark University, 1949, and an M.A. from Fletcher, 1950.

DAVID D. NEWSOM, a career diplomat, served as U.S. under secretary of state for political affairs from 1978 to 1981. Prior to that he was ambassador to the Philippines (1977–78), ambassador to Indonesia (1974–77), assistant secretary of state for African affairs (1969–74), and ambassador to Libya (1965–69). At Georgetown University since 1981, he is director of the Institute for the Study of Diplomacy and associate dean of the School of Foreign Service. He is president of the American Academy of Diplomacy and a board member of numerous international affairs organizations. Ambassador Newsom is a frequent contributor to foreign policy journals and the *Christian Science Monitor*. He has a B.A. degree from the University of California, Berkeley and an M.S. from the School of Journalism at Columbia University.

JOHN P. SALZBERG was special consultant, from 1973 to 1978, to the Subcommittee on International Organizations and Movements (chaired by Donald M. Fraser) of the House Committee on Foreign Affairs. He served as regional officer for African and East Asian affairs with the State Department Bureau of Human Rights and Humanitarian Affairs in 1978–81. Dr. Salzberg currently serves as executive director of William Penn House, a Quaker seminar and hospitality center in Washington, D.C. He has a Ph.D. in political science from New York University.

WILLIAM H. SULLIVAN was U.S. ambassador to Iran from June 1977 to April 1979. He was ambassador to the Philippines, 1973–77, and to Laos, 1964–69, and deputy assistant secretary of state for East Asian and Pacific affairs, 1969–73. He entered the Foreign Service in 1947, served in Calcutta, Tokyo, Rome and The Hague, and as deputy, then acting, U.S. representative at the Geneva Conference on Laos. His Washington assignments included that of special assistant to Secretary of State Dean Rusk and before that to Under Secretary W. Averell Harriman. Ambassador Sullivan currently serves as president of the American Assembly at Columbia University.

R. JOHN VINCENT is senior lecturer in international relations at the University of Keele in England. He is the author of *Nonintervention and International Order* (Princeton, 1974) and of two forthcoming books on human rights for the Royal Institute of International Affairs in London. He is editor of the *Review of International Studies*, the quarterly journal of the British International Studies Association.

Human Rights and Foreign Policy

Cyrus R. Vance

An address by the Secretary of State in the Carter administration at Law Day ceremonies at the University of Georgia School of Law at Athens, Georgia, on April 30, 1977 (text from press release 194). Published in Department of State Bulletin, *May 23, 1977, pp. 505–8.*

I speak today about the resolve of this Administration to make the advancement of human rights a central part of our foreign policy.

Many here today have long been advocates of human rights within our own society. And throughout our nation that struggle for civil rights continues.

In the early years of our civil rights movement, many Americans treated the issue as a "Southern" problem. They were wrong. It was and is a problem for all of us.

Now, as a nation, we must not make a comparable mistake. Protection of human rights is a challenge for *all* countries, not just for a few.

Our human rights policy must be understood in order to be effective. So today I want to set forth the substance of that policy and the results we hope to achieve.

Our concern for human rights is built upon ancient values. It looks with hope to a world in which liberty is not just a great cause, but the common condition. In the past, it may have seemed sufficient to put our name to international documents that spoke loftily of human rights. That is not enough. We will go to work, alongside other people and governments, to protect and enhance the dignity of the individual.

Let me define what we mean by "human rights."

First, there is the right to be free from governmental violation of the integrity of the person. Such violations include torture; cruel, inhuman, or degrading treatment or punishment; and arbitrary arrest or imprisonment. And they include denial of fair public trial and invasion of the home.

Second, there is the right to the fulfillment of such vital needs as food, shelter, health care, and education. We recognize that the fulfillment of this right will depend, in part, upon the stage of a nation's economic development. But we also know that this right can be violated by a government's action or inaction—for example, through corrupt official processes which divert resources to an elite at the expense of the needy or through indifference to the plight of the poor.

Third, there is the right to enjoy civil and political liberties: freedom of thought, of religion, of assembly; freedom of speech; freedom of the press; freedom of movement both within and outside one's own country; freedom to take part in government.

Our policy is to promote all these rights. They are all recognized in the Universal Declaration of Human Rights, a basic document which the United States helped fashion and which the United Nations approved in 1948. There may be disagreement on the priorities these rights deserve. But I believe that, with work, all of these rights can become complementary and mutually reinforcing.

The philosophy of our human rights policy is revolutionary in the intellectual sense, reflecting our nation's origin and progressive values. As Archibald MacLeish wrote during our Bicentennial a year ago: "... the cause of human liberty is now the one great revolutionary cause...."

President Carter put it this way in his speech before the United Nations:

All the signatories of the United Nations Charter have pledged themselves to observe and to respect basic human rights. Thus, no member of the United Nations can claim that mistreatment of its citizens is solely its own business. Equally, no member can avoid its responsibilities to review and to speak when torture or unwarranted deprivation occurs in any part of the world.

Since 1945, international practice has confirmed that a nation's obligation to respect human rights is a matter of concern in international law.

Our obligation under the United Nations Charter is written into our own legislation. For example, our Foreign Assistance Act now reads: "... a principal goal of the foreign policy of the United States is to promote the increased observance of internationally recognized human rights by all countries."

In these ways, our policy is in keeping with our tradition, our international obligations, and our laws.

In pursuing a human rights policy, we must always keep in mind the limits of our power and of our wisdom. A sure formula for defeat of our goals would be a rigid, hubristic attempt to impose our values on others. A doctrinaire plan of action would be as damaging as indifference.

We must be realistic. Our country can only achieve our objectives if we shape what we do to the case at hand. In each instance, we will consider these questions as we determine whether and how to act:

1. First, we will ask ourselves, what is the nature of the case that confronts us? For example:

What kinds of violations or deprivations are there? What is their extent? Is there a pattern to the violations? If so, is the trend toward concern for human rights or away from it?

What is the degree of control and responsibility of the government involved? And finally, is the government willing to permit independent outside investigation?

2. A second set of questions concerns the prospects for effective action:

Will our action be useful in promoting the overall cause of human rights? Will it actually improve the specific conditions at hand? Or will it be likely to make things worse instead?

Is the country involved receptive to our interest and efforts?

Will others work with us, including official and private international organizations dedicated to furthering human rights?

Finally, does our sense of values and decency demand that we speak out or take action anyway, even though there is only a remote chance of making our influence felt?

3. We will ask a third set of questions in order to maintain a sense of perspective:

Have we steered away from the self-righteous and strident, remembering that our own record is not unblemished?

Have we been sensitive to genuine security interests, realizing that outbreak of armed conflict or terrorism could in itself pose a serious threat to human rights?

Have we considered *all* the rights at stake? If, for instance, we reduce aid to a government which violates the political rights of its citizens, do we not risk penalizing the hungry and poor, who bear no responsibility for the abuses of their government?

If we are determined to act, the means available range from quiet diplomacy in its many forms, through public pronouncements, to withholding of assistance. Whenever possible, we will use positive steps of encouragement and inducement. Our strong support will go to countries that are working to improve the human condition. We will always try to act in concert with other countries, through international bodies.

In the end, a decision whether and how to act in the cause of human rights is a matter for informed and careful judgment. No mechanistic formula produces an automatic answer.

It is not our purpose to intervene in the internal affairs of other countries, but as the President has emphasized, no member of the United Nations can claim that violation of internationally protected human rights is solely its own affair. It is our purpose to shape our policies in accord with our beliefs and to state them without stridency or apology when we think it is desirable to do so.

Our policy is to be applied within our own society as well as abroad. We welcome constructive criticism at the same time as we offer it.

No one should suppose that we are working in a vacuum. We place great weight on joining with others in the cause of human rights.

The U.N. system is central to this cooperative endeavor. That is why the President stressed the pursuit of human rights in his speech before the General Assembly last month. That is why he is calling for U.S. ratification of four important human rights covenants and why we are trying to strengthen the human rights machinery within the United Nations.

And that is an important reason why we have moved to comply with U.N. sanctions against Rhodesia. In one of our first acts, this Administration sought and achieved repeal of the Byrd amendment, which had placed us in violation of these sanctions and thus in violation of international law. We are supporting other diplomatic efforts within the United Nations to promote basic civil and political rights in Namibia and throughout southern Africa.

Regional organizations also play a central role in promoting human rights. The President has announced that the United States will sign and seek Senate approval of the American Convention on Human Rights. We will continue to work to strengthen the machinery of the Inter-American Commission on Human Rights. This will include efforts to schedule regular visits to all members of the Organization of American States, annual debates on human rights conditions, and the expansion of the inter-American educational program on human rights.

The United States is seeking increased consultation with other nations for joint programs on economic assistance and more general efforts to promote human rights. We are working to assure that our efforts reach out to all, with particular sensitivity to the problems of women.

We will meet in Belgrade later this year to review implementation of the Final Act of the Conference on Security and Cooperation in Europe—the so-called Helsinki conference. We will take this occasion to work for progress there on important human issues: family reunification, binational marriage, travel for personal and professional reasons, and freer access to information.

The United States looks to use of economic assistance—whether bilateral or through international financial institutions—as a means to foster basic human rights.

— We have proposed a 20 percent increase in U.S. foreign economic assistance for fiscal year 1978.

— We are expanding the program of the Agency for International Development for "New Initiatives in Human Rights" as a complement to present efforts to get the benefits of our aid to those most in need abroad.

— The programs of the United States Information Agency and the State Department's Bureau of Educational and Cultural Affairs stress support for law in society, a free press, freedom of communication, an open educational system, and respect for ethnic diversity.

This Administration's human rights policy has been framed in collaboration and consultation with Congress and private organizations. We have taken steps to assure firsthand contact, consultation, and observation when Members of Congress travel abroad to review human rights conditions.

We are implementing current laws that bring human rights considerations directly into our decisions in several international financial institutions. At the same time, we are working with the Congress to find the most effective way to fulfill our parallel commitment to international cooperation in economic development.

In accordance with human rights provisions of legislation governing our security assistance programs, we recently announced cuts in military aid to several countries.

Outside the government, there is much that can be done. We welcome the efforts of individual American citizens and private organizations—such as religious, humanitarian, and professional groups—to work for human rights with commitments of time, money, and compassion.

All these initiatives to further human rights abroad would have a hollow ring if we were not prepared to improve our own performance at home. So we have removed all restrictions on our citizens' travel abroad and are proceeding with plans to liberalize our visa policies.

We support legislation and administrative action to expand our refugee and asylum policies and to permit more victims of repressive regimes to enter the United States. During this last year, the United States spent some $475 million on assistance to refugees around the world, and we accepted 31,000 refugees for permanent resettlement in this country.

What results can we expect from all these efforts?

We may justifiably seek a rapid end to such gross violations as those cited in our law: "torture or cruel, inhuman, or degrading treatment or punishment, (or) prolonged detention without charges...." Just last week our Ambassador at the United Nations, Andrew Young, suggested a series of new ways to confront the practice of torture around the world.

The promotion of other human rights is a broader challenge. The results may be slower in coming but are no less worth pursuing. And we intend to let other countries know where we stand.

We recognize that many nations of the world are organized on authoritarian rather than democratic principles—some large and powerful, others struggling to raise the lives of their people above bare subsistence levels. We can nourish no illusions that a call to the banner of human rights will bring sudden transformations in authoritarian societies.

We are embarked on a long journey. But our faith in the dignity of the individual encourages us to believe that people in every society, according to their own traditions, will in time give their own expression to this fundamental aspiration.

Our belief is strengthened by the way the Helsinki principles and the U.N. Declaration of Human Rights have found resonance in the hearts of people of many countries. Our task is to sustain this faith by our example and our encouragement.

In his inaugural address three months ago, President Carter said, "Because we are free we can never be indifferent to the fate of freedom elsewhere." Again, at a meeting of the Organization of American States two weeks ago, he said, "You will find this country...eager to stand beside those nations which respect human rights and which promote democratic ideals."

We seek these goals because they are right—and because we, too, will benefit. Our own well-being, and even our security, are enhanced in a world that shares common freedoms and in which prosperity and economic justice create the conditions for peace. And let us remember that we always risk paying a serious price when we become identified with repression.

Nations, like individuals, limit their potential when they limit their goals. The American people understand this. I am confident they will support foreign policies that reflect our traditional values. To offer less is to define America in ways we should not accept.

America fought for freedom in 1776 and in two World Wars. We have offered haven to the oppressed. Millions have come to our shores in times of trouble. In time of devastation abroad, we have shared our resources.

Our encouragement and inspiration to other nations and other peoples have never been limited to the power of our military or the bounty of our economy. They have been lifted up by the message of our Revolution, the message of individual human freedom. That message has been our great national asset in times past. So it should be again.

Human Rights and the Moral Dimension of U.S. Foreign Policy

George P. Shultz

An address by Secretary of State Shultz at the 86th Annual Washington Day Banquet of the Creve Coeur Club of Illinois, Peoria, Illinois, February 22, 1984. Published as Current Policy No. 551 by the United States Department of State Bureau of Public Affairs, Washington, D.C., 1984.

I would like to speak to you today about human rights and the moral dimension of U.S. foreign policy.

Americans have always been an introspective people. Most other nations do not go through the endless exercise of trying to analyze themselves as we do. We are always asking what kind of people we are. This is probably a result of our history. Unlike most other nations, we are not defined by an ancient common tradition or heritage or by ethnic homogeneity. Unlike most other countries, America is a nation consciously created and made up of men and women from many different cultures and origins. What unifies us is not a common origin but a common set of ideals: freedom, constitutional democracy, racial and religious tolerance. We Americans thus define ourselves not by where we come from but by where we are headed: our goals, our values, our principles, which mark the kind of society we strive to create.

This accounts in good part, I believe, for the extraordinary vitality of this country. Democracy is a great liberator of the human spirit, giving free rein to the talents and aspirations of individuals, offering every man and woman the opportunity to realize his or her fullest potential. This ideal of freedom has been a beacon to immigrants from many lands.

We are a people that never felt bound by the past but always had confidence that we could shape our future. We also set high standards for ourselves. In our own society, from Jefferson to Lincoln to the modern day, there have always been keepers of our conscience who measured our performance against our ideals and insisted that we do better. The revolution in civil rights is perhaps the most dramatic recent example, and it has given impetus to other revolutions, such as in women's rights. We are blessed with a society that is constantly renewing and improving itself by virtue of the standards it has set.

In foreign affairs, we do the same. In the 19th century, when we had the luxury of not being actively involved in world politics, we, nevertheless, saw ourselves as a moral example to others. We were proud when liberators like Simon Bolivar in Latin America or Polish patriots in Europe invoked the ideals of the American Revolution. In the 20th century, since Woodrow Wilson, we have defined our role in the world in terms of moral principles that we were determined to uphold and advance. We have never been comfortable with the bare concept of maintaining the balance of power, even though this is clearly part of our responsibility.

Americans can be proud of the good we have accomplished in foreign affairs.

- We have fought and sacrificed for the freedom of others.
- We helped Europe and Japan rebuild after World War II.
- We have given generously to promote economic development.
- We have been a haven for refugees.

Thus, moral values and a commitment to human dignity have been not an appendage to our foreign policy but an essential part of it, and a powerful impulse driving it. These values are the very bonds that unite us with our closest allies, and they are the very issues that divide us from our adversaries. The fundamental difference between East and West is not in economic or social policy, though those policies differ radically, but in the moral principles on which they are based. It is the difference between tyranny and freedom—an age-old struggle in which the United States never could, and cannot today, remain neutral.

But there has always been tension between our ideals and the messy realities of the world. Any foreign policy must weave together diverse strands of national interest: political objectives, military security, economic managment. All these other goals are important to people's lives and well-being. They all have moral validity, and they often confront us with real choices to make. As the strongest free nation, the United States has a complex responsibility to help maintain international peace and security and the global economic system.

At the same time, as one nation among many, we do not have the power to remake the planet. An awareness of our limits is said to be one of the lessons we learned from Vietnam. In any case, Americans are also a practical people and are interested in producing results. Foreign policy thus often presents us with moral issues that are not easy to resolve. Moral questions are more difficult to answer than other kinds of questions, not easier. How we respond to these dilemmas is a real test of our maturity and also of our commitment.

Approaches to Human Rights Policy

There are several different ways of approaching human rights issues, and some are better than others. One thing should be clear. Human rights policy should not be a formula for escapism or a set of excuses for evading problems. Human rights policy cannot mean simply dissociating or distancing ourselves from regimes whose practices we find deficient. Too much of what passes for human rights policy has taken the form of shunning those we find do not live up to internationally accepted standards. But this to me is a "cop-out"; it seems more concerned with making us feel better than with having an impact on the situation we deplore. It is really a form of isolationism. If some liberals advocate cutting off relationships with right-wing regimes—and some conservatives seek to cut off dealings with left-wing regimes—we could be left with practically no foreign policy at all. This is not my idea of how to advance the cause of human rights.

One unattractive example of this approach derives from theories of American guilt, originating in our domestic debate over Vietnam. There are those eager to limit or restrain American power because they concluded from Vietnam that any exercise of American power overseas was bound to end in disaster or that America was itself a supporter or purveyor of evil in the world. Human rights policy was seen by some as a way of restricting American engagement abroad. Perversely, in this way of thinking, a government friendly to us is subjected to more exacting scrutiny than others; our security ties with it are attacked; once such a government faces an internal or external threat, its moral defects are spotlighted as an excuse to desert it. This is not my view of human rights policy either.

At issue here is not so much a tactical disagreement over human rights policy but fundamentally different conceptions of America and its impact on the world. What gives passion to this human rights debate is that it is a surrogate for a more significant underlying contest over the future of American foreign policy.

There should be no doubt of President Reagan's approach—not isolationism or guilt or paralysis but, on the contrary, a commitment to active engagement, confidently working for our values as well as our interests in the real world, acting proudly as the champion of freedom. The President has said that "human rights means working at problems, not walking away from them." If we truly care about our values, we must be engaged in their defense—whether in Afghanistan and Poland, the Philippines and El Salvador, or Grenada. This is the President's philosophy: We are proud of our country and of what it stands for. We have confidence in our ability to do good. We draw our inspiration from the fundamental decency of the American people. We find in our ideals a star to steer by, as we try to move our ship of state through the troubled waters of a complex world.

So we consider ourselves activists in the struggle for human rights. As the President declared to the British Parliament on June 8, 1982: "We must be staunch in our conviction that freedom is not the sole prerogative of a lucky few but the inalienable and universal right of all human beings."

Goals and Techniques of Human Rights Policy

That was philosophy. But on a daily basis, we face practical issues and problems of human rights policy. On one level, human rights policy aims at specific goals. We try, for example, to use our influence to improve judicial or police practices in many countries—to stop murders, to eliminate torture or brutality, to obtain the release of dissidents or political prisoners, to end persecution on racial or other grounds, to permit free emigration, and so forth. Many American officials, including Vice President Bush and myself, have gone to El Salvador and denounced the death squads not only privately but publicly—all of which is having a positive effect. We have sought to promote an honest and thorough investigation of the murder of Philippine opposition leader Benigno Aquino.

President Reagan, during his visit to the Republic of Korea last November, publicly stated his belief in the importance of political liberalization. But we have also made our thoughts on specific cases known privately, and several of these approaches have been successful. In our contacts with the Soviets, we have pressed for the release of human rights activists and for freedom of emigration. There are literally hundreds of such examples of American action. Sometimes we make progress; sometimes we do not—proving only that we still have much to do. In this context, I must pay tribute to your distinguished Senator, Chuck Percy [Sen. Charles H. Percy, R-Ill.]. No one in the Senate has played a more important role than Chuck Percy in the struggle for the right of emigration for Soviet Jewry and other oppressed peoples, for religious freedoms, and for the release of prisoners of conscience.

The techniques of exerting our influence are well known. We try, without letup, to sensitize other governments to human rights concerns. Every year we put on the public record a large volume of country reports examining the practices of other countries in thorough and candid detail—the rights of citizens to be free from violations of the integrity of the person and the rights of citizens to enjoy basic civil and political liberties. The 1984 report has just been published—nearly 1,500 pages of facts about human rights around the world, something no other country undertakes. Twice each year, we also send the congressional Helsinki commission a public report thoroughly reviewing the record of Soviet and East European compliance with the human rights provisions of the Helsinki Final Act.

Wherever feasible, we try to ameliorate abuses through the kind of frank diplomatic exchanges often referred to as "quiet diplomacy." But where our positive influence is minimal, or where other approaches are unavailing, we may have no choice but to use other, more concrete kinds of leverage with regimes whose practices we cannot accept.

We may deny economic and military assistance, withhold diplomatic support, vote against multilateral loans, refuse licenses for crime control equipment, or take other punitive steps. Where appropriate, we resort to public pressures and public statements denouncing such actions as we have done in the case of the Salvadoran death squads, Iranian persecution of the Bahais, South African apartheid, and Soviet repression on Afghanistan.

Multilateral organizations are another instrument of our human rights policy. In the UN Commission on Human Rights, we supported a resolution criticizing martial law in Poland—the first resolution there against a Communist country. The United States has been active and vigorous in regional conferences and organizations, such as the Helsinki process and the Inter-American Commission on Human Rights. We regret that some multilateral organizations have distorted the purposes they were designed to serve—such as UNESCO [UN Educational, Scientific, and Cultural Organization], which has not been living up to its responsibility to defend freedom of speech, intellectual freedom, and human rights in general.

Friendly governments are often more amenable to traditional diplomacy than to open challenge, and we therefore prefer persuasion over public denunciations. But if we were seriously concerned about human rights abuses in friendly countries, our policy would be one-sided and cynical.

Thus, while the Soviet Union and its proxies present the most profound and far-reaching danger to human rights, we cannot let it appear—falsely—that this is our only human rights concern. It is not.

Dilemmas of Human Rights Policy

Clearly, there are limits to our ability to remake the world. In the end, sovereign governments will make their own decisions, despite external pressure. Where a system of government is built on repression, human rights will inevitably be subordinated to the perceived requirements of political survival. The sheer diversity and complexity of other nations' internal situations, and the problem of coping with them in a dangerous world, are additional limits. How we use our influence and how we reconcile political and moral interests are questions that call not for dogmatic conclusions but for painstaking, sober analysis—and no little humility.

The dilemmas we face are many. What, for instance, is the relationship between human rights concerns and the considerations of regional or international security on which the independence and freedom of so many nations directly depend? This issue recurs in a variety of forms.

There are countries whose internal practices we sometimes question but which face genuine security threats from outside—like South Korea—or whose cooperation with us helps protect the security of scores of other nations—like the Philippines. But it is also true that in many cases a concern for human rights on our part may be the best guarantee of a long-term friendly relationship with that country. There are countries whose long-term security will probably be enhanced if they have a more solid base of popular support and domestic unity. Yet there are also cases where regional insecurity weakens the chances for liberalization and where American assurance of security support provides a better climate for an evolution to democracy. Human rights issues occur in a context, and there is no simple answer.

In the Middle East, to take a very different example, we have no doubt of Israel's commitment to human rights and democratic values. It is those very values we appeal to when we express our concern for the human rights and quality of life of the Palestinian people in the West Bank and Gaza—a concern that exists side by side with our understanding of Israel's security needs and our conviction that the basic problem can only be resolved through negotiation.

Another question that arises is: Do we know enough about the culture and internal dynamics of other societies to be sure of the consequence of pressures we might bring? If we distance ourselves from a friendly but repressive government, in a fluid situation, will this help strengthen forces of moderation, or might it make things worse? Pressures on human rights grounds against the Shah, Somoza, or South Vietnam had justification but may also have accelerated a powerful trend of events over which we had little influence, ending up with regimes that pose a far greater menace not only to human rights in their own country but also to the safety and freedom of all their neighbors.

In some countries, harsh measures of repression have been caused—indeed, deliberately provoked—by terrorists, who waged deliberate warfare not only against the institutions of society—political leaders, judges, administrators, newspaper editors, as well as against police and military officials—but against ordinary citizens. Terrorism itself is a threat to human rights and to the basic right to civil peace and security which a society owes its citizens. We deplore all governmental abuses of rights, whatever the excuse. But we cannot be blind to the extremist forces that pose such a monumental and increasing threat to free government precisely because democracies are not well equipped to meet this threat. We must find lawful and legitimate means to protect civilized life itself from the growing problem of terrorism.

The role of Congress is another question. There is no doubt that congressional concerns and pressures have played a very positive role in giving impetus and backing to our efforts to influence other governments' behavior. This congressional pressure can strengthen the hand of the executive branch in its efforts of diplomacy. At the same time, there can be complications if the legislative instrument is too inflexible or heavy-handed, or, even more, if Congress attempts to take on the administrative responsibility for executing policy. Legislation requires that we withhold aid in extreme circumstances. If narrowly interpreted, this can lead us rapidly to a "stop-go" policy of fits and starts, all or nothing—making it very difficult to structure incentives in a way that will really fulfill the law's own wider mandate: to "promote and encourage increased respect for human rights and fundamental freedoms...."

In the case of El Salvador, the positive impact the Administration has had in its recent pressures against death squads should be a reminder that certification in its previous form is not the only, or even the most effective, procedure for giving expression to our objectives. Sometimes a change in approach is the most worthwhile course. We are ready to work cooperatively with the Congress on this issue, but it should be clear that the answers are not simple.

Finally the phenomenon of totalitarianism poses special problems. Sociologists and political theorists have recognized for decades that there is a difference between traditional, indigenous dictatorships and the more pervasively repressive totalitarian states, fortified by modern technology, mass parties, and messianic ideology. Certainly, both are alien to our democratic ideals. But in this year of George Orwell, 1984, we cannot be oblivious to the new 20th century phenomenon.

Suppression of religion because it represents an autonomous force in a society; abuse of psychiatric institutions as instruments of repression; the use of prison labor on a mass scale for industrial construction—these and other practices are typical of the modern Marxist-Leninist state. Totalitarian regimes pose special problems not only because of their more systematic and thorough repression but also because of their permanence and their global ambitions. In the last decade we have seen several military regimes and dictatorships of the right evolve into democracies—from Portugal, Spain, and Greece to Turkey and Argentina. No Communist state has evolved in such a manner—though Poland attempted to.

And the Soviet Union, most importantly and uniquely, is driven not only by Russian history and Soviet state interest but also by what remains of its revolutionary ideology to spread its system by force, backed up by the greatest military power of any tyranny in history.

I raise these issues not to assert answers but to pose questions. These are complexities that a truly moral nation must face up to if its goal is to help make the world a better place.

Human Rights and Democracy

The Reagan Administration approaches the human rights question on a deeper level. Responding to specific juridical abuses and individual cases, as they happen, is important, but they are really the surface of the problem we are dealing with. The essence of the problem is the kind of political structure that makes human rights abuses possible. We have a duty not only to react to specific cases but also to understand, and seek to shape, the basic structural conditions in which human rights are more likely to flourish.

This is why President Reagan has placed so much emphasis on democracy: on encouraging the building of pluralistic institutions that will lead a society to evolve toward free and democratic forms of government. This is long-term, positive, active strategy for human rights policy.

It is not a utopian idea at all. For decades, the American labor movement has worked hard in many countries assisting the growth and strengthening of free labor unions—giving support and advice, teaching the skills of organizing and operating. In Western Europe after World War II, it was the free labor unions, helped in many cases by free unions here, that prevented Communist parties from taking over in several countries. Today, free political parties in Western Europe give similar fraternal assistance to budding parties and political groups in developing countries, helping these institutions survive or grow in societies where democratic procedures are not as firmly entrenched as in our own.

The new National Endowment for Democracy, proposed by President Reagan and now funded with the bipartisan support of the Congress, represents an imaginative and practical American effort to help develop the tools of democracy. Just as our traditional aid programs try to teach economic and agricultural skills, so our new programs will try to transfer skills in organizing elections, in campaigning, in legal reform, and other skills which we take for granted but which are basic to free, pluralistic societies.

Through the endowment, our two major political parties, along with labor, business, and other private groups, will assist countries and groups that seek to develop democratic institutions and practices in their own societies. The President is also directing AID [Agency for International Development], USIA [U.S. Information Agency], and other agencies to strengthen their programs for democracy, such as support for free labor movements, training of journalists, and strengthening judicial institutions and procedures. Sen. Percy also deserves particular credit here for his cosponsorship of the Kassebaum-Percy Human Rights Fund for South Africa, which will channel $1.5 million to private and community organizations in South Africa working for human rights.

It may not seem romantic or heroic to train African magistrates in Zimbabwe, provide technical help to the Liberian Constitution Commission, help publish a revised penal code in Zaire, help finance the education and research program of the Inter-American Institute of Human Rights in Costa Rica, or help provide international observers for free elections in El Salvador—but these programs help create the institutional preconditions for democracy. Democracy and the rule of law are the only enduring guarantee of human rights.

We should never lose faith in the power of the democratic idea. Democracies may be a minority in the world at large, but it is not true that they must always be so. Freedom is not a culture-bound Western invention but an aspiration of peoples everywhere—from Barbados to Botswana, from India to Japan.

In Latin America, for example, where the news is so much dominated by conflict, there is, in fact, an extraordinary trend toward democracy. Twenty-seven nations of Latin America and the Caribbean are either democratic or are formally embarked on a transition to democracy—representing almost 90 percent of the region's population, as compared with some 50 percent less than 10 years ago. And the trend has been accelerating.

Between 1976 and 1980, two Latin American nations, Ecuador and Peru, elected civilian presidents who successfully replaced military presidents. Since 1981, however, El Salvador, Honduras, Bolivia, and most recently Argentina have moved from military rule to popularly elected civilian governments.

Brazil is far along the same path. The people of Grenada have had restored to them the right to be the arbiters of their own political future. Uruguay has a timetable for a transition to democracy, and its parties have returned to independent activity. Pressure for return to civilian rule is being felt in Chile and Guatemala. This leaves only Cuba, a Marxist-Leninist state; Nicaragua, which has been steadily moving in that direction; and a handful of dictatorships outside this pattern.

This trend toward democracy, which reflects the most profound aspirations of the people of Latin America, has received wholehearted and effective encouragement from the Reagan Administration. Dictatorship in any form, leftist or rightist, is anathema in this hemisphere, and all states within the region have a responsibility to see that dictatorship gives way to genuine pluralist democracy.

Nor is the trend toward democracy confined to Latin America. In the Philippines, for example, the democratic tradition of that republic is evident in the strong popular pressure for free elections and a revitalized Congress. The government has begun to respond to these aspirations, and we are encouraging it to continue this hopeful process so important to the long-term stability of the Philippines. Likewise in the Republic of Korea, we are encouraged by President Chun [Doo Hwan]'s commitment to undertake in the next few years the first peaceful, constitutional transfer of power in Korea's modern history.

The Moral Commitment of the United States

A policy dedicated to human rights will always face hard choices. In El Salvador, we are supporting the moderates of the center, who are under pressure from extremists of both right and left; if we withdrew our support, the moderates would be the victims, as would be the cause of human rights in that beleaguered country. The road will be long and hard, but we cannot walk away from our principles.

The cause of human rights is at the core of American foreign policy because it is central to America's conception of itself. These values are hardly an American invention, but America has perhaps been unique in its commitment to base its foreign policy on the pursuit of such ideals. It should be an everlasting source of pride to Americans that we have used our vast power to such noble ends. If we have sometimes fallen short, that is not a reason to flagellate ourselves but to remind ourselves of how much there remains to do.

This is what America has always represented to other nations and other peoples. But if we abandoned the effort, we would not only be letting others down, we would be letting ourselves down.

Our human rights policy is a pragmatic policy which aims not at striking poses but at having a practical effect on the well-being of real people. It is a tough-minded policy, which faces the world as it is, not as we might wish or imagine it to be. At the same time, it is an idealistic policy, which expresses the continuing commitment of the United States to the cause of liberty and the alleviation of suffering. It is precisely this combination of practicality and idealism that has marked American statemanship at its best. It is the particular genius of the American people.

Appendix D

Pertinent U.S. Legislation

Legislation enacted by the United States Congress in the 1970s, and subsequently amended and updated, has authorized or required U.S. administrations to apply human rights criteria to programs of military assistance, military sales, police assistance, export credits, and trade and economic assistance not specifically addressed to "basic human needs"; to establish administrative machinery and programs to achieve these goals; and to report annually on the human rights situations in all UN member countries. What follows is not an exhaustive list of every statute concerning human rights, but rather the principal enactments that form an important part of the basis of human rights diplomacy.

The format, subject characterizations and citations used here are derived primarily from *U.S. Legislation Relating Human Rights to U.S. Foreign Policy*, Third Edition, September 1982 ($15), prepared by the International Human Rights Law Group, 733 15th Street, N.W. Suite 1000, Washington, DC 20005. That compilation also contains the legislative texts and is indexed both by title of statute and by subject. An updated edition to be published in late 1986 will provide post-1982 details that may be missing from the list that follows. (This list *does* incorporate some later legislation, such as the human rights amendments enacted in the International Security and Development Cooperation Act of 1985.)

I. Foreign Assistance and Trade Restrictions

Prohibition against Foreign Assistance to Governments with Political Prisoners

Section 32 of the Foreign Assistance Act of 1973

Cite as: FOREIGN ASSISTANCE ACT OF 1973, PL 93-189, §32, 22 U.S.C. 2151 note (1976).

Note on abbreviations:

Fed. Reg.	*Federal Register*
PL	*Public Law Number*
Stat.	*United States Statutes at Large*
U.S.C.	*United States Code*

223

Prohibition against Security Assistance to Gross Violators of Human Rights

Section 502B of the Foreign Assistance Act of 1961, as amended

Cite as: FOREIGN ASSISTANCE ACT OF 1961, PL 87-195, §502B, 22 U.S.C. 2304 (Supp. II 1978)(added by FOREIGN ASSISTANCE ACT OF 1974, PL 93-559, §46, 88 Stat. 1815, as amended, INTERNATIONAL SECURITY ASSISTANCE AND ARMS EXPORT CONTROL ACT OF 1976, PL 94-329, §301(a), 90 Stat. 748, as amended, FOREIGN RELATIONS AUTHORIZATION ACT, FISCAL YEAR 1978, PL 95-105, §109(a)(3), 91 Stat. 846 (1977), as amended, INTERNATIONAL SECURITY ASSISTANCE ACT OF 1978, PL 95-384, §§6(a)-(e), 10(b)(1), 12(b), 92 Stat. 731, 732, 735 & 737, as amended, INTERNATIONAL DEVELOPMENT COOPERATION ACT OF 1979, PL 96-53, §511, 93 Stat. 380, as amended, INTERNATIONAL SECURITY ASSISTANCE ACT OF 1979, PL 96-92, §4, 93 Stat. 702, as amended, INTERNATIONAL SECURITY AND DEVELOPMENT COOPERATION ACT OF 1980, PL 96-533, §701(b), 94 Stat. 3156; §704, 94 Stat. 3157, as amended, INTERNATIONAL SECURITY AND DEVELOPMENT COOPERATION ACT OF 1985, PL 99-83, §1201, 99 Stat. 276).

Prohibition against Foreign Assistance for Police Training

Section 660 of the Foreign Assistance Act of 1961, as amended (1974)

Cite as: FOREIGN ASSISTANCE ACT OF 1961, PL 87-195, §660, 22 U.S.C. 2420 (1976)(added by FOREIGN ASSISTANCE ACT OF 1974, PL 93-559, §30(a), as amended, INTERNATIONAL SECURITY AND DEVELOPMENT COOPERATION ACT OF 1985, PL 99-83, §711, 99 Stat. 243-44).

Freedom of Emigration in East-West Trade (Jackson-Vanik Amendment)

Sections 402 and 409 of the Trade Act of 1974

Cite as: TRADE ACT OF 1974, PL 93-618, §§402, 409, 19 U.S.C. 2432, 2439 (1976).

Prohibition against Foreign Assistance to Gross Violators of Human Rights (Harkin Amendment)

Section 116 of the Foreign Assistance Act of 1961, as amended (1975)

Cite as: FOREIGN ASSISTANCE ACT OF 1961, PL 87-195, §116, 22 U.S.C. 2151 note (Supp. II 1978) (added by INTERNATIONAL DEVELOPMENT AND FOOD ASSISTANCE ACT OF 1975, PL 94-161, §310, 89 Stat. 849, as amended, INTERNATIONAL DEVELOPMENT AND FOOD ASSISTANCE ACT OF 1977, PL 95-88, §111, 91 Stat. 537, as amended, FOREIGN RELATIONS AUTHORIZATION ACT, FISCAL YEAR 1978, PL 95-105, §109(a)(2), 91 Stat. 846 (1977), as amended, INTERNATIONAL DEVELOPMENT AND FOOD ASSISTANCE ACT OF 1978, PL 95-424, §109(1), 92 Stat. 947, as amended, INTERNATIONAL DEVELOPMENT COOPERATION ACT OF 1979, PL 96-53, §504, 93 Stat. 378, as amended, INTERNATIONAL SECURITY AND DEVELOPMENT COOPERATION ACT OF 1980, PL 96-533, §701(a), 94 Stat. 3156, as amended, INTERNATIONAL SECURITY AND DEVELOPMENT AND COOPERATION ACT OF 1981, PL 97-113, §306, 95 Stat. 1533, as amended, DEPARTMENT OF STATE AUTHORIZATION ACT, FISCAL YEARS 1984 AND 1985, PL 98-164, §§1002(a)(1), 1002(a)(3), 97 Stat. 1052).

Prohibition against Agricultural Commodity Sales to Gross Violators of Human Rights

Section 112 of the Agricultural Trade Development and Assistance Act of 1954, as amended (1977)

Cite as: AGRICULTURAL TRADE DEVELOPMENT AND ASSISTANCE ACT OF 1954, PL 83-480, §1112, 7 U.S.C. 1712 (Supp. II 1978)(added by the INTERNATIONAL DEVELOPMENT AND FOOD ASSISTANCE ACT OF 1977, PL 95-88, §203, 91 Stat. 545, as amended, INTERNATIONAL SECURITY AND DEVELOPMENT COOPERATION ACT OF 1980, PL 96-533, §701(c), 94 Stat. 3156).

International Military Education and Training: Human Rights Curriculum

Section 543 of the Foreign Assistance Act of 1961, as amended (1978)

Cite as: FOREIGN ASSISTANCE ACT OF 1961, PL 87-195, §543, 22 U.S.C. 2347b (Supp. II 1978) (added by INTERNATIONAL SECURITY ASSISTANCE ACT OF 1978, PL 95-384, §11(b)(3), 92 Stat. 736).

Prohibition against Foreign Assistance Used to Violate Universal Declaration of Human Rights

Section 511 of the Foreign Assistance and Related Programs Appropriations Act, 1982 [in effect since 1979 under continuing resolutions]

Cite as: FOREIGN ASSISTANCE & RELATED PROGRAMS APPROPRIATIONS ACT, FY 1982, PL 97-121, §511, 95 Stat. 1655 (1981).

Export-Import Bank: Human Rights Considerations

Section 2(b)(1)(B) of the Export-Import Bank Act of 1945, as amended (1978)

Cite as: EXPORT-IMPORT BANK ACT OF 1945, PL 79-173, §2(b)(1)(B), 12 U.S.C. 635(b)(1)(B) (Supp. II 1978) (as amended, EXPORT-IMPORT BANK ACT AMENDMENTS OF 1978, PL 95-630, §1904, 92 Stat. 3724).

Overseas Private Investment Corporation: Human Rights Considerations

Section 239(i) of the Foreign Assistance Act of 1961, as amended (1978)

Cite as: FOREIGN ASSISTANCE ACT OF 1961, PL 87-195, §239(i), 22 U.S.C. 2199 (Supp. II 1978) (added by the OVERSEAS PRIVATE INVESTMENT CORPORATION ACT OF 1978, PL 95-268, §8, 92 Stat. 216, as amended, OVERSEAS PRIVATE INVESTMENT CORPORATION AMENDMENTS ACT OF 1981, PL 97-65, §8(3), 95 Stat. 1024).

Overseas Private Investment Corporation: Reporting Requirement

Section 240A of the Foreign Assistance Act of 1961, as amended (1978)

Cite as: FOREIGN ASSISTANCE ACT OF 1961, PL 87-195, §240A, 22 U.S.C. 2200a

(Supp. II 1978) (as amended, OVERSEAS PRIVATE INVESTMENT CORPORATION AMENDMENTS ACT OF 1978, PL 95-268, §10, 92 Stat. 216).

Foreign Intimidation and Harassment of Individuals in the United States

Section 6 of the Arms Export Control Act, as amended (1981)

Cite as: ARMS EXPORT CONTROL ACT, as amended §6, (added by the INTERNATIONAL SECURITY AND DEVELOPMENT COOPERATION ACT OF 1981, PL 97-113, §115, 95 Stat. 1528) 22 U.S.C. 2756.

Prohibition against Assistance to any Communist Country

Section 620(f) of the Foreign Assistance Act of 1961 as amended

Cite as: FOREIGN ASSISTANCE ACT OF 1961, PL 87-195, §620(f), 22 U.S.C. 2370 (added by FOREIGN ASSISTANCE ACT OF 1962, PL 87-565, §301(d)(3), 76 Stat. 255, as amended, INTERNATIONAL SECURITY AND DEVELOPMENT COOPERATION ACT OF 1985, PL 99-83, §1202).

Waiver under the Trade Act of 1974 with Respect to the Socialist Republic of Romania*

Cite as: Executive Order 11854, 40 Fed. Reg. 18391 (1975).

Waiver under the Trade Act of 1974 with Respect to the Hungarian People's Republic*

Cite as: Executive Order 12051, 43 Fed. Reg. 15131 (1978).

Waiver under the Trade Act of 1974 with Respect to the People's Republic of China*

Cite as: Executive Order 12167, 44 Fed. Reg. 61167 (1979).

Crime Control Equipment: Export Licensing Requirement

Section 6(j) of the Export Administration Act of 1979

Cite as: EXPORT ADMINISTRATION ACT OF 1979, PL 96-72, §6(j), 93 Stat. 503 (1979).

Regulations Relating to Section 6(j) of the Export Administration Act

Section 376.14(a), Crime Control and Detection Commodities

Cite as: 15 C.F.R. [*Code of Federal Regulations*] §376.14(a), as amended at 47 Fed. Reg. 9203 (March 4, 1982).

---

*Waivers are extended annually by Presidential Determination unless specifically prohibited by Congressional action.

II. Special Authority to Waive Human Rights Restrictions

Special Authority for Emergency Requirements

Section 506 of the Foreign Assistance Act of 1961, as amended (1979). In accordance with Section 652, Foreign Assistance Act of 1961, as amended (1972)

Cite as: FOREIGN ASSISTANCE ACT OF 1961, PL 87–195, §506, 22 U.S.C. 2318 (as amended, FOREIGN ASSISTANCE ACT OF 1967, PL 90-137, §201(j)(1), 81 Stat. 445, as amended, INTERNATIONAL SECURITY ASSISTANCE AND ARMS EXPORT CONTROL ACT OF 1976, PL 94-329, §102, 90 Stat. 729, as amended, INTERNATIONAL SECURITY ASSISTANCE ACT OF 1979, PL 96-92, §5(b), 93 Stat. 702); and FOREIGN ASSISTANCE ACT OF 1961, PL 87-195, §652, 22 U.S.C. 2411 (as amended, FOREIGN ASSISTANCE ACT OF 1971, PL 92-226, §304(a)(1), 86 Stat. 20).

Special Authority for Security Interests

Section 614 of the Foreign Assistance Act of 1961, as amended (1980)

Cite as: FOREIGN ASSISTANCE ACT OF 1961, PL 87–195, §614, 22 U.S.C. 2364 (as amended, INTERNATIONAL SECURITY AND DEVELOPMENT COOPERATION ACT OF 1980, PL 96-533, §117(a), 94 Stat. 3140).

III. Restrictions on United States Participation in International Financial Institutions

International Financial Institutions: United States Must Oppose Loans to Gross Violators of Human Rights

Section 701 of the International Financial Institutions Act, as amended

Cite as: INTERNATIONAL FINANCIAL INSTITUTIONS ACT, PL 95-118, §701, 22 U.S.C. 262d (Supp. II 1978), as amended, INTER-AMERICAN AND ASIAN DEVELOPMENT BANKS AND AFRICAN DEVELOPMENT FUND, PL 96-259, §§501(a),(b), 94 Stat. 431-32, as amended, PL 97-375, §211, 96 Stat. 1826, as amended, SUPPLEMENTAL APPROPRIATIONS ACT, 1984, PL 98-181, §1004(1),(2), 97 Stat. 1286.

International Financial Institutions: Development of a Standard to Protect Human Rights

Section 703 of the International Financial Institutions Act

Cite as: INTERNATIONAL FINANCIAL INSTITUTIONS ACT, PL 95-118, §703, 22 U.S.C. 262c note (Supp. II 1978).

Human Rights and Basic Needs Considerations

Section 507 of the Foreign Assistance and Related Programs Appropriations Act of 1978

Cite as: FOREIGN ASSISTANCE AND RELATED PROGRAMS APPROPRIATIONS ACT OF 1978, §507, 22 U.S.C. 262d-1.

International Financial Institutions: Implementing General Human Rights Provisions

Section 705 of the International Financial Institutions Act, as amended (1980)

Cite as: INTERNATIONAL FINANCIAL INSTITUTIONS ACT, PL 95-118, §705, 22 U.S.C. 262d note (Supp. II 1978)(as amended, PL 96-259, §501(c), 94 Stat. 432).

IV. General Human Rights Legislation

Reaffirmation of Support for Religious Freedom

Section 501 of the Foreign Assistance Act of 1964

Cite as: FOREIGN ASSISTANCE ACT OF 1964, PL 88-633, §501, 78 Stat. 1009, 22 U.S.C. 2151 note.

Establishment of an Assistant Secretary of State for Human Rights and Humanitarian Affairs

Section 624(f) of the Foreign Assistance Act of 1961, as amended (1977)

Cite as: FOREIGN ASSISTANCE ACT OF 1961, PL 87-195, §624(f), 22 U.S.C. 2384(f) (Supp. II 1978) (as amended, FOREIGN RELATIONS AUTHORIZATION ACT, FISCAL YEAR 1978, PL 95-105, §109(a)(1)(A), 91 Stat. 846).

Establishing a Commission on Security and Cooperation in Europe

An Act to Establish a Commission on Security and Cooperation in Europe

Cite as: PL 94-304, 90 Stat. 661, as amended, PL 94-534, 90 Stat. 2495, PL 95-426, 92 Stat. 963 at 992, PL 96-60, 93 Stat. 395 at 403, as amended, AN ACT TO PROVIDE THAT THE CHAIRMANSHIP OF THE COMMISSION...SHALL ROTATE BETWEEN MEMBERS [OF] THE HOUSE AND...SENATE, PL 99-7, 99 Stat. 18.

Genocide Disassociation Proposal

Section 5(b) of the Bretton Woods Agreements Act Amendments, 1978

Cite as: BRETTON WOODS AGREEMENTS ACT AMENDMENTS, 1978, PL 95-435, §5(b), 22 U.S.C. 2151 note (1979).

Interagency Group on Human Rights: Report Requirement

Section 710 of the International Security and Development Cooperation Act of 1980

Cite as: INTERNATIONAL SECURITY AND DEVELOPMENT COOPERATION ACT OF 1980, PL 96-533, §710, 94 Stat. 3160 (1980).

Reaffirmation of Support for Human Rights Provisions

Section 713 of the International Security and Development Cooperation Act of 1981

Cite as: INTERNATIONAL SECURITY AND DEVELOPMENT COOPERATION ACT OF 1981, PL 97-113, §713, 95 Stat. 1548 (1981).

U.S. Government Opposition to the Practice of Torture

Joint Resolution regarding the implementation of the policy of the United States Government in opposition to the practice of torture by any foreign government

Cite as: PL 98-447 [H. J. Res. 605], 98 Stat. 1721, approved October 4, 1984.

V. Country Specific Legislation

Argentina: Establishment of Certification Procedure

Sections 725(b),(c) of the International Security and Development Cooperation Act of 1981

Cite as: INTERNATIONAL SECURITY AND DEVELOPMENT COOPERATION ACT OF 1981, PL 97-113, §§725(b),(c), 95 Stat. 1553-54, 22 U.S.C. 2370 note (1981).

Central America: Respect for Human Rights

Chapter 6 of the Foreign Assistance Act of 1961, as amended (1985)

Cite as: FOREIGN ASSISTANCE ACT OF 1961, PL 87-195, §§461-64 (added by IN-TERNATIONAL SECURITY AND COOPERATION ACT OF 1985, PL 99-83, 99 Stat. 234).

Chile: U.S. Support of International Humanitarian Initiatives

Section 35 of the Foreign Assistance Act of 1973

Cite as: FOREIGN ASSISTANCE ACT OF 1973, PL 93-189, §35, 87 Stat. 714, 22 U.S.C. 2151 note (1976).

Chile: Establishment of Certification Procedure

Section 726(b) of the International Security and Development Cooperation Act of 1981

Cite as: INTERNATIONAL SECURITY AND DEVELOPMENT COOPERATION ACT OF 1981, PL 97-113, §726(b), 95 Stat. 1554, 22 U.S.C. 2370 note (1981).

Cuba: Human Rights Considerations in Future Negotiations

Section 511(b) Foreign Relations Authorization Act, Fiscal Year 1978

Cite as: FOREIGN RELATIONS AUTHORIZATION ACT, FISCAL YEAR 1978, PL 95-105,§511(b), 91 Stat. 844 (1977).

Cuba, Vietnam, and Cambodia: Foreign Assistance Restrictions

Section 717 of the International Security and Development Cooperation Act of 1980

Cite as: INTERNATIONAL SECURITY AND DEVELOPMENT COOPERATION ACT OF 1980, PL 96-533, §717, 94 Stat. 3161, 22 U.S.C. 2151 note (1980).

El Salvador: Establishment of Certification Procedures

Section 728 of the International Security and Development Cooperation Act of 1981

Cite as: INTERNATIONAL SECURITY AND DEVELOPMENT COOPERATION ACT OF 1981, PL 97-113, §728, 45 Stat. 1555-57, 22 U.S.C. 2370 note (1981).

El Salvador: Promotion of Human Rights through Economic and Military Assistance

Section 727 of the International Security and Development Cooperation Act of 1981

Cite as: INTERNATIONAL SECURITY AND DEVELOPMENT COOPERATION ACT OF 1981, PL 97-113, §727, 95 Stat. 1554-55 (1981).

El Salvador: Case-by-Case Review of Petitions for Extended Voluntary Departure

Section 731 of the International Security and Development Cooperation Act of 1981

Cite as: INTERNATIONAL SECURITY AND DEVELOPMENT COOPERATION ACT OF 1981, PL 97-113, §731, 95 Stat. 1557, 8 U.S.C. 1157 note (1981).

Guatemala: Human Rights Considerations in U.S. Assistance to Guatemala

Section 703 of the International Security and Development Cooperation Act of 1985

Cite as: INTERNATIONAL SECURITY AND DEVELOPMENT COOPERATION ACT OF 1985, PL 99-83, §703, 99 Stat. 239.

Haiti: Promoting the Development of the Haitian People and Providing for Orderly Emigration from Haiti

Section 721 of the International Security and Development Cooperation Act of 1981

Cite as: INTERNATIONAL SECURITY AND DEVELOPMENT COOPERATION ACT OF 1981, PL 97-113, §721, 95 Stat. 1557, 22 U.S.C. 2151 note (1981)(as amended, INTERNATIONAL SECURITY AND DEVELOPMENT COOPERATION ACT OF 1985, PL 99-83, §705, 99 Stat. 241-42).

Laos, Kampuchea, and Afghanistan: Condemnation of Use of Chemical and Toxin Weapons

Section 716 of the International Security and Development Cooperation Act of 1981

Cite as: INTERNATIONAL SECURITY AND DEVELOPMENT COOPERATION ACT OF 1981, PL 97-113, §716, 95 Stat. 1548-49 (1981).

Lebanon: Consideration of Human Rights Principles in Policy Formulation

Section 715 of the International Security and Development Cooperation Act of 1981

Cite as: INTERNATIONAL SECURITY AND DEVELOPMENT COOPERATION ACT OF 1981, PL 97-113, §715, 95 Stat. 1548 (1981).

Libya, Iraq, South Yemen, Angola, Cambodia, Cuba, Laos, the Socialist Republic of Vietnam, and Syria: Restrictions on Foreign Assistance

Section 513 of the Foreign Assistance and Related Programs Appropriations Act, 1982

Cite as: FOREIGN ASSISTANCE AND RELATED PROGRAMS APPROPRIATIONS ACT, PL 97-121, §513, 95 Stat. 1647 (1982).

Mozambique: Restrictions on Foreign Assistance

Section 512 of the Foreign Assistance and Related Programs Appropriations Act, 1982

Cite as: FOREIGN ASSISTANCE AND RELATED PROGRAMS APPROPRIATIONS ACT, PL 97-121, §512, 95 Stat. 1647 (1982).

Nicaragua: Restrictions on Security Assistance

Section 119 of the International Security and Development Cooperation Act of 1980

Cite as: INTERNATIONAL SECURITY AND DEVELOPMENT COOPERATION ACT OF 1980, PL 96-533, §119, 94 Stat. 3141, 22 U.S.C. 2151 note (1980).

Nicaragua: Restrictions on Foreign Assistance

Section 724 of the International Security and Development Cooperation Act of 1981

Cite as: INTERNATIONAL SECURITY AND DEVELOPMENT COOPERATION ACT OF 1981, PL 97-113, §724, 95 Stat. 1552-53 (1981).

The Philippines: Restrictions on Foreign Assistance and Arms Export

Section 901 of the International Security and Development Cooperation Act of 1985

Cite as: INTERNATIONAL SECURITY AND DEVELOPMENT COOPERATION ACT OF 1985, PL 99-83, §901, 99 Stat. 266-67.

South Africa: Prohibition against Export-Import Bank Assistance (Evans Amendment)

Section 2(b)(9) of the Export-Import Bank Act of 1945, as amended

Cite as: EXPORT-IMPORT BANK ACT OF 1945, PL 79-173, §2(b)(9), 12 U.S.C. 635(b)(9) (Supp. II 1978)(added by EXPORT-IMPORT BANK ACT AMENDMENTS OF 1978, PL 95-630, §1915, 92 Stat. 3727, as amended, EXPORT-IMPORT BANK ACT AMENDMENTS OF 1983, PL 98-181, title VI, §619(d)(1), 97 Stat. 1261).

South Korea: Concern over Human Rights Conditions

Section 412 of the International Security Assistance and Arms Export Control Act of 1976, as amended

Cite as: INTERNATIONAL SECURITY ASSISTANCE AND ARMS EXPORT CONTROL ACT OF 1976, PL 94-329, §412, 22 U.S.C. 2428 note (1976).

Uganda and Cambodia: Export Restrictions

Section 610 of the Foreign Relations Authorization Act, Fiscal Year 1979

Cite as: FOREIGN RELATIONS AUTHORIZATION ACT, FISCAL YEAR 1979, PL 95-426, §610, 22 U.S.C. 2151 note (Supp. II 1978)(as amended, PL 97-241, §505(a)(2), 96 Stat. 299).

Uganda: Foreign Assistance Restrictions

Section 719 of the International Security and Development Cooperation Act of 1980

Cite as: INTERNATIONAL SECURITY AND DEVELOPMENT COOPERATION ACT OF 1980, PL 96-533, §719, 94 Stat. 3162 (1980).

Vietnam, Cambodia and Cuba: Foreign Assistance Restrictions

Section 602 of the International Development and Food Assistance Act of 1978

Cite as: INTERNATIONAL DEVELOPMENT AND FOOD ASSISTANCE ACT OF 1978, PL 95-424, §602, 22 U.S.C. 2151 note (Supp. II 1978)(as amended, PL 96-67, §1(a), 93 Stat. 415 (1979)).

VI. Legislation No Longer in Force

Impact on Foreign Relations of Reports on Human Rights Practices: Report Requirement

Section 504(b) of the International Development Cooperation Act of 1979

Cite as: INTERNATIONAL DEVELOPMENT COOPERATION ACT OF 1979, PL 96-53, §504(b), 22 U.S.C. 2151 note (1979)(repealed, 1981).

International Monetary Fund Supplemental Financing Facility: Human Rights Considerations

Section 31 of the Bretton Woods Agreements Act, as amended

Cite as: BRETTON WOODS AGREEMENTS ACT, PL 79-171, §31, 22 U.S.C. 286e-10 (Supp. II 1978)(added by BRETTON WOODS AGREEMENTS ACT AMENDMENTS, 1978, PL 95-435, §4, 92 Stat. 1052 (1978)) (repealed, 1981).

Argentina: Foreign Assistance Restrictions

Section 620B of the Foreign Assistance Act of 1961, as amended

Cite as: FOREIGN ASSISTANCE ACT OF 1961, PL 87-195, §620B, 22 U.S.C. 2372 (Supp. II 1978)(added by INTERNATIONAL SECURITY ASSISTANCE ACT OF 1977, PL 95-92, §11, 91 Stat. 619, as amended, INTERNATIONAL SECURITY ASSISTANCE ACT OF 1978, PL 95-384, §12(c)(1), 92 Stat. 737)(repealed, 1981).

Chile: Military and Economic Assistance Restrictions

Section 406 of the International Security Assistance and Arms Export Control Act of 1976, as amended

Cite as: INTERNATIONAL SECURITY ASSISTANCE AND ARMS EXPORT CONTROL ACT OF 1976, PL 94-329, §406, 22 U.S.C. 2370 note (Supp. II 1978)(as amended by INTERNATIONAL SECURITY ASSISTANCE ACT OF 1978, PL 95-384, §§10(b)(5), 12(c)(5), 92 Stat. 735, 737)(repealed, 1981).

Nicaragua: Foreign Assistance Restrictions

Section 533 of the Foreign Assistance Act of 1961, as amended

Cite as: FOREIGN ASSISTANCE ACT OF 1961, PL 87-195, §533 (added by INTERNATIONAL SECURITY AND DEVELOPMENT COOPERATION ACT OF 1980, PL 96-533, §202, 94 Stat. 3142-44 (1980)(amended and restated, 1981). [See "Nicaragua: Restrictions on Foreign Assistance," section V of this appendix.]

South Korea: Restrictions on Military Assistance

Section 26 of the Foreign Assistance Act of 1974

Cite as: FOREIGN ASSISTANCE ACT OF 1974, PL 93-559, §26, 88 Stat. 1809 (repealed, 1981).

Uganda: Import Restrictions

Sections 5(a),(c),(e) of the Bretton Woods Agreements Act Amendments, 1978

Cite as: BRETTON WOODS AGREEMENTS ACT AMENDMENTS, 1978, PL 95-435, §§5(a),(c),(e), 22 U.S.C. 2151 note (1979)(Repealed, 1979).

Uganda: Export Restrictions

Section 4 of the Export Administration Act of 1969, as amended

Cite as: EXPORT ADMINISTRATION ACT OF 1969, §4(m), 50 U.S.C. app. 2403m (Supp. II 1978)(added by BRETTON WOODS AGREEMENTS ACT AMENDMENTS, 1978, PL 95-435, §5(d), 92 Stat. 1052 (1978))(repealed 1979).

Zimbabwe: Reports on Internal Situation Pursuant to Grant of Assistance

Section 720 of the International Security and Development Cooperation Act of 1980

Cite as: INTERNATIONAL SECURITY AND DEVELOPMENT COOPERATION ACT OF 1980, PL 96-533, §720, 94 Stat. 3162 (1980)(repealed, 1981).

*   *   *

Following are a few other useful sources of information on human rights legislation:

U.S. Congress. House. Committee on Foreign Affairs. *Human Rights Documents: Compilation of Documents Pertaining to Human Rights.* U.S. Laws on Human Rights, Basic U.N. Human Rights Instruments, U.N. Instruments in Selected Human Rights Areas, Regional Human Rights Instruments, War Crimes and International Humanitarian Laws (Laws of Armed Conflict), and Human Rights Bodies Established by U.S. Laws or Multilateral Instruments. Committee Print. September 1983.

U.S. Congress. Senate. Committee on Foreign Relations. House. Committee on Foreign Affairs. *Legislation on Foreign Relations Through 1984.* Current

Legislation and Related Executive Orders. Volumes I and II. Joint Committee Print. March 1985.

Cohen, Stephen B. "Conditioning U.S. Security Assistance on Human Rights Practices." *The American Journal of International Law* 76 (April 1982): 246-79.

Appendix E

Human Rights Organizations

A Selected List

Private nongovernmental organizations concerned with the protection of human rights provide important support for human rights policies and their implementation. Some are international in scope, some focus on specific countries or regions; still others focus on specific professions, religious, ethnic, or labor concerns. Public education and legislative lobbying are the main activities of many of these groups.

Among the many hundreds of human rights groups in the United States and worldwide are some that provide invaluable support to diplomatic efforts through impartial observations and reports that document human rights violations and bring them to the attention of governments and international organizations for action. Others create pressures on governments by mobilizing public concern on behalf of victims of human rights abuses. What follows is only a partial listing of some of the principal international and U.S.-based organizations conducting such human rights activities. (Headquarters are shown in parentheses.)

International groups, most with U.S. affiliates

Amnesty International (London)
Anti-Slavery Society for the Protection of Human Rights (London)
Inter-American Press Association (Miami)
International Commission of Jurists (Geneva)
International Committee of the Red Cross (Geneva)
International Confederation of Free Trade Unions (Brussels)
International League for Human Rights (New York)
International PEN, Writers in Prison Committee (London)
Ligue français pour la défense des droits de l'homme et du citoyen (Paris)

Minority Rights Group (London)
Survival International (London)
World Federation of United Nations Associations (Geneva)
World Conference on Religion and Peace (New York)
World Council of Churches (Geneva)
World Jewish Congress (Geneva)

U.S. groups

American Association for the Advancement of Science [AAAS] Clearinghouse
    on Persecuted Foreign Scientists (Washington, D.C.—hereinafter DC)
American Bar Association Committees on International Human Rights (DC)
American Federation of Labor–Congress of Industrial Organizations [AFL–
    CIO], its auxiliary programs for Africa, Asia and Latin America, and
    member unions' international affairs departments (DC)
American Jewish Committee/Jacob Blaustein Institute for the Advancement of
    Human Rights (New York City—hereinafter NY)
American Psychiatric Association, Committee on International Abuse of
    Psychiatry and Psychiatrists (DC)
Americas Watch (NY)
Association of American Publishers, International Freedom to Publish
    Committee (NY)
Committee of Concerned Scientists (NY)
Committee to Protect Journalists (NY)
Council on Hemispheric Affairs (DC)
Freedom House (NY)
Friends Committee on National Legislation (DC)
Fund for Free Expression (NY)
Human Rights Working Group of the Coalition for a New Foreign and Military
    Policy and its member organizations (DC)
International Human Rights Law Group (DC)
Joint Baltic American National Committee (Rockville, Maryland)
Lawyers' Committee for Civil Rights Under Law, Southern Africa Project (DC)
Lawyers' Committee for International Human Rights (NY)
National Academy of Sciences, Committee on Human Rights (DC)
National Conference on Soviet Jewery (NY)
National Council of Churches USA, Division of Overseas Ministries, Human
    Rights Office (NY)
North American Coalition for Human Rights in Korea (DC) and numerous
    similar groups focusing on human rights in specific countries
Palestine Human Rights Campaign (Chicago)
U.S. Catholic Conference, Office of International Justice and Peace (DC)
U.S. Helsinki Watch Committee (NY)
Washington Office on Africa (DC)

Washington Office on Latin America (DC)
World Peace Through Law Center (DC)

Sources of Additional Information

Several directories listing hundreds of organizations document the proliferation in recent years of organizations concerned with the protection and promotion of human rights. The United States, Canada, Great Britain, Switzerland, France and other West European countries predominate in these lists, but over 400 organizations in Asia, Africa and Latin America now appear that are concerned with human rights and social justice in their own societies or internationally. Following are some of the useful sources of information on these groups.

* **Conference of Non-Governmental Organizations in Consultative Status with the United Nations Economic and Social Council (CONGO)**, Subcommittee on Human Rights. Office of the President (through 1/89), Palais des Nations, CH-1211, Geneva 10, Switzerland.

* **Human Rights Internet (HRI)**
c/o Harvard Law School, Pound Hall, Room 401
Cambridge, Massachusetts 02138

    HRI Directories:

    North American Human Rights Directory, A Guide to Over 700 Organizations Based in the U.S. and Canada Concerned with Human Rights and Social Justice. Edited by Laurie S. Wiseberg and Hazel Sirett. 1984.

    Human Rights Directory: Western Europe, A Directory of Organizations in Western Europe Concerned with Issues of Human Rights and Social Justice. Edited by Laurie S. Wiseberg and Hazel Sirett. 1982.

    Human Rights Directory: Latin America, Africa, Asia, A Directory of Organizations in Latin America and the Caribbean, Africa, the Middle East, Asia and the Pacific, Concerned with Issues of Human Rights and Social Justice. Edited by Laurie S. Wiseberg and Harry M. Scoble. 1981.

    Human Rights Directory: Eastern Europe. Forthcoming 1986.

    Human Rights Internet Reporter. Bimonthly since 1976. Covers the activities of nongovernmental organizations, recent publications research in progress etc.

    Note: HRI Directories, Reporters, and extensive library resources can be obtained from HRI via computer database and/or microfiche (documentation only). Telephone (617) 495–9924.

* ***The Human Rights Handbook: A Guide to British and American International Human Rights Organisations.*** Compiled by Marguerite

Garling for the Writers and Scholars Educational Trust (London). New York: Facts on File, 1979.

• An ongoing study of U.S.-based nongovernmental organizations actively concerned with international human rights by Lowell W. Livezy of Princeton University (Princeton, New Jersey 08544).

Other Books of Interest
from the Institute for the Study of Diplomacy and University Press of America

CASE STUDIES IN DIPLOMACY

U.N. Security Council Resolution 242: A Case Study in Diplomatic Ambiguity
by Lord Caradon, Arthur J. Goldberg, Mohamed El-Zayyat and Abba Eban
Resolution of the Dominican Crisis, 1965: A Study in Mediation
by Audrey Bracey, with concluding chapter by Martin F. Herz
Mediation of the West New Guinea Dispute, 1962: A Case Study
by Christopher J. McMullen, with Introduction by George C. McGhee
Resolution of the Yemen Crisis, 1963: A Case Study in Mediation
by Christopher J. McMullen
American Diplomats and the Franco-Prussian War: Perceptions from Paris and Berlin
by Patricia Dougherty, O.P.
Conference Diplomacy—A Case Study: The World Food Conference, Rome, 1974
by Edwin McC. Martin
Conference Diplomacy II—A Case Study: The UN Conference on Science and
Technology for Development, Vienna, 1979
by Jean M. Wilkowski, with Foreword by John W. McDonald, Jr.

SYMPOSIA ON PROBLEMS AND PROCESSES OF DIPLOMACY

The Modern Ambassador: The Challenge and the Search
edited by Martin F. Herz, with Introduction by Ellsworth Bunker
Diplomats and Terrorists: What Works, What Doesn't—A Symposium
edited by Martin F. Herz
Contacts with the Opposition—A Symposium
edited by Martin F. Herz
The Role of Embassies in Promoting Business—A Symposium
edited by Martin F. Herz, with Overview by Theodore H. Moran
Diplomacy: The Role of the Wife—A Symposium
edited by Martin F. Herz
The Consular Dimension of Diplomacy—A Symposium
edited by Martin F. Herz

EXEMPLARY DIPLOMATIC REPORTING SERIES & OCCASIONAL PAPERS

David Bruce's "Long Telegram" of July 3, 1951
by Martin F. Herz
A View from Tehran: A Diplomatist Looks at the Shah's Regime in 1964
by Martin F. Herz
A View from Yenan
by John K. Emmerson
The North-South Dialogue and the United Nations
by John W. McDonald, Jr.
Making the World a Less Dangerous Place: Lessons Learned from a Career in
Diplomacy
by Martin F. Herz

DIPLOMATIC AND CONTEMPORARY HISTORY

U.S.-Soviet Summits: An Account of East-West Diplomacy at the Top, 1955-1985
by Gordon R. Weihmiller and Dusko Doder
215 Days in the Life of an American Ambassador
by Martin F. Herz
First Line of Defense—Forty Years' Experiences of a Career Diplomat
by John Moors Cabot
The Vietnam War in Retrospect
by Martin F. Herz